The Therapeutic Recreation Stress Management Primer

by

Cynthia Mascott

The Therapeutic Recreation Stress Management Primer

by

Cynthia Mascott

Venture Publishing, Inc.

State College, Pennsylvania

Venture Publishing, Inc.
1999 Cato Avenue
State College, PA 16801
Phone: (814) 234-4561
Fax: (814) 234-1651

Production Manager: Richard Yocum
Manuscript Editing: Michele L. Barbin
Cover by Echelon Design

Library of Congress Catalogue Card Number 2004103846
ISBN 1-892132-44-3

*This book is dedicated to the loving memory of my aunt,
Meta Fleisher, and to my dear friend, Julie Parrish—
equally bold, beautiful, and brave.*

Meta

Julie

Table of Contents

Section I
Relaxation Techniques

Acknowledgments

First and foremost, I would like to thank my editor at Venture Publishing, Michele Barbin, for her fine editorial supervision and sense of humor throughout the writing of this book. It has been a pleasure working with her. I am particularly appreciative of the psychiatric rehabilitation staff at Los Angeles County & University of Southern California Healthcare Network for all of their encouragement during the past year and for being there for me, always.

I would like to acknowledge a number of important people who have molded my career in the therapeutic recreation field. Thanks to Leslie Horowitz, who in 1984, hired me as a Recreation Therapy Aide when I virtually had no experience and who changed my life. Also thanks to Lora Saavedra who steered me toward graduate school and Kathy Halberg at the University of Oregon who mentored me there and continues to be an ongoing professional support. I have had several supervisors in the past 20 years who have been exceptionally wonderful and who had the courage to allow me to grow professionally. Thanks to Mead Jackson, Kathleen Austria, Iris Lee Knell, Brian Toomey, and Brian Maxfield. What a difference it has made in my career to have you all in my life.

There were many people who helped me with this book. I would like to thank Ulla Anneli, for her technical assistance and modeling on the adaptive yoga section of the book. Special thanks to Laura Leyva for the tai chi chapter of the book. I would like to thank Charlie Bolding and Robbie Harris, Stella Beltran, and Cathy Earhart for their assistance with the stretching and adaptive tai chi sections of the book during our lunch hours. Lori Pond also contributed to the Yoga chapter. Thanks to John Keller for our time at Tower Records and for his expertise as a composer and music fanatic (not to mention a lifetime of enduring friendship). My sister, Holly Nadler, was of particular help in the classical music section of the book. (She's the intellectual in the family.) I also would like to thank

Kim and Roger Selbert for the use of their lovely yard during the tai chi photo shoot.

Of course I would like to thank my mother for being my first line editor, reminding me to dot my *i*s and cross my *t*s before sending my manuscript off to the publishers.

Last but not least, I want to acknowledge the amazing clients I have worked with over the years. They have taught me so much. I have become the therapist I am today because of them. I wish all of my clients, past and present, Godspeed.

Introduction

Guess what? We all live under a lot of stress whether we want to or not. The nature of living is such that if something good or bad happens, we manifest the event by feeling stress. This means our bodies feel stress whether we are promoted or fired, fall in love or out of love, and so forth. Not only that, our environment is stressful. This is particularly true in urban areas where traffic, noise, and crime can be pervasive.

Stress is a consequence of living, and in many ways we have little control over it. However we are able as human beings to control the ways in which we react to stress.

The role of the therapeutic recreation specialist (TRS) is to provide various activities to engage the client in therapeutic/rehabilitative, education/preventative, and recreational activities. Teaching stress management skills can be utilized throughout the continuum.

In therapeutic recreation, TRSs work with individuals who are often in crisis. Whether someone has suffered a stroke; suffers from mental illness, developmental disabilities, or physical impairment(s); or has had a substance abuse problem, the TRS's mission is to improve the client's quality of life.

While there is more than enough information about stress management for the lay person, TRSs often have to adapt material when providing a stress management component to their program. *The Therapeutic Recreation Stress Management Primer* is written specifically for TRSs. Since TRSs work with a variety of populations, the stress management techniques provided in this primer include adaptations specific to special populations. If a client has limited physical functioning due to an illness or injury, the lesson plan suggests adaptations for physical alterations. For those who suffer from mental illness, developmental disabilities, or brain injury, the plan suggests cognitive adjustments. *The Therapeutic Recreation Stress Management Primer* provides two types of stress management assessments—textual and pictorial—which take into account the client's cognitive abilities/limitations.

The stress management techniques and activities in this primer are categorized as follows: relaxation techniques, exercise, and coping skills and wellness. Physical and cognitive adaptations are provided for each activity.

Relaxation Techniques

Meditation: One of the most powerful stress-busting activities, meditation, involves learning how to live in the moment through becoming still and letting go of negative thoughts and feelings. Meditation can be used with all populations served by TRSs.

Breathing: Learning how to take deep breaths is a surefire way of decreasing stress. Teaching clients how to breathe from the diaphragm can help them learn to become calmer and more relaxed.

Progressive Relaxation: This activity involves concentrating on a certain part of the body and willing it to rest until the entire body feels peaceful.

Self-Hypnosis: Hypnosis involves invoking a flow state of being. By learning how to enter a hypnotic state, the mind is able to subconsciously make the necessary changes to improve quality of life.

Creative Visualization: By entering an imagined place of peace and beauty, the mind is able to calm itself and bring about a new sense of hope and promise.

Aromatherapy: The effects of some calming herbs and oils decrease the stress response by evoking an individual's senses.

Acupressure: For centuries, the Chinese have used acupressure and acupuncture to stimulate energy sources in the body to give the mind and body a chance to heal itself.

Autogenics: The purpose of autogenics is to induce the relaxation response by visualizing various sensations in the body, for example, heaviness in the neck, shoulders, and limbs; warmth in the limbs; a calm heartbeat; relaxed breathing; and coolness of the forehead.

Music: By using soothing music, it's possible to produce the relaxation response. The simple act of listening to music can slow the heart rate and induce a sense of peace and wholeness.

Exercise

Beginning an Exercise Program: This chapter provides tips for how to begin an exercise program, and includes an exercise diary and a list of suggested exercises, although multitudes of exercises are available.

Stretching Exercises: Exercise is an important element in most TR departments. While activities may need to be adapted, clients will feel significantly better if they can pursue an exercise program. Stretching exercises can be done in a standing position, lying down, or in a chair and can be used with the elderly and some physically challenged individuals.

Tai Chi: Tai chi has been practiced in Asia for centuries. It involves making slow but artful movements which will exercise clients' minds, bodies, and souls.

Yoga: This type of exercise is also good for the mind, body, and soul. Yoga involves concentrating on a series of graceful movements. A proven stress buster, yoga can be adapted for people who are physically challenged, and simplified for people with cognitive problems.

Coping Skills and Wellness

Coping Skills and Wellness (Cognitive Behavior Techniques): Is the glass half full—or is it half empty? Many clients are stuck in negative-thinking patterns. By learning new behaviors and thought processes, clients will feel much better about themselves and their situation.

Social Support: It is critical for clients to get needed social support to enhance their health and emotional well-being. This section includes tips on developing a social support network, and a resource guide of support groups available in the community.

Smoking Cessation: The health hazards regarding smoking are numerous. If a client is a smoker and wants to stop, this section includes current information regarding smoking cessation that can help.

Substance Abuse: It is important for clients to look at their relationship to alcohol and/or drugs. Substance abuse can exacerbate existing medical problems.

This section includes tips on the recovery process along with a recovery resource guide available to clients.

Nutrition: Learning how to eat a healthy diet is a pivotal component in becoming healthier. Many clients have never developed good eating habits, or have had problems with either weight loss or weight gain since they became ill or injured.

Sleep Hygiene: Good sleep habits are critical for people who have struggled with stress. By examining an individual's sleeping patterns, changes can be made which will improve the possibility of getting a good night's sleep.

I have been a therapeutic recreation specialist for many years, and have worked with many populations. My particular interest is helping people learn new stress management skills. Many of my clients have either lost the ability to deal with stress, are overwhelmed with losses they have sustained because of a physical or mental crisis or condition, or they never learned good stress management skills in the first place.

Chapter One
Getting Started

Stress and Your Client

Wouldn't it be nice if TRSs could regulate a client's mood and health by just waving a magic wand?

More than likely, TRSs have wished it was that easy. Most clients are in the midst of a life change, whether they have sustained an injury, have a physical or mental illness, are young and having adjustment problems, or are dealing with aspects of growing older. When clients are in an acute state of distress, they often feel as if they are in stress overload. TRSs encourage clients to learn stress management techniques, but people don't always know how to decrease the amount of stress they are feeling.

Unfortunately, this book cannot offer any magical answers, but it does provide techniques to help clients feel much better by managing stress in their lives.

What Is Stress?

Stress can be defined as the physiological and psychological response to change. Stress occurs in our daily lives and can be exacerbated during times of change.

Understanding how human beings respond to stress, both physiologically and psychologically, can help TRSs become more effective therapists. First and foremost, it is important to understand that there are a variety of reasons why clients experience stress. As stated earlier, clients are often in an acute state of stress. Assisting them in coming to terms with their physical or health problem(s) is our primary goal. When clients experience negative feelings, they may feel mental or physical discomfort. Even when a client's health situation has stabilized, if he or she continues to view the situation as stressful, his or her body will continue to respond to that perceived stress.

In 1925 Hans Seyle, an Austrian-Canadian physician, began to research the causes of stress. He believed that a body reacts to stress the same way it reacts to danger by going through various biochemical changes, which he called the general adaptation syndrome (GAS; see Figure 1.1, p. 2).

Seyle's general adaptation syndrome is defined as the total organism's nonspecific response to stress. The response occurs in three stages:

1. *Alarm reaction* in which the body recognizes the stressor and the pituitary-adrenocortical system responds by producing the hormones essential for either fight or flight. In this stage the heart rate increases, blood sugar is elevated, pupils dilate, and digestion slows.

2. *Resistance* or *adaptive stage* where the body begins to repair the effect of arousal. Acute stress symptoms diminish or disappear. If, however, the stress continues, adaptation fails in its attempt to maintain the defense.

3. *Exhaustion stage* occurs when the body can no longer respond to the stress. As a consequence, one or several of a great variety of diseases (e.g., emotional disturbances, cardiovascular and renal disease, certain asthmas) may develop. (Seyle, 1984)

In the first stage, the autonomic nervous system activates. The body assumes a fight-or-flight reaction, whereby the heartbeat accelerates, blood pressure levels elevate, more blood flows to the muscles, and the lungs dilate to increase respiratory effort. In the second phase, known as the resistance phase, the body continues to fight the stress even though the effects of the fight-or-flight response is no longer present. This can affect both the body's immune and neuroendocrine systems. In the final stage, exhaustion, the body becomes weakened and energy is depleted from prolonged exposure to the stressor.

```
                          STRESSFUL EVENTS
```

| • Hypothalamus
• Pituitary
(located in the brain) | | • Alarm
• Mobilization
• Adaptation | • Fight-or-flight
behavior |

| • Autonomic
nervous system | • Adrenal Glands
Cortex (corticoids)
Medulla (ACTH) | • Prolonged
adaptation | • Temporary
adaptation |

| • Overall body
effects | • Thymus | • Exhaustion
• Symptomatology
• Illness | • Return to normal
equilibrium |

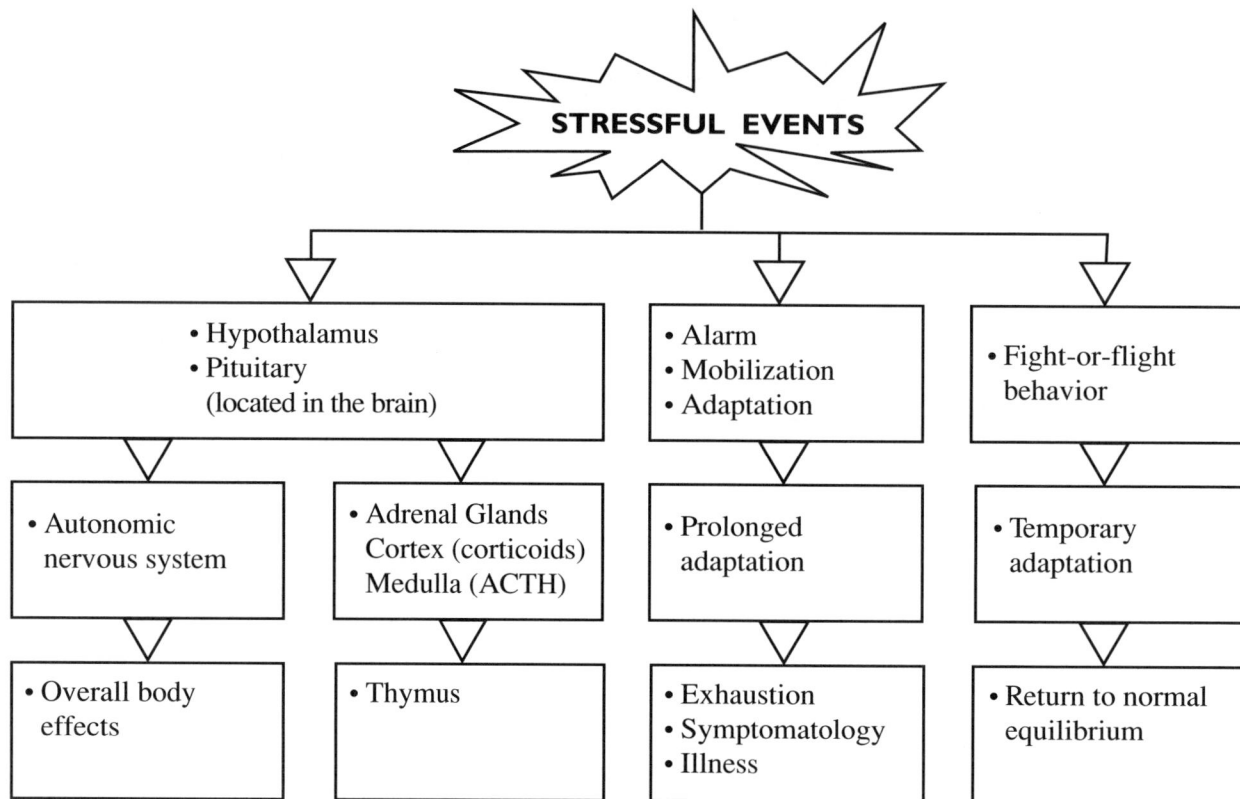

Figure 1.1 Physiological response to stress and Seyle's general adaptation syndrome

The Brain's Response to Acute Stress

In response to stress, the brain activates the hypothalamic-pituitary-adrenal (HPA) system. The HPA system triggers the production of steroid hormones. The anterior portion of the pituitary gland is influenced by the hypothalamus and causes the adrenal cortex to release hormones into the bloodstream. One of the groups of hormones, the glucocorticoids, increases the amount of blood sugar in the body which is trying to adapt to the perceived stress. By releasing more blood sugar, the body has more energy and it facilitates blood circulation. On the downside, however, these hormones reduce resistance to infection and reduce the body's ability to repair tissue damage.

During an acute response to stress, the brain releases neurotransmitters such as dopamine, norepinephrine, and epinephrine (also called adrenaline). The neurotransmitters activate an area inside the brain called the *amygdala*. This in turn triggers an emotional response to the stressful event which can result in problems with short-term memory, concentration, inhibition, and rational response.

The human body is very intricate. Each and every day, the body reacts to a variety of stressors. Each body wants to maintain an equilibrium, known as homeostasis. In other words, homeostasis is the body's thermostat. In response to stress, or even perceived stress, the body tries to adapt by going through numerous physiological and psychological changes. It tries to maintain balance, but because it feels under attack it fights back in ways which may result in one feeling worse instead of better. Even the perception of feeling stressed can result in the body going into overdrive. Stress affects the central nervous system, adrenal system, and cardiovascular system. These effects can result in headaches, indigestion, depression, insomnia, and a host of other stress-related symptoms.

Acute Stress Disorder and Posttraumatic Stress Disorder

According to the *Diagnostic and Statistical Manual of Mental Disorders IV* (*DSM-IV*), "the essential feature of acute stress disorder is the development of characteristic anxiety, dissociative and other symptoms that occurs within one month after exposure to an extreme traumatic event." Symptoms of acute stress disorder include: a subjective sense of numbing, detachment or absence of emotional responsiveness, a reduction in awareness of one's surroundings (e.g., "being in a daze"), derealization, depersonalization, and/or dissociative amnesia (i.e., inability to recall an important aspect of trauma).

According to the *DSM-IV*, posttraumatic stress disorder (PTSD) is "the development of characteristic symptoms following exposure to an extreme stressor involving direct-person experience of an event that involves actual or threatened death or serious injury, or threat to one's physical integrity." Symptoms of PTSD include: difficulty falling or staying asleep, irritability or outbursts of anger, difficulty concentrating, hypervigilance, and/or exaggerated startle response.

The role of the TRS is to work with the treatment team to determine whether the client meets the criteria for either acute stress disorder or posttraumatic stress disorder. Once this determination has been made, the appropriate intervention can be implemented. Teaching stress reduction techniques is a critical component of working with individuals with these diagnoses.

Chronic Stress

Although not listed in the *DSM-IV* as an Axis-I diagnosis, many clients experience chronic stress. It can occur when there appears to be no solution to a problem. Individuals who are medically compromised, have mental health problems, or have experienced personal changes in living and work situations often feel as if they are living with unrelenting stress. Chronic stress can also occur when stressors accumulate. As long as the mind perceives a threat, the body remains in a state of crisis. If the stress response remains aroused, the body may not recover its sense of equilibrium. A prolonged stress response may worsen preexisting health problems. Furthermore, as the body continues to release and deplete the neurotransmitter norepinephrine, depression may result.

Related Risk Factors

Stressful life situations are a way of life. Some situations increase susceptibility to stress. How someone responds to a stressor, however, can be influenced by such factors as:

- the family environment,
- personality traits,
- financial status,
- living in an urban area,
- isolation from others,
- age (e.g., the elderly, adolescents),
- education level,
- employment status (e.g., unemployed, overworked), and
- whether or not one has health insurance.

Signs and Symptoms

Stress affects an individual's cognitive, physical, emotional, and behavioral functioning in many ways. Some signs and symptoms include:

Related Cognitive Symptoms

- Forgetfulness
- Inability to concentrate
- Disorganized thought processes
- Preoccupation
- Lack of attention to detail
- Blocking
- Blurred vision
- Negative self-talk
- Decreased coordination
- Slowed psychomotor responses

Related Physical Indicators

- Increased heart rate
- Elevated blood pressure
- Tightness of chest, neck, jaw, and back muscles
- Shallow breathing
- Insomnia or fatigue
- Headaches
- Stomach upset (e.g., diarrhea, constipation)
- Chronic pain
- Urinary tract problems
- Immune system compromised
- Susceptible to minor illnesses

Related Emotional Indicators

- Depression
- Withdrawal
- Anxiety
- Decreased self-esteem
- Diminished interests

- Restlessness
- Nightmares
- Impatience
- Obsessive thinking
- Crying
- Helplessness
- Isolation from others

Behavioral Symptoms

- Impatience
- Compulsive behavior
- Hostility/anger
- Withdrawal
- Overeating, smoking, substance abuse
- Loss of appetite
- Aggressive behavior
- Isolation
- Prone to accidents

The Relaxation Response

Whereas humans often have little to no control over the stressors of modern-day living, they do have control over how they allow themselves to react to stressors and control over how they choose alternative activities which will increase their sense of well-being rather than diminish it.

Herbert Benson, a Harvard trained and affiliated physician, in his pivotal book *The Relaxation Response* (1975) felt that by using simple meditative techniques an individual could successfully reverse the fight-or-flight response. Benson believes that the body can calm itself. By activating the relaxation response, the body is able to:

- decrease its heart rate,
- decrease blood pressure,
- decrease muscle tension,
- decrease breathing rate, and
- decrease mental arousal.

Such changes in the body can literally reverse the negative ramifications of stress. The relaxation response also assists in allowing the individual to view himself or herself as having some sort of control over the environment.

The relaxation response can be evoked through the stress management techniques outlined in this book. By understanding the concept of the relaxation response, TRSs can assist their clients in increasing their sense of well-being. (See Figure 1.2)

Flow

When an individual is completely immersed in an activity, there is no room in his or her awareness to worry, feel "stressed out," or otherwise deal with conflict or life's difficulties. The flow experience occurs when outside distractions become erased by participation in an activity or event which captures a person's body, mind, and soul. Mihaly Csikszentmihalyi, in his instrumental book, *Flow: The Psychology of Optimal Experience* (1990) describes such activities as skiing, playing a game, the runners' high, or even conversing with a friend as "flow" experiences. TRSs often use the theory of flow in their programming. When conducting a stress management group, it is important to educate your clients about the flow experience. By providing clients with the opportunity to participate in a number of stress reduction activities and addressing the fact that they have let go of their issues/problems, clients can reenter this state of well-being during the group activity as well as on their own after treatment.

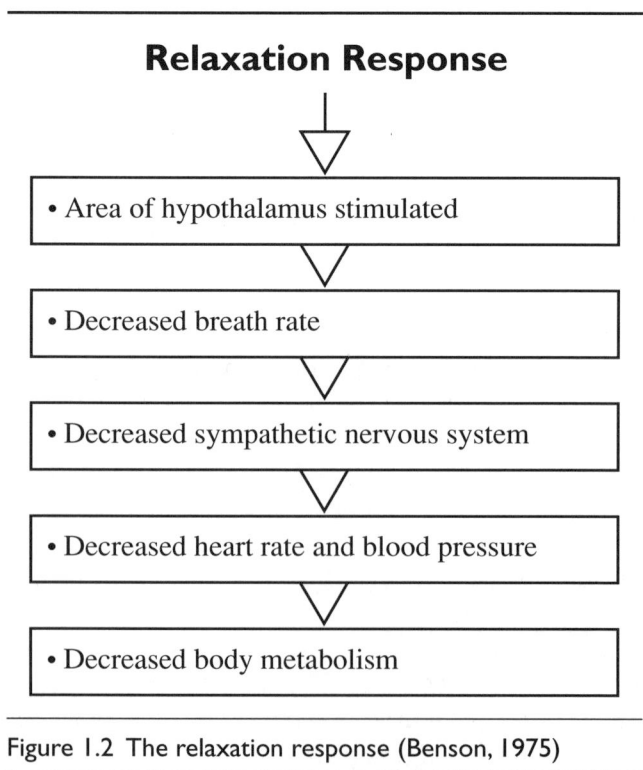

Relaxation Response

```
        Relaxation Response
               |
               ▽
  ┌────────────────────────────────────┐
  │ • Area of hypothalamus stimulated  │
  └────────────────────────────────────┘
               ▽
  ┌────────────────────────────────────┐
  │ • Decreased breath rate            │
  └────────────────────────────────────┘
               ▽
  ┌────────────────────────────────────┐
  │ • Decreased sympathetic nervous system │
  └────────────────────────────────────┘
               ▽
  ┌────────────────────────────────────┐
  │ • Decreased heart rate and blood pressure │
  └────────────────────────────────────┘
               ▽
  ┌────────────────────────────────────┐
  │ • Decreased body metabolism        │
  └────────────────────────────────────┘
```

Figure 1.2 The relaxation response (Benson, 1975)

Locus of Control

Does an individual have control over his or her environment? This is an age-old question which does not have a ready answer. Natural disasters, political upheaval, even traffic and environmental noise are beyond the control of an individual. When people are in crisis, they often report feeling helpless and out of control. To a certain extent, perception of control varies from one individual to another. In regard to stress management, people who express a high sense of internal locus of control report feeling less stress. The role of the TRSs during stress management groups, therefore, is to educate clients that while they may not have control over their health problems, life events, and so forth, they do have control over choosing activities which will help them decrease the amount of stress they are experiencing and increase their sense of locus of control.

The Role of the TRS in Stress Management

TRSs wear many hats. As the team member who is most likely to breathe life into a program, the TRS helps the client make the necessary life changes he or she needs to make. TRSs laugh and cry and share the most intimate moments with their clients. The TRS can teach stress management techniques to a variety of populations, including people with physical challenges, people with psychiatric illness, people with substance addiction(s), people with developmental disabilities, and people who are experiencing transitional stress, such as adolescents and the elderly.

People With Physical Challenges

TRSs often work with people who are physically challenged. A number of circumstances can compromise an individual's physical abilities. Some individuals have experienced a traumatic event such as an accident, burn, or assault. Disease-related conditions such as a stroke, diabetes, or multiple sclerosis impair one's ability to move.

People with physical challenges are often bewildered by their circumstances. Where once they walked and enjoyed life without restrictions, they now have to come to terms with many adjustments. The impact on their lives is astounding. Learning stress management techniques is critical. TRSs are trained *to see the abilities of their clients rather than their disabilities.*

It is important when treating people with physical challenges to continue to emphasize abilities over disabilities. Like the little train engine that said "I think I can…I know I can," TRSs must encourage clients to make adjustments and to pursue an active lifestyle. Stress management methods, such as meditation, relaxation exercises, and deep-breathing techniques are within most clients' abilities and can be helpful to people with physical challenges.

Other conditions, such as cancer, heart disease, lupus, and scleroderma, can also compromise an individual's physical abilities. Again, the amount of stress related to acute or chronic stages of any illnesses can be enormous. For these individuals, learning new stress management techniques can help them improve their own quality of life and reenter life in the community.

People With Mental Illness

People with mental illness often suffer from mood and cognition problems. TRSs who work in the mental health field often work with people who are schizophrenic, bipolar, or suffer from a major depressive disorder.

People with schizophrenia often have thought-process problems and can be very disorganized in their thinking. It is important to provide information to people with schizophrenia in a clear, concise manner. While most people with schizophrenia may have a full physical range of motion, following simple directions may be difficult, and the confusion in which they live can play havoc on their ability to deal with stress.

Bipolar disorder also affects an individual's ability to think clearly. With mood fluctuations being a major aspect of this illness, the TRS must provide equal measures of structure and caring.

Depression is one of the leading illnesses worldwide. When an individual is in the midst of a major depressive episode, even simple tasks seem overwhelming. These individuals feel very sad and lonely and have difficulty expressing their thoughts and feelings. Their whole system has slowed down. Learning stress management techniques can help individuals with depression feel that they have more control over their lives and assists them in subduing some of their feelings of hopelessness.

People With Substance Addictions

Just like the riddle: "What came first, the chicken or the egg?" it's difficult to determine whether people with substance addictions use substances to deal with stress or whether the prolonged use of drugs and/or alcohol causes stress. Either way, once people with substance addictions have become sober, they will find that their perception about stress has changed.

The bad news is that addictive chemicals taken alter the body's functioning. People with substance addictions must learn how to manage stress without chemicals. The good news is—once they start practicing sober stress management techniques—they are going to feel a lot better.

People With Developmental Disabilities

The term *developmental disability* is primarily used to describe individuals who have either a significant intellectual and/or social impairment that has limited their development since birth or an early age. In addition to intellectual limitations, individuals with developmental disabilities may have problems with chronic medical conditions and physical disabilities as well.

Individuals who are developmentally delayed must deal with numerous issues. Mental retardation can impair a person's ability to learn. People with mental retardation are often quite concrete in their thinking process and are delayed in achieving developmental skills such as walking, feeding, talking, and dressing. Social skills problems and low self-esteem are issues most individuals with developmental disabilities must face. Stress management techniques for this population should be tailored to the individual's ability to process new information. Lesson plans need to be simplified, and goals need to be reachable.

Adolescents

Adolescents are at a crossroad. With one foot still in childhood and the other stepping into adulthood, it's often a difficult adjustment. Teens who seek out treatment usually have experienced unresolved family issues, problems in school, and mood fluctuations. Stress management is critical for adolescents. They have too much energy and have not yet learned how to deal with stress. Physical activities such as tai chi, martial arts, and yoga; time management; and assertion training have been used successfully with adolescents.

Aging Populations

TRSs are instrumental in helping seniors come to grips with the concerns that they face. Most seniors have

sustained a tremendous amount of loss. Some have lost their lifelong spouse or partner and/or are dealing with their own physical or mental decline. The world around them is moving quickly, yet their lives seem to be standing still. Teaching stress management techniques to the elderly is critical. Physical activities like yoga can be simplified so that seniors can achieve a feeling of success. Playing music from the seniors' earlier days while teaching them relaxation techniques can give them a sense of familiarity.

Working with clients who have Alzheimer's disease can be challenging. The importance of providing relaxation activities cannot be overlooked. Simple, familiar activities, such as rolling yarn or folding clothing, can decrease an individual's level of anxiety. When programming for people with dementia, TRSs must be sure to simplify instructions.

To Change or Not To Change?

TRSs often work as agents of change for their clients, yet it is critical to understand that some clients may resist change. James Prochaska, John Norcross, and Carlo DiClemente documented in their book *Changing for Good* (1994) that people will make changes when they are ready, willing, and able. Prochaska, Norcross, and DiClemente identified six stages of change: precontemplation, contemplation, preparation, action, maintenance, and relapse/recycle. The client's location in this cycle will determine his or her willingness to change his or her behavior (see Figure 1.3).

TRSs can assign appropriate groups once they have assessed the client's level of willingness to change. Recommendations for types of groups follow.

Precontemplation

During this stage, the client does not perceive himself or herself as having a problem. Psychoeducational classes are recommended at this stage to provide relevant information about the benefits of change. Confrontation of the client is not recommended at this stage.

Contemplation

Clients during this stage are beginning to recognize that change is necessary. In a push-pull mode the clients may well change their mind as they grapple with issues regarding changing a behavior or circumstance. Psy-

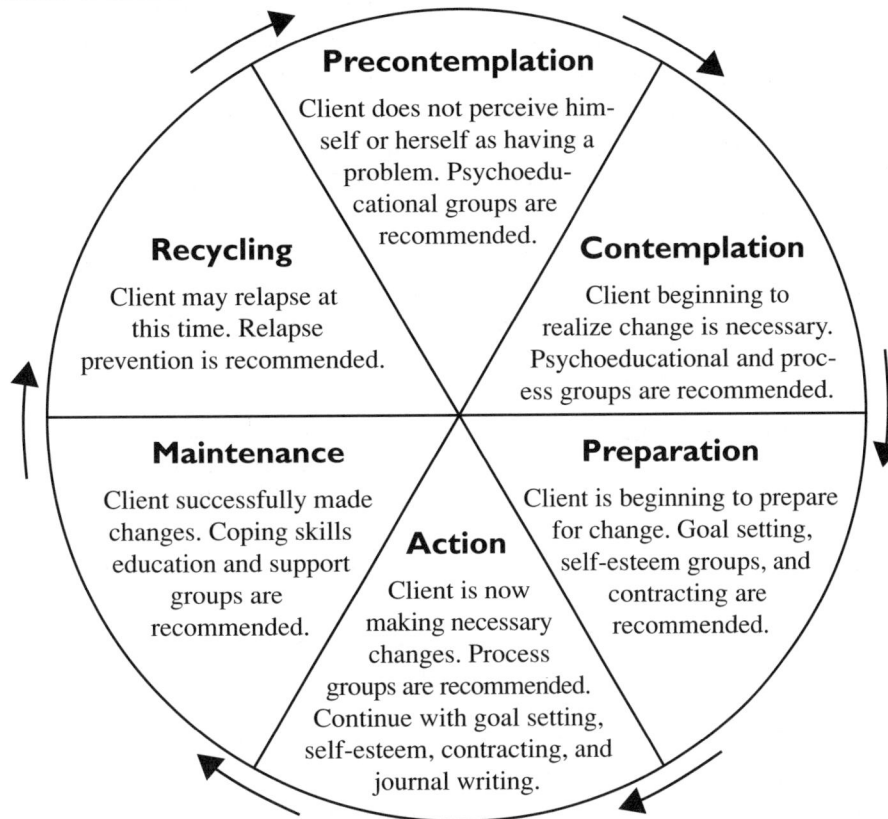

Precontemplation
Client does not perceive himself or herself as having a problem. Psychoeducational groups are recommended.

Contemplation
Client beginning to realize change is necessary. Psychoeducational and process groups are recommended.

Recycling
Client may relapse at this time. Relapse prevention is recommended.

Preparation
Client is beginning to prepare for change. Goal setting, self-esteem groups, and contracting are recommended.

Maintenance
Client successfully made changes. Coping skills education and support groups are recommended.

Action
Client is now making necessary changes. Process groups are recommended. Continue with goal setting, self-esteem, contracting, and journal writing.

Figure 1.3 The cycle of change (Prochaska & Norcross, 1975)

choeducational and process groups should be utilized at this time.

Preparation

During this stage, the client is beginning to prepare for change. Treatment groups utilizing goal setting, self-esteem, and contracting are recommended at this stage of change.

Action

The client is now in the process of making the necessary changes he or she has decided to make. The TRS should continue to work with the client on goal setting, self-esteem building, and contracting. Journal writing and process groups are also recommended at this stage.

Maintenance

At this level of change, the clients have begun a journey in which they are beginning to recover from the life circumstances which caused their pain. The TRS needs to teach the client coping skills during this stage of change to enhance their choice to change their lifestyles. Support group involvement is recommended at this time.

Relapse/Recycling

It is not uncommon for people to relapse after making necessary changes. At this point in treatment, the TRS should work with the client to determine the risk factors and triggers which can lead to a relapse.

Emotional Stages of Change

Elisabeth Kubler-Ross, in her book *On Death and Dying* (1969) wrote about the emotional stages that people with terminal illness often experience. Kubler-Ross' stages have been used to explain the emotional states that people experience when confronted with a traumatic physical, mental, or life event as well.

TRSs can gain an understanding of their client's current emotional state by understanding these emotional stages: denial, anger, bargaining, depression, and acceptance.

Denial

During this stage, an individual has difficulty accepting that they have a problem or are sick. Providing support is recommended at this stage although with people who abuse substances, an intervention is sometimes used to break down the person's defenses.

Anger

After experiencing denial, individuals often become angry and form a "Why me?" mentality. Support is recommended at this emotional stage. Using a confrontational approach is contraindicated.

Bargaining

Individuals at this emotional stage will try to make bargains with themselves and others, and even to God. Bargaining is a form of postponing the inevitable. A client at this stage may exhibit "good behavior" with the hope that somehow the situation will pass. TRSs may want to use a cognitive approach when treating a client at this stage.

Depression

During this stage, the individual is beginning to recognize the severity of his or her situation which often results in depression. Treatment intervention should include support and recognition of the client's sadness or loss. A "cheer up" stance may exacerbate the client's depression, however.

Acceptance

After the journey through the first four stages, an individual can get to a point where he or she accepts the reality of their situation. Process groups should be provided at this stage. If possible, support group participation is recommended.

In conclusion, the Alcoholics Anonymous slogan, "Today is the first day of the rest of your life" says it all. As TRSs, it is our mission to help clients live the best possible life that they can. We teach hope. We give clients a chance to improve their quality of life. When clients begin to look at their stress-related issues and begin to make changes, we are doing our job.

Self-Assessments

Prior to beginning a stress management program with a client, gathering a baseline assessment regarding each client's perception of his or her current stress level is recommended. This can be achieved by providing the client with a self-assessment tool. These self-assessments (beginning on p. 10) can help clients identify their current stressors; the ways in which stress affects them physically, mentally, and spiritually; and defines some "stress busters" they may find useful.

The TRS should ask each client to complete a self-assessment. This will help the TRS to begin a dialogue about stress management with the client. Additionally, it will help the TRS to get an idea about the activities which are best-suited for each client.

Assessments can be completed either individually or in a group setting. The Consequences of Stress Self-Assessment is designed for clients who have full cognition and are interested in an in-depth self-analysis of common stress management issues.

Several populations are taken into account in the assessments that follow. Self-assessments are provided for:

- all populations (SAGP),
- adolescents (SAAY),
- people with mental health issues (SAMH),
- people with substance abuse issues (SASB),
- people who are physically challenged (SAPH), and
- people who are aging (SAOA).

These stress indicator checklists can help clients determine their physical and mental symptoms of stress. The stress buster checklist will give clients an opportunity to become familiar with some stress reduction activities. The pictorial self-assessments (SAPIC) use illustrations or photographs to help TRSs communicate with clients whose verbal skills or cognitive abilities are limited.

The Stress Meter

The stress meter (page 25) provides clients with a visual aid to indicate a "before" and "after" score of their individual stress levels. Ask clients to fill in the box which represents their current level of stress prior to the stress management exercise, and repeat this request after completing the exercise.

Pulse

Clients can also measure their heartbeat before and after an stress management exercise to help them determine the effectiveness of the exercise.

Two simple methods can be used to check one's heart rate. One method checks the pulse at the wrist (i.e., radial pulse). The other is at the neck (i.e., carotid pulse). For a radial pulse check, have the client use the tips of his or her index and middle fingers. The radial artery can be found on the thumb side of either wrist. It lies just a little below the base of the thumb. The pulsing artery will be felt when the fingers are in the right place.

The carotid pulse check can be taken in the place just below the jaw along the windpipe and along the throat. Suggest that the client use his or her first and middle fingers and to press gently just until they can feel the pulse.

Use a digital watch or the second hand on a traditional watch to time the client's pulse for six seconds while they count, then multiply the count by ten.

References

American Psychological Association (1994). *Diagnostic and statistical manual of mental disorders (4th ed.)*. Washington, DC: Author.

Benson, H. (1975). *The relaxation response*. New York, NY: William Morrow and Co.

Csikszentmihalyi, M. (1990). *Finding flow: The psychology of engagement with everyday life*. New York, NY: Basic Books.

Kubler-Ross, E. (1969). *On death and dying*. New York, NY: Macmillian Publishing Co.

Prochaska, J., Norcross, J., and DiClemente. (1994). *Changing for good*. New York, NY: William Morrow and Co.

Seyle, H. (1984). *The stress of life (Rev. ed.)*. New York, NY: McGraw-Hill.

Consequences of Stress Self-Assessment

Instructions: Many life situations can result in increased stress. Since you have been sick or injured, you are more than likely experiencing a tremendous amount of stress. Take a moment to complete this assessment.

Check off the stressful situations which have occurred during the past three years:

❐ Depression

❐ Loneliness

❐ Substance abuse

❐ Problems in the workplace

❐ Family problems

❐ Spouse or partner being under stress

❐ Recent death of someone close to you

❐ Lack of motivation

❐ Problems with healthcare

❐ Not enough time for yourself

❐ Weight gain or loss

❐ Legal problems

❐ Financial problems

❐ Unable to work

❐ Moving

❐ Medication problems

❐ Losing contact with family or friend

❐ Starting a new relationship

❐ Divorce or separation

❐ Getting back together with a partner or spouse

❐ Going back to school

❐ Retirement

❐ Beginning and/or staying sober

❐ Decrease in recreation involvement

❐ Change in sleeping habits

❐ Difficulty finding good help

❐ Being hospitalized

❐ Living in a hospital environment

❐ Dealing with insurance companies

❐ Difficulty with getting dressed, showered, etc.

❐ Difficulty with getting shopping done

❐ Unable to drive

❐ Lack of public transportation

❐ Unable to pursue former recreational interests

❐ Not feeling well

❐ Fatigue

Now take some time to score your test.

If you scored between 0–12:
You have some stress in your life but the amount of stress is manageable. You may still want to look at the ways in which stress interferes with your life and decide on a stress management regime that will suit you.

If you scored between 13–24:
You are experiencing a moderate amount of stress and it's strongly recommended that you make some lifestyle changes. The consequences of your medical problems have caught up with you. It may take some time to sort things out. Speak to a therapist, family members and/or friends about the changes you plan to make. In a Catch-22 situation, you have a lot of stressors in your life which can cause more stress. This is why a book like this one is so important in your recovery. By identifying your stressors, recognizing how they have affected you mentally and physically and then learning stress management techniques, you will begin to feel a lot better.

If you scored 25–36:
You have experienced a number of very stressful life events and you will need to make some very important changes in your life. It is critical that you begin to develop a strong support network. Finding a support group will help you recognize that you are not alone. People who have also had your problems are the best source for giving you support and guidance A therapist can also help you sort out what has happened to you. Over a period of time, you can begin to become more actively involved with your friends and family members.

You are going to feel overwhelmed at times. Try to remember to live in the moment. Schedule a time each day where you allow yourself to become worry-free. Begin a stress management program which includes an activity which will help you feel more relaxed such as breathing exercises, meditation, or massage.

Don't get stuck in a rut where you think that your life will never be okay. Many of my clients have gone on after treatment to lead happy and fulfilling lives. So can you!

Effects of Stress on Your Mind, Body, and Soul

This survey will help you identify how stress is manifested in your mind, body and soul. Again, check off each box which pertains to your life in the last three years.

Part A—Your Mind
- ❐ I am depressed a lot of the time.
- ❐ I often feel anxious.
- ❐ I often have paranoid thoughts.
- ❐ I feel tense most of the time.
- ❐ I often feel hopeless.
- ❐ Sometimes I see things that are not really there.
- ❐ I often have racing thoughts.
- ❐ I find it difficult to concentrate.
- ❐ I often have difficulty expressing my thoughts and feelings.

Part B—Your Body
- ❐ I often get headaches.
- ❐ I often have stomach problems like diarrhea and indigestion.
- ❐ I often have many aches and pains.
- ❐ I often feel dehydrated.

- ❐ I often eat too much.
- ❐ I often have trouble sleeping.
- ❐ I feel tense much of the time.
- ❐ I often lose my appetite.
- ❐ I feel unstable physically.
- ❐ I frequently feel fatigued.
- ❐ I generally feel unwell.
- ❐ I often clench my fists.
- ❐ My neck is often stiff.

Part C—The Soul
- ❐ I often feel hopeless.
- ❐ I frequently feel disconnected from people, places, and things.
- ❐ I have not developed a spiritual life.
- ❐ I don't have a clue about the meaning of life.
- ❐ I don't take time to appreciate nature.

You don't need to score this survey, but you may want to take some time to review it. By recognizing where you are most vulnerable in regards to stress, you can start making the necessary changes toward a healthier lifestyle.
If you had a number of "mind" complaints:

Depression is very common when you have lived through a traumatic medical problem. You may have an underlying depression which never was treated. Additionally, some of your medication can negatively affect your brain chemistry resulting in a depressive episode. Speak to your doctor about the medications you are taking and be sure to read all of the literature about your medications. A pharmacist can also help you determine whether your depression is a result of the medications you are on. Furthermore, if you have experienced a lot of negative consequences, such as losing a job, spouse or friends because of your medical problems, you may be experiencing a situational depression. Seeking out a psychotherapist may be a very good idea. A therapist can help you sort out your feelings and emotions.
If you had a number of physical complaints:

It would be an excellent idea to make an appointment with your doctor. Ask for a thorough physical. Even if your doctor gives you a clean bill of health, you may have a number of psychosomatic symptoms. This is not unusual. Because or your medical problems, you may experience a heightened awareness of your body, even those parts of your body which are not affected by your physical problems. Many of my clients said that once they recognized which part of their body was feeling out of whack, they felt better by finding stress management techniques which worked for their specific complaints. As you begin your own stress management program you will become more aware of your body and begin to respect it.
If you have a number of "soul" complaints:

First and foremost, getting sick or sustaining an injury directly affects the spirit. Don't despair. From your pain and grief you can rise anew. You may want to spend time with your priest, minister, rabbi or spiritual advisor. Spiritual renewal is an important part of the recovery process. Give yourself time to renew your spirit. Remember, your soul has the capacity to heal.

Stress Busters

Check off the activities you'd like to pursue to help decrease your stress level:

- ❐ Yoga
- ❐ Meditation
- ❐ Deep breathing exercises
- ❐ Music
- ❐ Aromatherapy
- ❐ Acupuncture/Acupressure
- ❐ Creative visualization
- ❐ Exercise
- ❐ Tai chi
- ❐ Taking walks
- ❐ Reading
- ❐ Art work
- ❐ Sauna
- ❐ Steam bath
- ❐ Baths
- ❐ Progressive relaxation
- ❐ Biofeedback
- ❐ Spiritual retreats
- ❐ Nature

Stress Test Self-Assessment

Check all the stressors that apply to you.

❒ A recent illness

❒ A divorce, separation or break-up

❒ Family problems

❒ Spouse or partner under stress or ill

❒ Recent death of a loved one

❒ Loneliness

❒ Moving to a new location

❒ Weight gain or loss

❒ Being in debt

❒ Feeling overwhelmed

❒ Relationship problems

❒ Worrying about our society

❒ Unemployed

❒ New job

❒ Job stress/problems

❒ Anniversary of a beloved's death

❒ Money issues

❒ Pregnancy

❒ Dealing with the medical establishment

❒ Substance abuse problems

❒ Substance abuse problems of family member or friend

❒ Starting a new relationship

❒ Change in a family member's health

❒ Going back to school

❒ Change in financial status

❒ Falling in love

❒ Becoming or staying sober

❒ Sleeping problems

❒ Lack of education

❒ Being in school

❒ Worrying a lot

❒ Wanting to eat but on a diet

❒ Someone telling you what to do

❒ Threat of war

❒ Violence in neighborhood

❒ Lack of recreation involvement

❒ Boredom

❒ Depression

❒ Anxiety

❒ Mental health issues

❒ Unresolved family issues

❒ Change in living situation

❒ Making new friends

❒ Needing to borrow money

❒ Anger issues

❒ Not enough time

❒ Too much time

❒ Waiting in a long line

❒ Being hospitalized

❒ Legal problems

❒ Friend or family member with mental health problem

❒ Friend or family member with financial problems

❒ Transportation problems

❒ Going back to work

❒ Holidays

❒ Neighbors are too loud

❒ Medication issues

❒ Sexual problems

❒ Motivation problems

❒ Unable to relax

❒ Feeling isolated

❒ Worrying about appearance

Number of boxes checked _____

0–20   Mild Stress
21–40 Moderate Stress
41–60 Extreme Stress

Form SAGP

Stress Test Self-Assessment

Check all the stressors that apply to you.

❐ A recent illness
❐ Your parents have divorced or separated
❐ Family problems
❐ Family member under stress or ill
❐ Recent death of a loved one
❐ Loneliness
❐ Moving to a new location
❐ Starting at a new school
❐ Weight gain or loss
❐ Poor grades
❐ New job
❐ School stress/problems
❐ Money issues
❐ Pregnancy
❐ Social problems at school
❐ Dropped out of school
❐ Substance abuse problems
❐ Anniversary of a friend or family member's death
❐ Substance abuse problems of family member or friend
❐ Starting a new relationship
❐ Going back to school
❐ Parents have financial problems
❐ Parents have marital problems
❐ Falling in love
❐ Becoming or staying sober
❐ Sleeping problems
❐ Problems getting along with brother or sister
❐ Dealing with stepfamily members

❐ Worrying a lot
❐ Wanting to eat but on a diet
❐ Dealing with social service agency
❐ Someone telling you what to do
❐ Threat of war
❐ Violence in neighborhood
❐ Lack of recreation involvement
❐ Boredom
❐ Depression
❐ Anxiety
❐ Mental health issues
❐ Unresolved family issues
❐ Change in living situation
❐ Making new friends
❐ Anger issues
❐ Not enough time
❐ Too much time
❐ Waiting in a long line
❐ Being hospitalized
❐ Legal problems
❐ Getting into verbal fights with friends
❐ Getting into physical fights with friends
❐ Transportation problems
❐ Having to take medications
❐ Holidays
❐ Neighbors are too loud
❐ Looking for a job
❐ Job problems
❐ Motivation problems
❐ Unable to relax

Number of boxes checked _____

0–20 Mild Stress
21–40 Moderate Stress
41–60 Extreme Stress

Form SAAY

Stress Test Self-Assessment

Check all the stressors that apply to you.

❐ A recent illness

❐ A divorce, separation, or break-up

❐ Family problems

❐ Spouse or partner under stress or ill

❐ Recent death of a loved one

❐ Loneliness

❐ Moving to a new location

❐ Weight gain or loss

❐ Unemployed

❐ New job

❐ Job stress/problems

❐ Anniversary of a beloved's death

❐ Money issues

❐ Pregnancy

❐ Dealing with the medical establishment

❐ Substance abuse problems

❐ Substance abuse problems of family member or friend

❐ Starting a new relationship

❐ Change in a family member's health

❐ Going back to school

❐ Homelessness

❐ Change in financial status

❐ Falling in love

❐ Becoming or staying sober

❐ Sleeping problems

❐ Lack of education

❐ Being in school

❐ Worrying a lot

❐ Wanting to eat but on a diet

❐ Someone telling you what to do

❐ Threat of war

❐ Violence in neighborhood

❐ Lack of recreation involvement

❐ Boredom

❐ Depression

❐ Anxiety

❐ Dealing with social service agencies

❐ Getting or staying on SSI

❐ Unresolved family issues

❐ Change in living situation

❐ Making new friends

❐ Needing to borrow money

❐ Anger issues

❐ Not enough time

❐ Too much time

❐ Waiting in a long line

❐ Being hospitalized

❐ Legal problems

❐ Friend or family member with mental health problem

❐ Friend or family member with financial problems

❐ Transportation problems

❐ Going back to work

❐ Holidays

❐ Neighbors are too loud

❐ Medication issues

❐ Sexual problems

❐ Worrying about appearance

❐ Feeling isolated

❐ Motivation problems

❐ Unable to relax

Number of boxes checked _____

    0–20 Mild Stress
    21–40 Moderate Stress
    41–60 Extreme Stress

Form SAMH

Stress Test Self-Assessment

Check all the stressors that apply to you.

- ❏ A recent hospitalization
- ❏ A divorce, separation, or break-up
- ❏ Family problems
- ❏ Spouse or partner under stress or ill
- ❏ Recent death of a loved one
- ❏ Loneliness
- ❏ Moving to a new location
- ❏ Weight gain or loss
- ❏ Unemployment
- ❏ New job
- ❏ Job stress/problems
- ❏ Anniversary of a beloved's death
- ❏ Money issues
- ❏ Pregnancy
- ❏ Dealing with the medical establishment
- ❏ Substance abuse problems
- ❏ Substance abuse problems of family member or friend
- ❏ Starting a new relationship
- ❏ Change in a family member's health
- ❏ Have been jailed for a substance abuse problem
- ❏ Homelessness
- ❏ Change in financial status
- ❏ Charged with a DUI
- ❏ Becoming or staying sober
- ❏ Sleeping problems
- ❏ Lack of education
- ❏ Problems at school
- ❏ Worrying a lot
- ❏ Liver disease
- ❏ Someone telling you what to do

- ❏ History of seizures
- ❏ Violence in neighborhood
- ❏ Lack of recreation involvement
- ❏ Boredom
- ❏ Depression
- ❏ Anxiety
- ❏ Dealing with social service agencies
- ❏ Getting or staying on SSI
- ❏ Unresolved family issues
- ❏ Change in living situation
- ❏ Friends all use drugs or alcohol
- ❏ Needing to borrow money
- ❏ Anger issues
- ❏ Not enough time
- ❏ Too much time
- ❏ History of stroke
- ❏ Being hospitalized
- ❏ Legal problems
- ❏ Friend or family member with mental health problem
- ❏ Friend or family member with financial problems
- ❏ Transportation problems
- ❏ Going back to work
- ❏ Holidays
- ❏ Delirium tremens
- ❏ Medication issues
- ❏ Sexual problems
- ❏ Worrying about appearance
- ❏ Feeling isolated
- ❏ Motivational problems
- ❏ Got the shakes

Number of boxes checked _____

- 0–20   Mild Stress
- 21–40 Moderate Stress
- 41–60 Extreme Stress

Stress Test Self-Assessment

Check all the stressors that apply to you.

❒ A recent illness
❒ A recent injury/accident
❒ A divorce, separation, or break-up
❒ Family problems
❒ Spouse or partner under stress or ill
❒ Recent death of a loved one
❒ Loneliness
❒ Moving to a new location
❒ Weight gain or loss
❒ Unemployed
❒ New job
❒ Job stress/problems
❒ Anniversary of a beloved's death
❒ Money issues
❒ Pregnancy
❒ Dealing with the medical establishment
❒ Substance abuse problems
❒ Substance abuse problems of family member or friend
❒ Starting a new relationship
❒ Change in a family member's health
❒ Going back to school
❒ Physical pain or discomfort
❒ Change in financial status
❒ Falling in love
❒ Becoming or staying sober
❒ Sleeping problems
❒ Lack of education
❒ Being in school
❒ Worrying a lot
❒ Wanting to eat but on a diet
❒ Someone telling you what to do

❒ Threat of war
❒ Violence in neighborhood
❒ Lack of recreation involvement
❒ Boredom
❒ Depression
❒ Anxiety
❒ Mental health issues
❒ Unresolved family issues
❒ Change in living situation
❒ Making new friends
❒ Limited physical abilities
❒ Change in appearance
❒ Needing to borrow money
❒ Anger issues
❒ Not enough time
❒ Too much time
❒ Waiting in a long line
❒ Being hospitalized
❒ Legal problems
❒ Friend or family member with mental health problem
❒ Friend or family member with financial problems
❒ Transportation problems
❒ Going back to work
❒ Holidays
❒ Neighbors are too loud
❒ Medication issues
❒ Sexual problems
❒ Motivation problems
❒ Unable to relax

Number of boxes checked _____

0–20 Mild Stress
21–40 Moderate Stress
41–60 Extreme Stress

Form SAPH

Stress Test Self-Assessment

Check all the stressors that apply to you.

- ❒ A recent illness
- ❒ A divorce, separation, or break-up
- ❒ Family problems
- ❒ Spouse or partner under stress or ill
- ❒ Recent death of a loved one
- ❒ Loneliness
- ❒ Moving to a new location
- ❒ Weight gain or loss
- ❒ Unemployed
- ❒ New job
- ❒ Job stress/problems
- ❒ Anniversary of a beloved's death
- ❒ Money issues
- ❒ Retirement
- ❒ Dealing with the medical establishment
- ❒ Substance abuse problems
- ❒ Substance abuse problems of family member or friend
- ❒ Starting a new relationship
- ❒ Change in a family member's health
- ❒ Fatigue
- ❒ Being in debt
- ❒ Feeling overwhelmed
- ❒ Forgetfulness
- ❒ Limited physical abilities
- ❒ Worrying about societal problems
- ❒ Change in appearance
- ❒ Change in financial status
- ❒ Falling in love
- ❒ Becoming or staying sober
- ❒ Sleeping problems
- ❒ Lack of education

- ❒ Lack of social support
- ❒ Worrying a lot
- ❒ Wanting to eat but on a diet
- ❒ Someone telling you what to do
- ❒ Threat of war
- ❒ Violence in neighborhood
- ❒ Lack of recreation involvement
- ❒ Boredom
- ❒ Depression
- ❒ Anxiety
- ❒ Mental health issues
- ❒ Unresolved family issues
- ❒ Change in living situation
- ❒ Change in social activities
- ❒ Needing to borrow money
- ❒ Anger issues
- ❒ Not enough time
- ❒ Too much time
- ❒ Waiting in a long line
- ❒ Being hospitalized
- ❒ Legal problems
- ❒ Friend or family member with mental health problem
- ❒ Friend or family member with financial problems
- ❒ Transportation problems
- ❒ Holidays
- ❒ Neighbors are too loud
- ❒ Medication issues
- ❒ Motivation problems
- ❒ Unable to relax

Number of boxes checked _____

> 0–20 Mild Stress
> 21–40 Moderate Stress
> 41–60 Extreme Stress

Form SAOA

Pictorial Stress Test—Your Body

When you get stressed, it can make you feel sick. Check off the problems you have experienced.

❏ Headaches

❏ Depression/Sad

❏ Stiff Neck

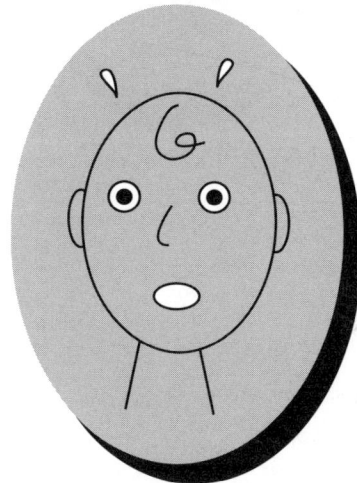

❏ Anxiety

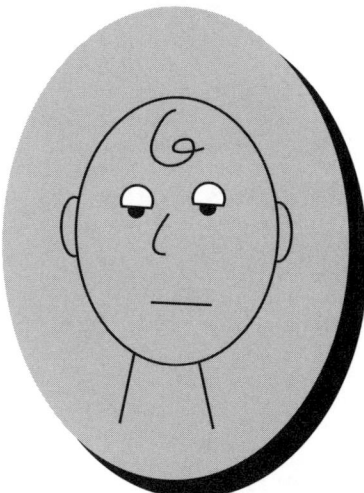

❏ Tired

❏ Insomnia/Can't sleep

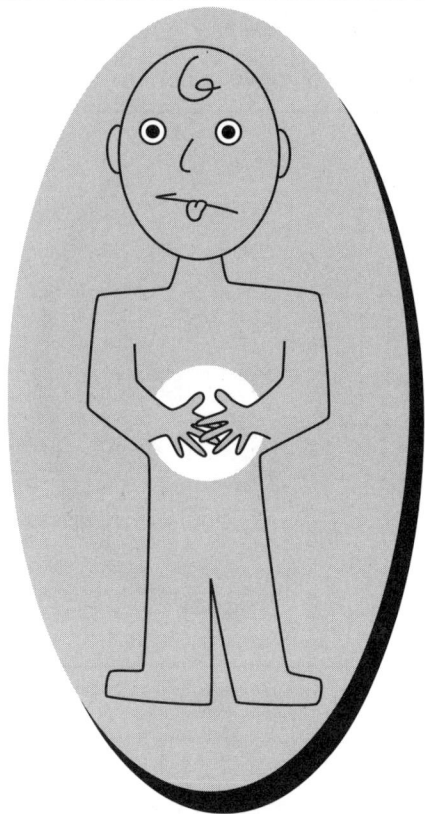

❏ Stomach problems like diarrhea and indigestion

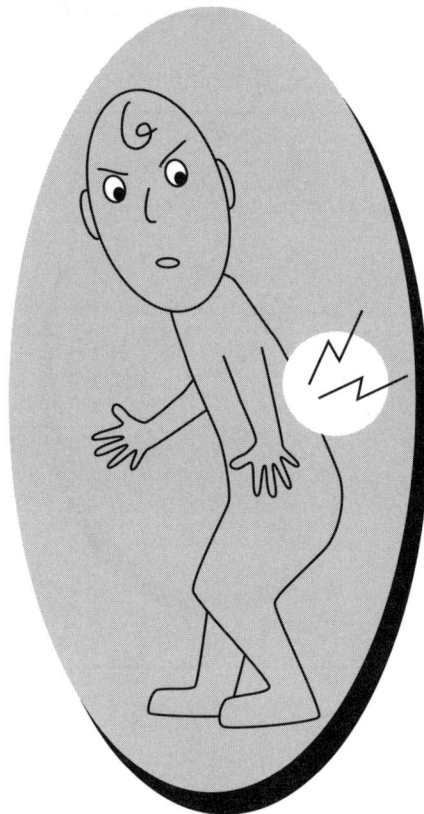

❏ Backache

Pictorial Stress Test—Causes

What causes stress for you? Check the boxes of the things that cause stress for you.

❐ Yelling

❐ Crowds

❐ Traffic

❐ Being sick

❐ Money problems

❐ Being sad

❐   Being lonely/isolated

❐   Too much television

❐   Feeling too fat or too thin

❐   Broken heart

Pictorial Stress Busters

There are a lot of activities you can do to make yourself feel better. Check off the ones you would like to try.

❏   Going to the beach

❏   Going to the mountains

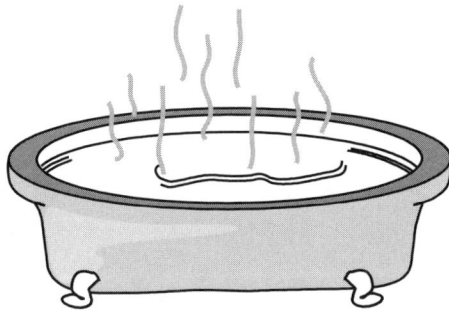

❏   Taking a bath

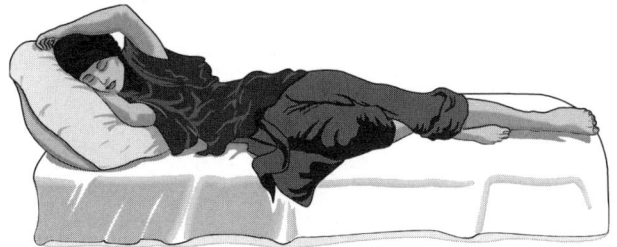

❏   Taking a nap

❏   Listening to soft music

❏   Taking a walk

❏   Yoga

❏   Tai chi

Form SAPICsb

❐   Exercise

❐   Daydreaming

Stress Meter

Instructions: Prior to beginning a stress management activity, measure your level of stress in the "before" section by taking your pulse and/or shading in the appropriate box on the stress meter. Once you have completed your stress management activity, fill in the box in the "after" section of the stress meter and take your pulse again. Did you notice a drop in your stress level? Did you notice a reduction of heart rate? Discuss.

Pulse before activity: _____ bpm

Pulse after activity: _____ bpm

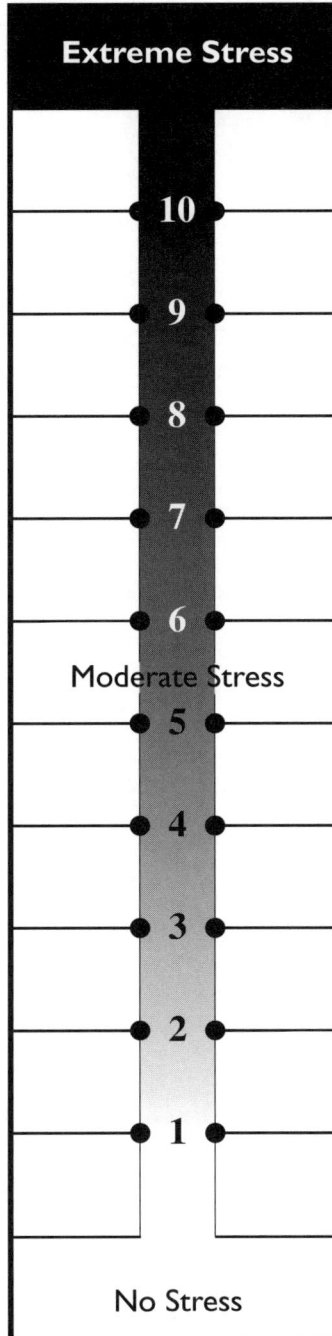

Before   After

Extreme Stress

10

9

8

7

6

Moderate Stress

5

4

3

2

1

No Stress

Discussion, comments and/or other thoughts:

Section I
Relaxation Techniques

Chapter Two
Meditation

Meditation has become one of the most popular forms of stress reduction worldwide. It has been a way of life in the Eastern world for thousands of years. Western cultures have become more aware of meditation as a form of stress reduction, particularly in the last twenty years.

Meditation has been used effectively in the treatment and prevention of the following disorders:

- high blood pressure
- heart disease
- migraine headaches
- autoimmune disease
- diabetes
- arthritis
- cancer
- obsessive-compulsive disorders
- depression
- anxiety
- substance abuse
- anger management

Research has shown that meditation alters the body's physiological response to stress by:

- slowing the heartbeat and breathing mechanism;
- reducing oxygen consumption (by 20%);
- inducing brainwave changes, including lower alpha states;
- boosting the immune system; and
- enhancing personal development.

In a study conducted at the Harvard Mind-Body Medical Institute in 2000, researchers used functional magnetic resonance imagine (fMRI) to establish that meditation activates brain structures involved in attention and in controlling the autonomic nervous system.

Transcendental meditation, which primarily focuses on breathing or repetition of a word or phrase, has a beneficial impact on cardiovascular functioning at rest and during acute laboratory stress in adolescents at-risk for hypertension (Barnes, Treiber & Davis, 2001).

Research conducted at the Australian College of Maharishi Vedic Medicine found that transcendental meditation showed promise as a preventive and treatment for coronary heart disease. Transcendental meditation is associated with decreased hypertension and atherosclerosis, improvement in patients with heart disease, decreased hospitalization rates, and reductions of other risk factors including smoking behaviors and high cholesterol (King, Carr & Cruz, 2002).

Meditation also proved beneficial for a group of patients with irritable bowel syndrome (IBS) who took part in a research study at the Center for Stress and Anxiety Disorders at SUNY Albany. Researchers found that continued use of meditation was particularly effective in reducing symptoms of pain and bloating in patients with IBS (Keefer & Blanchard, 2002).

Furthermore, in a study conducted with institutionalized male Thai juvenile delinquents, 70% of the boys described feelings of contentment and calm after participating in a meditation program (Witoonchart & Bartless, 2002).

Implementation

Meditation can be used effectively in therapeutic recreation programs with most populations. Children and adolescents are natural meditators. Adults may also enjoy meditation, but it may take more practice. You may want to work with clients on an individual basis, but meditation can also be used in group settings.

The first meditation provided in this book uses a leaf as its central focus. If possible, gather leaves prior to the activity. You can substitute a flower, piece of fruit, or any pretty object. A photograph or illustration may also be used with minor script adjustments.

The second meditation uses the sun as a focal point. Ideally, this meditation should be conducted outdoors but can be used indoors as well.

The third meditation calls for the use of a mantra. A mantra is a saying or phrase which is used over and over, as in a chant. While "om" is the most often used mantra, you can use another word or phrase which would better suit your clientele. For instance, if you are working with a group of agitated teens, the word "peace" may be a better idea. For a group of clients with compromised health, the word "health" or "healing" may be effective.

Decrease outside stimuli during this activity. If possible, conduct the group in a clinic or in a conference room where environmental stimuli can be controlled. Dim the lights or only use lamps with 25- or 40-watt bulbs. Turn off the television and overhead lighting. If you plan to use meditation in a hospital room, be sure to dim the lights and make sure the client is as comfortable as possible.

If you decide to use background music, choose instrumental tapes or CDs rather than music with lyrics.

For clients with adequate cognitive abilities, ask them to use the Stress Meter before and after the activity to determine whether they have experienced a reduction in stress.

For best results a short stretch and breathing exercise prior to starting the meditation exercise will help clients relax.

Be sure to pause for at least 10 to 15 seconds when three dots (…) appear in the script and 30 to 45 seconds between paragraphs or logical pausing points. If you feel more comfortable, tape the script prior to the session thereby allowing yourself the chance to modify the script if applicable or to add your own thoughts/ideas.

Consider photocopying the meditation scripts for clients to encourage them to try to do the exercises on their own. For best results, recommend that they use this technique three times a day, particularly when waking up and just before going to bed.

Special Populations

These exercises are not recommended for people who are actively hallucinating. Clients will need to be able to sit still for about a half hour, therefore meditation exercises are not recommended for agitated clients or you should limit the length of the exercise to a much shorter time frame.

If your clients are ambulatory, you might want to use mats for the group. Suggest that your clients sit in a cross-legged position and assume a meditative pose with their palms up and resting on their knees.

While ideally you would want your clients to meditate for about 20 to 30 minutes, you may want to start with five-minute sessions until they are more comfortable with the process. Remind your client that some thoughts will more than likely enter their minds and for them not to worry about this at first. In each meditation, the clients will be told repeatedly to acknowledge when they are thinking or worrying, but to then let go of their thoughts and worries.

Recommended Reading

Barnes, V.A., Treiber, F.A., and Davis, H. (2001). Impact of transcendental meditation on cardiovascular function at rest and during acute stress in adolescents with high normal blood pressure. *Journal of Psychosomatic Research, 51*(4), 597–605.

Harvard Women's Health Watch. (2001). Is meditation good medicine? Retrieved April 22, 2003, from http://www.health.harvard.edu/medline/Women/W101d.html

Keefer, L. and Blanchard, E.B. (2002). A one-year follow-up of relaxation response meditation as a treatment for irritable bowel syndrome. *Behavior Research and Therapy, 40*(5), 541–546.

King, M.S., Carr, T., and D'Cruz, C. (2002). Transcendental meditation, hypertension and heart disease. *Australian Family Physician, 31*(2), 164–168.

Osho. (1993). *The everyday meditator*. Rutland, UK: Charles E. Tuttle Co.

Witoonchart, C. and Bartlet, L. (2002). The use of a meditation programme for institutionalized juvenile delinquents. *Journal of the Medical Association of Thailand, 85*(2), S790–793.

Meditation Script 1
Befriend a Leaf

We are going to take a short journey. You are going to feel a sense of relaxation you have not felt before starting this meditation.

Take a leaf from the pile and place it in your lap... Take a moment to become familiar with your leaf. Turn it over and see the leaf from both sides... Know that every leaf is unique... A leaf is one of nature's miracles... Look at the colors in the leaf... Notice the intricate patterns on the leaf... Feel its texture... Bring it to your nose and smell it... Breathe in... Breathe out...

As you look at your leaf, begin to let go of your worries and thoughts. If a worry enters your mind, concentrate on the leaf. Say hello to whatever thoughts enter your mind, but then say goodbye to them. Allow your thoughts to move through your mind and then gently reintroduce yourself to the leaf...

The leaf is very beautiful... The leaf is your friend... You are one with the leaf... Take some time to really become familiar with the leaf...

[Allow the clients 5–10 minutes to meditate on their own.]

When you are ready, wait for a minute before you come out of the meditation. Gently take in your surroundings. Stretch. Breathe in. Breathe out.

Meditation Script 2
The Golden Light

Close your eyes. When you breathe in, visualize a golden light entering your body. Envision the sunlight as it flows into your body through the top of your head. Imagine the first rays of sun in the morning, all golden and fresh and beautiful. Allow the light to enter your body. It enters through your head then moves into your arms… you feel peaceful… The light warms up your torso, then radiates down your legs until it reaches your toes. You are the golden light of the sun. As thoughts enter your mind, let the glow of the golden sunlight greet your thoughts and then let your thoughts go… You are the golden light on the sun… Your thoughts may come and go. You are the golden light of the sun…

Meditation Script 3
The Mantra

Today you are going to find your own mantra—a saying or word that has a special meaning just for you. For some people, the word "om," meaning "life force," is a mantra they like to use. The word or saying can be anything. It can be the name of a place, person, thing, or a saying that bespeaks happiness and positive energy. You decide what you want your mantra to be. Take a moment to decide on a mantra. If you would like to write it down, you can do so now.

My mantra: _____

_____

You can ask your therapist or peer for help with your mantra if you like.

Now we're going to do a meditation using your mantra:

> Relax and close your eyes. Say your mantra… Repeat it… Listen to yourself as you say your mantra. As you repeat your mantra, thoughts may move into your mind, but let them go… Like clouds in the sky, thoughts will pass by, but then they will go… Whenever you get lost in your thoughts, repeat your mantra… Listen to yourself as you say your mantra… Let your thoughts go… Repeat your mantra… Let your thoughts go… Repeat your mantra…

Chapter Three
Breathing

While most people take breathing for granted, by learning how to breathe properly, wonderful changes can take place. With each breath of air, the body obtains oxygen and releases carbon dioxide. Poor breathing habits such as shallow breathing make it harder for the body to deal with stress. Improper breathing can worsen anxiety, panic attacks, depression, muscles tension, headaches, and fatigue.

Learning how to breathe correctly through breathing exercises has been found to be effective in the treatment of:

- anxiety disorders
- agoraphobia
- panic attacks
- depression
- muscle tension
- headaches
- fatigue

Benefits of breathing exercises include:

- Warms and energizes the body
- Prevents colds and congestion
- Improves digestion
- Changes brain and tissue chemistry by inducing the relaxation response
- Induces positive changes in attitude and mood
- Stimulates the body's self-healing abilities
- Induces muscular relaxation
- Calms the nervous system
- Balances the left and right side of the brain
- Stabilizes blood pressure

At the Department of Nursing at the College of Allied Health Sciences at Thomas Jefferson University in Philadelphia, Pennsylvania, a group of nursing students took part in a study to determine the effectiveness of a variety of stress management techniques. It was found that deep abdominal breathing was associated with a significant reduction in physiological responsivity (i.e., skin temperature) relative to baseline (Forbes & Pekala, 1993).

Breathing techniques have been incorporated into childbirth for many years. According to Herbert Benson, M.D., and Eileen M. Stuart, RCN, in *The Wellness Book: The Comprehensive Guide to Maintaining Health and Treating Stress-Related Illness* (1993), "Through breathing techniques, you can actually learn to uncouple the sensations of pain from the emotional reactions, tensions, and fears that tend to accentuate pain."

Implementation Concerns

Decrease outside stimulus during this activity, and conduct this group in a clinic or in a conference room if possible. Dim the lights or use lamps with 25- or 40-watt bulbs. Turn off the television and overhead lighting.

If you decide to use background music, choose instrumental tapes or CDs rather that music with lyrics. These tapes and CDs are available at most music and New Age stores.

Explain to clients that you are going to guide them through a series of breathing exercises to help them decrease their stress level. For clients with adequate cognitive abilities, ask them to fill in the Stress Meter before and after the activity to determine whether they have experienced a reduction in stress. Heart-rate monitoring can also be used to assess your clients' stress level.

Special Considerations

These exercises should be performed gradually and slowly to develop the body's tolerance to increased energy and cleansing activity.

Caution clients to report any discomfort or dizziness. If they do, they may be "pushing it" and will need the stop the exercise for the day.

Implementation

Although breathing is one of the most natural functions of living, some clients may become self-conscious while teaching them breathing exercises. Therefore it may be a good idea to begin a breathing regimen with clients using the basic breathing exercises. These first two simple breathing exercises may also be used successfully with clients who have limited cognition.

Be sure to pause for at least three to five seconds when three dots (…) appear in the script to give the clients time to respond. If it makes you feel more comfortable, tape the script prior to the session thereby allowing yourself the chance to modify the script (if applicable) or to add you own thought/ideas.

Recommended Resources

Benson, H and Stuart, E.M. (1993). *The wellness guide: The comprehensive guide to maintaining health and treating stress-related illness.* New York, NY: Simon & Schuster.

Forbes, E.J. and Pekala, R.J. (1993). Psychophysiological effects of several stress management techniques. *Psychological Reports, 72*(1), 19–27.

Freeman, R. (2002). *Yoga breathing* [audiotape]. Boulder, CO: Sounds True.

Gabriel, S. (2002). *Breathing for life.* North Berjen, NJ: Basic Health Publications.

Basic Breathing Exercises

Timed Breathing

Instruct clients to sit or lie quietly while you time their breathing for a three-minute interval. Encourage them to pay attention to their breath while breathing normally and naturally.

Counting the Breath

Encourage clients to sit or lie quietly while you lead them counting to five, three times:

One:	Inhale…exhale
Two:	Inhale…exhale
Three:	Inhale…exhale
Four:	Inhale…exhale
Five:	Inhale…exhale

Repeat:

One:	Inhale…exhale
Two:	Inhale…exhale
Three:	Inhale…exhale
Four:	Inhale…exhale
Five:	Inhale…exhale

Repeat:

One:	Inhale…exhale
Two:	Inhale…exhale
Three:	Inhale…exhale
Four:	Inhale…exhale
Five:	Inhale…exhale

As a variation, you may use the vowels (a-e-i-o-u), repeating them three times.

Intermediate Breathing Exercises

Three-Part Breathing

Choose a comfortable seated position, keeping the spine straight and shoulders relaxed.

Place the palm of your hand on your abdomen to check the movement of the diaphragm and stomach muscles. Inhale deeply and feel the abdominal muscles relax and expand. You will notice that your fingers part as the stomach moves outward.

Continue to inhale, filling the mid-chest; feel how the rib cage is expanding. Finally, inhale into the upper chest; feel the collar bones gently rising.

Exhale in reverse order, first from the upper chest, the collar bone relaxing. Then, exhale from the chest, feeling the rib cage relax. Finally exhale from the abdomen by contracting the stomach muscles to force out any remaining air. Notice how your fingers come together as the stomach deflates.

As the stomach muscles relax, another inhalation naturally flows into the stomach. Begin the second round.

Repeat six times.

Skull Shining

This technique should only be performed with an empty stomach so try to wait at least two hours after eating.

Choose a comfortable seated position, preferably one of the cross-legged postures. Keep the spine straight and shoulders relaxed.

Begin with a full inhalation into the abdomen by expanding the stomach muscles. Quickly contract the stomach muscles, forcing the exhalation through the nose, almost like a sneeze. This forceful exhalation is followed by a rapid inhalation into the abdomen, accomplished once again by expanding or puffing out the stomach muscles.

Repeat the short, forceful inhalation and exhalation six times using the stomach muscles as a "pump" while concentrating all breathing activity in the solar plexus.

Take a few normal breaths between rounds.

Repeat five times.

Bellows Breath

Sit in a comfortable position with a straight spine and relax your shoulders. Inhale normally, with a relaxed inflow of air. In the beginning, is it helpful to place your hands on the abdomen to ensure proper contraction and relaxation of the stomach muscles.

Start with a full breath into the abdomen. Your belly should be "puffed out," drawing the breath as low as possible into the body.

Quickly contract the stomach muscles, forcing the exhalation out through the nose. You may give your stomach muscles a little push with your hand to accomplish this until it becomes natural.

As you relax the tensed stomach muscles, the inhalation is naturally drawn back down into the abdomen; you are ready to begin the second exhalation. Limit each round to 10–12 exhalations, ending each round with a full exhalation.

Take a few normal breaths between rounds.

Repeat three times.

Alternate Nostril Breathing

Use once three-part breathing is mastered. Alternate nostril breathing is one of the most powerful of all breathing techniques, but can be the most difficult to master.

Sit in a comfortable position with a straight spine and relaxed shoulders. Make your right hand into a fist. Release the thumb and last two fingers so that the ring fingers and "pinky" form a "V."

Inhale deeply and slowly using three-part breathing. Close the right nostril with the thumb and exhale through the left, again using the three-part exhalation. Then inhale through the left nostril, close off the left nostril with the two fingers, release the thumb and exhale through the right. Inhale, close off the thumb while releasing the fingers and exhale though the left.

Continue in this manner: exhale, change.

The breathing should be effortless. *Any strain is likely to produce discomfort or dizziness.*

Once you get the hang of this exercise, close your eyes and allow your awareness to become centered within. Finish with an exhalation through the right nostril (remember that you began your exhaling through the left). Sit quietly with your eyes closed for a few minutes. Start participating for only a minute or less, then gradually increase to five-minutes sessions.

Chapter Four
Progressive Relaxation

Progressive relaxation will allow clients the opportunity to recognize the difference between tension and relaxation in each of the major muscle groups. This will allow the client to be able to identify chronic trouble spots and consciously let go of the tension in that area. The client will be able to bring his or her muscles to a deeper state of relaxation after tensing the muscles first. Progressive relaxation has been used to treat the following conditions:

- panic disorders
- anxiety disorders
- headaches
- migraines
- back and joint pain
- epilepsy
- insomnia
- heart disease
- cancer

The benefits of progressive relaxation include:

- Changes the brain and tissue chemistry by inducing the relaxation response
- Regulates unwanted tension in the voluntary and involuntary muscles
- Improves ability to handle stress
- Reduces anxiety

A research project at the Department of Surgery at the Tseung Kwan O Hospital in Hong Kong found that progressive muscle relaxation training (PMRT) helped decrease anxiety and improve the quality of life in colorectal cancer patients after stoma surgery (Cheung, Molassiotis & Chang, 2003).

Similar results were found at the Hebrew University School of Nursing in Jerusalem, Israel, where patients with advanced cancer reported a decrease in anxiety and depression after taking part in a PMRT program (Sloman, 2002).

A decrease in pain levels were reported by gynecological and obstetric patients participating in a progressive relaxation study conducted at the University of Sao Paulo, Riberirao Preto College of Nursing, WHO Collaborating Centre for Nursing Research Development, Brazil (de Paula, de Carvalho & dos Santos, 2002).

In a pilot study at Kent State University College of Nursing in Ohio, patients enrolled in a cardiac rehabilitation program reported a high degree of subjective satisfaction and a reduction in stress levels in their lives after completing a PMRT program (Wilk & Turkoski, 2001).

At the Department of Clinical Psychology at the University of Southern Mississippi, researchers interested in determining the physiological changes that take place during an Abbreviated Progressive Relaxation Training (APRT) program studied 46 experimental subjects who completed two APRT sessions. Fifteen control subjects were asked to sit quietly for an equal amount of time but received no other interventions. Laboratory findings showed a significantly lower postintervention heart rate, lower state of anxiety, perceived stress, and salivary cortisol in the experimental subjects (Pawlow & Jones, 2002).

Implementation Concerns

Decrease outside stimulus during this activity, and conduct this group in a clinic or conference room if possible. Dim the lights or use lamps with 25- or 40-watt bulbs. Turn off the television and overhead lighting.

If you decide to use background music, choose instrumental tapes or CDs rather than music with lyrics. These tapes and CDs are available at most music and New Age stores.

For clients with adequate cognitive abilities, ask them to use the Stress Meter before and after the activity to determine whether they have experienced a reduction in stress.

For best results a short stretch and breathing exercise prior to starting the progressive relaxation exercise will help relax your clients.

Be sure to pause for at least three to five seconds when three dots (...) appear in the scripts and 15 to 30 seconds between paragraphs or logical pausing points.

Special Considerations

If your client has physical limitations, alter the exercise in order for him or her to have a successful experience. Prior to the exercise, determine the adaptation(s) needed.

This activity should be used with caution if your client has an illness causing psychotic symptoms as this exercise can lead to an out-of-body state.

Deep relaxation can cause variation in blood pressure. Therefore, when concluding this exercise, allow participants time to adjust back to a normal activity level.

Recommended Resources

Bernstein, D. (2000). *New directions in progressive relaxation training: A guidebook for helping professionals.* Westport, CT: Praeger.

Cheung, Y.L., Molassiotis, A., and Chang, A.M. (2003). The effect of progressive muscle relaxation training on anxiety and quality of life after stoma surgery in colorectal cancer patients. *Psycho-oncology, 12*(3), 254–266.

de Paula, A.A., de Carvallio, E.C., and dos Santos, C.B. (2002). The use of the "progressive muscle relaxation" technique for pain relief in gynecology and obstetrics. *Revista Latino-Americana de Enfermagem, 10*(5), 654–659.

Lazarus, J. (2000). *Stress relief and relaxation techniques.* Berkeley, CA: McGraw Hill/Contemporary.

Pawlow, L.A. and Jones, G.E. (2002). The impact of abbreviated progressive muscle relaxation on salivary cortisol. *Biological Psychology, 60*(1), 1–16.

Sloman, R. (2002). Relaxation and imagery for anxiety and depression control in community patients with advanced cancer. *Cancer Nursing, 25*(6), 432–435.

Wilk, C. and Turkoski, B. (2001). Progressive muscle relaxation in cardiac rehabilitation: A pilot study. *Rehabilitation Nursing, 26*(6), 238–242.

Progressive Relaxation Script

As you begin, you are going to experience the tension in your feet. You are going to stretch them out and hold the tension for 10 to 12 seconds. Stretch your feet… As you hold your feet, squeeze them, hold the tension and force the toes to curl as tightly as you can. Relax your feet.

Take a deep breath. Breathe in, hold, and exhale. You have become more relaxed… In just a few minutes you are going to feel more comfortable, more relaxed as you continue with this exercise.

Take a deep breath… Hold it while you stretch out your feet, again. Hold the tension. Become aware of the tension, push your toes out, push your heels up… Hold the tension… Exhale. As you exhale, let go of the tension in your feet. Relax your feet.

Take a deep breath. Breathe in, hold it, and exhale. You have become more relaxed… In just a few minutes you are going to feel more comfortable, more relaxed as you continue with this exercise.

Now we will be working on your calves. Feel the tension in your calves. Take a deep breath… Hold your breath while you tense your calf muscles. Hold the tension. Become aware of the tension… Hold the tension… Exhale. As you exhale, let go of the tension in your calves.

Take a deep breath. Breathe in, hold it, and exhale. You have become more relaxed… In just a few minutes you are going to feel more comfortable, more relaxed as you continue with this exercise.

Now we will be working on your thighs and quadriceps. Feel the tension in your thighs and quadriceps. Take a deep breath… Hold your breath while you tense your thighs and quadriceps. Hold the tension. Become aware of the tension… Hold the tension… Exhale. As you exhale, let go of the tension in your thighs and quadriceps.

Take a deep breath. Breathe in, hold it, and exhale. You have become more relaxed… In just a few minutes you are going to feel more comfortable, more relaxed as you continue with this exercise.

Now we will be working on your stomach and lower back. Feel the tension in your stomach and lower back. Take a deep breath… Hold your breath while you pull in your stomach and abdomen. Hold the tension. Become aware of the tension… Hold the tension… Exhale. As you exhale, let go of the tension in your stomach and lower back.

Take a deep breath. Breathe in, hold it, and exhale. You have become more relaxed… In just a few minutes you are going to feel more comfortable, more relaxed as you continue with this exercise.

Now we will be working on your chest and back. Feel the tension in your chest and back. Take a deep breath… Hold your breath while you pull in your chest and back. Hold the tension. Become aware of the tension… Hold the tension… Exhale. As you exhale, let go of the tension in your stomach and lower back .

Take a deep breath. Breathe in, hold it, and exhale. You have become more relaxed… In just a few minutes you are going to feel more comfortable, more relaxed as you continue with this exercise.

Now we will be working on your hands. Breathe in, hold your breath as you make a fist with both of your hands at the same time. Hold the tension… Squeeze your fists as tightly as you can. Exhale. Relax your hands.

Breathe in and hold your breath as you open your fingers slowly… Extend each finger one finger at a time… Exhale… Relax your fingers and palms.

Take a deep breath. Breathe in, hold it, and exhale. You have become more relaxed… In just a few minutes you are going to feel more comfortable, more relaxed as you continue with this exercise.

Next, we are going to concentrate on the your upper back, shoulders, and neck. Inhale. Lift your shoulders toward the top of your head and squeeze your neck tightly. Squeeze… Squeeze… Exhale… Relax…

Let it all go… Let go of all of your tension… Let go of the stress… of your pains… your troubles… your worries… your problems… you feel completely relaxed and safe…

Now we will concentrate on your facial muscles. Inhale. Hold the tension in your mouth… Squeeze your lips together… Squeeze… Now exhale…

Now clench your jaw… Inhale… Hold on to the tension… Focus on the clenching of your jaw… Now breathe out through your teeth… Relax…

Relax. Let it all go… Let go of all of your tension… Let go of the stress… of your pains… your troubles… your worries… your problems… You feel completely relaxed and safe…

Now we are going to concentrate in your eyes. Inhale… Squeeze your eyes together… Squeeze your eyes tight, very tight… Now exhale… Relax…

Now we are going to hold the tension in our mouth, jaws, eyes, in our entire face… Inhale… Squeeze… Squeeze… Now exhale.

Relax. Let it all go… Let go of all of your tension… Let go of the stress… of your pains… of your troubles…

We are now going to hold the tension in our entire body… Hold your body tight. Now inhale… Squeeze… Squeeze… Exhale… Relax…

You are entirely relaxed. You have let go of all of your tension. You feel as if you are floating on a cloud. Begin to notice your breath as you lay quietly. Breathe in, breathe out. Breathe in, breathe out… Let your mind go… Let it go…

[pause for 3 to 5 minutes]

You are now completely relaxed… You have treated yourself… You have let go of all of your tension, your worries, your fears. You feel completely renewed. You are filled with hope… Stay with that hope…

Soon you will be getting up and going on with your day. Know that you can always return to this exercise, any time, any day, to help you feel invigorated. Now stretch your body one more time before sitting up. Stretch… Stretch…

[pause for thirty seconds]

When you are ready, sit up…

Chapter Five
Self-Hypnosis

Self-hypnosis can help clients enter a deep, relaxed state. Human beings have a built-in capacity to enter a "flow" or trance state whereby they are able to suspend their awareness of the world around them. Hypnosis can be defined as a condition resembling sleep in which the objective manifestations of the mind are more or less inactive, accompanied by an increased susceptibility to suggestions (Taber, 2001).

Self-hypnosis as a therapeutic tool draws on this capacity for hypnotic states by using a variety of methods which induce a deep, relaxed state. It has been used effectively to treat individuals with the following problems:

- headaches
- chronic muscle tension
- depression
- smoking cessation
- chronic pain
- chronic fatigue syndrome
- insomnia
- weight control

The psychological and physiological benefits of self-hypnosis include:

- Changes in brain and tissue chemistry by inducing the relaxation response
- Reduces tension of voluntary and involuntary muscles
- Induces positive changes in attitude and mood
- Stimulates the body's self-healing abilities

In a study conducted at the Biobehaviorial Medicine Program, Cancer Prevention and Control, Derald H. Ruttenberg Cancer Center, Mount Sinai School of Medicine in New York, hypnosis was used as a non-pharmacological means for managing adverse surgical side effects. The results indicated that patients in the hypnosis treatment groups had better clinical outcomes than 89% of the patient in the control group (Montgomery, Winkel, Silverstein & Bovbjerg, 2002).

In a study conducted at the Cystic Fibrosis Center at SUNY Upstate Medical University in Syracuse, New York, self-hypnosis was used effectively with patients with cystic fibrosis. The study concluded that self-hypnosis can help patients with cystic fibrosis to quickly learn to enhance their control over discomfort associated with therapy and disease (Anbar, 2000).

According to a group of researchers at the California School of Professional Psychology in Fresno, California, HIV patients who had taken part in a twelve-week self-hypnosis program reported using significantly less pain medication during the treatment phase (Langenfeld, Cipani & Borckardt, 2002). Since stress is known to compromise the immune system, these results suggest that stress management to reduce arousal of the nervous system and anxiety would be an appropriate components of a treatment regimen of HIV infection (Taylor, 1995).

Implementation Concerns

Decrease outside stimulus during this activity, and conduct this group in a clinic or conference room if possible. Dim the lights or use lamps with 25- or 40-watt bulbs. Turn off the television and overhead lighting.

If you decide to use background music, choose instrumental tapes or CDs rather than music with lyrics. If you are planning to use one of the guided imagery lesson plans which take place in a natural setting (e.g., forest, beach, lake), choose a tape or CD with corresponding nature sounds. These tapes and CDs are available at most music and New Age stores.

Explain to the clients that you are going to guide them through a visualization which uses natural settings to help them decrease their stress level.

For clients with adequate cognitive abilities, ask them to use the Stress Meter before and after the activity to determine whether they have experienced a reduction in stress. The clients may also monitor their heart rates before and after the activity to assess stress reduction.

For best results a short stretch and breathing exercise prior to starting the self-hypnosis exercise will help to relax your clients.

Be sure to pause for at least three to five seconds when three dots (…) appear in the scripts and 10 to 15 seconds between paragraphs or logical pausing points.

Consider photocopying the self-hypnosis scripts for the clients, and encourage them to try to do the exercises on their own. For best results, recommend that they use this technique three times a day, particularly when waking up and just before going to bed.

Special Populations

This exercise is not recommended for people who are actively hallucinating. Clients will need to be able to sit still for about a half hour, therefore, self-hypnosis exercises are not recommended for agitated clients or you may limit the length of the exercise to a much shorter time frame.

Recommended Reading

Bernstein, D.A., Borkoves, D., and Stevens, H.H. (2002). *New directions for progressive relaxation training: A guide for helping professionals.* Westport, CT: Praeger Trade.

References

Anbar, R. D. (2001). Self-hypnosis for the treatment of functional abdominal pain in childhood. *Clinical Pediatrics, 40*(8), 447–451.

Langenfeld, M.C., Cipani, E., and Borckardt, J.J. (2002). Hypnosis for the control of HIV/AIDS-related pain. *International Journal of Clinical and Experimental Hypnosis, 50*(2), 170–188.

Montgomery, G.H., David, D., Winkel, G., Silverstein, J.H., and Bovbjerg, D.H. (2002). The effectiveness of adjunctive hypnosis with surgical patients: A meta-analysis. *Anesthesia and Analgesia, 94*(6), 1639–1645.

Taber's cyclopedic medical dictionary (19th ed.). (2001). Philadelphia, PA: F.A. Davis.

Taylor, D.N. (1995). Effects of a behavioral stress management program on anxiety, mood, self-esteem, and T-cell count in HIV-positive men. *Psychological Reports, 76*(2), 451–457.

Self-Hypnosis Script I
General Relaxation

You are about to descend a spiral staircase. It is very beautiful with a lovely alabaster banister and thick, red carpeting down the middle of the staircase. There are twenty-five steps from the top of the staircase to the landing. Every time you descend another five steps, you will feel more and more relaxed…

First, get into a relaxed position. Stretch your arms to the ceiling, stretch… Stretch. Now take in a couple of deep breaths. Breathe in… Hold… Breathe out… Breathe in… Hold… Breathe out. One more time, breathe in… Hold… Breathe out… Now close your eyes…

Imagine that you are at the top of the staircase. You place your hand on the banister. Now begin to walk down each step, slowly. When you reach the twentieth step, you are going to feel more relaxed. Now begin to walk down each step… 24… 23… 22… 21… 20…

You are feeling more relaxed. Your body feels heavy. Your mind is calm. You feel very relaxed… You are feeling more relaxed, deeper and deeper, relaxed… You are feeling heavier in all parts of your body. Your body feels heavy. Your mind feels calm. You are going deeper and deeper into a completely relaxed state…

Now we will walk down another five steps… 19… 18… 17… 16… 15… The calm you are feeling is a calm you didn't know was possible… You are feeling very relaxed… You notice how restful you feel in this relaxed state, you notice how relaxed you feel in your shoulders… arms… legs… feet and toes… You are completely relaxed.

You will now descend another five steps… 14… 13… 12… 11… 10…

You are in a very deepened relaxation state. You feel very relaxed. Your body and mind are very calm… You notice that you are breathing more comfortably… You take a deep, slow… breath… Notice how a deep, relaxed feeling spreads throughout your body…

Now you will descend another five steps… 9… 8… 7… 6… 5…

You are very relaxed and calm. You are very relaxed and calm… You feel yourself sinking further and further, heavier and heavier, into a deeply relaxed state. You are almost at the bottom of the staircase.

You are going to descend the last five steps. When you reach the bottom of the staircase, you will feel completely relaxed and calm… 4… 3… 2… 1… You are at the bottom of the stairs. You feel completely relaxed and calm.

You are in a very deep state of relaxation. You continue to feel completely relaxed… Let your mind drift… Notice how relaxed you feel…

[pause for about three minutes]

It is time now to say goodbye to this relaxed state. Know that you can always return here. You can imagine yourself descending the staircase whenever you feel the need to become relaxed. This place of relaxation is your own special place. You can return to this place whenever you want to feel a deep sense of relaxation.

In a few moments, you are going to walk back up the staircase. When you reach the top you will be completely awake. When you reach the top of the stairs you will feel refreshed and alert. The closer you get to the top of the staircase, the more awake you will feel… 1… 2… 3… 4… 5… You are beginning to awaken… 6… 7… 8… 9… 10… You are beginning to awaken… 11… 12… 13… 14… 15… You are beginning to awaken… 16… 17… 18… 19… 20… You are almost awake… 21… 22… 23… 24… 25… Open your eyes… You are completely awake… You feel renewed and refreshed… Now take a deep, refreshing breath—an awakening breath… You feel clear and alert…

Self-Hypnosis Script 2
Improved Health

You are about to descend a spiral staircase. It is very beautiful with a lovely alabaster banister and thick, red carpeting down the middle of the staircase. There are twenty-five steps from the top of the staircase to the landing. Every time you descend another five steps, you will feel more and more relaxed… healthier and healthier…

First, get into a relaxed position. Stretch your arms to the ceiling, stretch… Stretch. Now take in a couple of deep breaths. Breathe in… Hold… Breathe out… Breathe in… Hold… Breathe out. One more time, breathe in… Hold… Breathe out… Now close your eyes.

Imagine that you are at the top of the staircase. You place your hand on the banister. Now begin to walk down each step, slowly. When you reach the twentieth step, you are going to feel more relaxed. Now begin to walk down each step… 24… 23… 22… 21… 20…

You are feeling more relaxed. Your body feels heavy. Your mind is calm. You feel very relaxed… You are feeling more relaxed, deeper and deeper, relaxed… You are feeling heavier in all parts of your body. Your body feels heavy. Your mind feels calm. You are going deeper and deeper into a completely relaxed state…

You are feeling healthy… You are feeling healthier and healthier… Your body feels refreshed. Listen to you heart beat… Thank your heart for the life it brings you… Listen to your heart beat…

Now we will walk down another five steps… 19… 18… 17… 16… 15… The calm you are feeling is a calm you didn't know was possible… You are feeling very relaxed… Your mind feels completely relaxed. You praise your mind for all of your thoughts and ideas. You recognize how intricate your mind is. Your mind can help heal you. You thank your mind for giving you your perceptions of life around you… Your mind is still and content…

You will now descend another five steps… 14… 13… 12… 11… 10…

You are in a very deepened relaxation state. You feel very relaxed. Your body and mind are very calm… You notice that you are breathing more comfortably… You take a deep… slow… breath… Notice how a deep, relaxed feeling spreads throughout your body… You visualize your lungs as they give you the breath of life. You feel the sensation of your lungs as you breathe in and out. You thank your lungs for giving you the breath of life…

Now you will descend another five steps… 9… 8… 7… 6… 5…

You are very relaxed and calm. You are very relaxed and calm… You feel yourself sinking further and further, heavier and heavier, into a deeply relaxed state. You are almost at the bottom of the staircase. You notice how restful you feel in this relaxed state, you notice how relaxed you feel in your shoulders… arms… legs… feet and toes… You are completely relaxed. Your body feels so strong and able. Your body is the miracle of your life… Thank your body…

You are going to descend the last five steps. When you reach the bottom of the staircase, you will feel completely relaxed and calm… 4… 3… 2… 1… You are at the bottom of the stairs. You feel completely relaxed and calm. You are in a very deep state of relaxation. You continue to feel completely relaxed… Let your mind drift… Notice how relaxed you feel… Notice how healthy you feel. You thank your heart, mind, and body for feeling so healthy.

[pause for about three minutes]

It is time now to say goodbye to this relaxed state. Know that you can always return here. You can imagine yourself descending the staircase whenever you feel the need to become relaxed and to feel healthy. This place of relaxation and health is your own special place. You can return to this place whenever you want to feel a deep sense of relaxation and health.

In a few moments, you are going to walk back up the staircase. When you reach the top you will be completely awake. When you reach the top of the stairs you will feel refreshed and alert. The closer you get to the top of the staircase, the more awake you will feel… 1… 2… 3… 4… 5… You are beginning to awaken… 6… 7… 8… 9… 10… You are beginning to awaken… 11… 12… 13… 14… 15… You are beginning to awaken… 16… 17… 18… 19… 20… You are almost awake… 21… 22… 23… 24… 25… Open your eyes… You are completely awake… You feel renewed and refreshed… Now take a deep refreshing breath—an awakening breath… You feel clear and alert… You feel completely well…

Self-Hypnosis Script 3
Your Special Place

Choose a special place or destination before you start.

You are about to descend a spiral staircase. It is very beautiful with a lovely alabaster banister and thick, red carpeting down the middle of the staircase. There are twenty-five steps from the top of the staircase to the landing. Every time you descend another five steps, you will feel more and more relaxed…

First, get into a relaxed position. Stretch your arms to the ceiling, stretch… Stretch. Now take in a couple of deep breaths. Breathe in… Hold… Breathe out… Breathe in… Hold… Breathe out. One more time, breathe in… Hold… Breathe out. Now close your eyes…

Imagine that you are at the top of the staircase. You place your hand on the banister. Now begin to walk down each step, slowly. When you reach the twentieth step, you are going to feel more relaxed. Now begin to walk down each step… 24… 23… 22… 21… 20…

You are feeling more relaxed. Your body feels heavy. Your mind is calm. You feel very relaxed… You are feeling more relaxed, deeper and deeper, relaxed… You are feeling heavier in all parts of your body. Your body feels heavy. Your mind feels calm. You are going deeper and deeper into a complete relaxed state…

Now we will walk down another five steps… 19… 18… 17… 16… 15… The calm you are feeling is a calm you didn't know was possible… You are feeling very relaxed… Your mind feels completely relaxed. You are going to go to your special place. Envision your special place… Notice your surroundings… You look a see that very special place and you feel so happy… Say hello to your special place…

You will now descend another five steps… 14… 13… 12… 11… 10…

You are in a very deepened relaxation state. You feel very relaxed. Your body and mind are very calm… You notice that you are breathing more comfortably… You take a deep, slow… Breath… Notice how a deep, relaxed feeling spreads throughout your body… You are in your special place and you feel completely safe. It is your own special place… Use your senses to imagine your special place… Use your eyes to see your special place… Use your nose to smell the special place… Use your hands to touch the special place… Use your ears to hear your special place…

Now you will descend another five steps... 9... 8... 7... 6... 5...

You are very relaxed and calm. You are very relaxed and calm... You feel yourself sinking further and further, heavier and heavier, into a deeply relaxed state. You are in your special place... Stay in your special place... You feel so wonderful and safe... Continue to visualize your special place...

You are going to descend the last five steps. When you reach the bottom of the staircase, you will feel completely relaxed and calm... 4... 3... 2... 1... You are at the bottom of the stairs. You feel completely relaxed and calm. You are in a very deep state of relaxation. You continue to feel completely relaxed... Let your mind drift in your special place...

[pause for about three minutes]

It is time now to say goodbye to this relaxed state. Know that you can always return here. You can imagine yourself descending the staircase whenever you feel the need to become relaxed... You can return to your special place whenever you want to feel a deep sense of relaxation and well-being...

In a few moments, you are going to walk back up the staircase. When you reach the top you will be completely awake. When you reach the top of the stairs you will feel refreshed and alert. The closer you get to the top of the staircase, the more awake you will feel... 1... 2... 3... 4... 5... You are beginning to awaken... 6... 7... 8... 9... 10... You are beginning to awaken... 11... 12... 13... 14... 15... You are beginning to awaken... 16... 17... 18... 19... 20... You are almost awake... 21... 22... 23... 24... 25... Open your eyes... You are completely awake... You feel renewed and refreshed... Now take a deep refreshing breath—an awakening breath... You feel clear and alert... You feel completely well...

Self-Directed Self-Hypnosis Worksheet

Prior to going into a self-hypnotic state, determine a goal you would like to obtain.

1. My goal is: _____

    _____

    _____

2. Now rewrite the goal, using the following suggestions:

    a. You want the goal to be written in the present tense.

    b. Make the goal as action-oriented as possible.

    c. Use positive statements. The unconscious mind can't process the negatives.

    Rewrite the goal: _____

    _____

    _____

3. Read the goal to yourself five times. Set the paper aside.

4. Begin the self-hypnosis process.

Self-Hypnosis Script 4
Self-Directed Self-Hypnosis Script

You are about to descend a spiral staircase. It is very beautiful with a lovely alabaster banister and thick, red carpeting down the middle of the staircase. There are twenty-five steps from the top of the staircase to the landing. Every time you descend another five steps, you will feel more and more relaxed... Healthier and healthier...

First, get into a relaxed position. Stretch your arms to the ceiling, stretch... Stretch. Now take in a couple of deep breaths. Breathe in... Hold... Breathe out... Breathe in... Hold... Breathe out. One more time, breathe in... Hold... Breathe out. Now close your eyes.

Imagine that you are at the top of the staircase. You place your hand on the banister. Now begin to walk down each step, slowly. When you reach the twentieth step, you are going to feel more relaxed. Now begin to walk down each step... 24... 23... 22... 21... 20...

You are feeling more relaxed. Your body feels heavy. Your mind is calm. You feel very relaxed... You are feeling more relaxed, deeper and deeper relaxed... You are feeling heavier in all parts of your body. Your body feels heavy. Your mind feels calm. You are going deeper and deeper into a completely relaxed state...

Envision yourself reaching your goal. How do you feel? Imagine yourself having reached the goal. You feel wonderful. You are feeling very positive.

Now we will walk down another five steps... 19... 18... 17... 16... 15... The calm you are feeling is a calm you didn't know was possible... You are feeling very relaxed... Your mind feels completely relaxed. You praise yourself for reaching your goal. You thank yourself for reaching your goal. You are feeling content...

You will now descend another five steps... 14... 13... 12... 11... 10...

You are in a very deepened relaxation state. You feel very relaxed. Your body and mind are very calm... You notice that you are breathing more comfortably... You take a deep... slow... breath... Notice how a deep, relaxed feeling spreads throughout your body... You envision yourself having reached your goal. You are feeling physically and mentally renewed.

Now you will descend another five steps... 9... 8... 7... 6... 5...

You are very relaxed and calm. You are very relaxed and calm... You feel yourself sinking further and further, heavier and heavier, into a deeply relaxed state. You are almost at the bottom of the staircase. You notice how restful you feel in this relaxed state, you notice how relaxed you feel in your shoulders... arms... legs... feet and toes. You are completely relaxed. Recall your goal and repeat it to yourself, envisioning yourself at that goal.

You are going to descend the last five steps. When you reach the bottom of the staircase, you will feel completely relaxed and calm... 4... 3... 2... 1... You are at the bottom of the stairs. You feel completely relaxed and calm. You are in a very deep state of relaxation. You continue to feel completely relaxed... Let your mind drift... Notice how relaxed you feel... Notice how wonderful you feel having reached your goal. Thank yourself for reaching the goal.

[pause for about three minutes]

It is time now to say goodbye to this relaxed state. Know that you can always return here. You can imagine yourself descending the staircase whenever you feel the need to become relaxed and to reach your goal. This place of relaxation and reaching your goals is your own special place. You can return to this place whenever you want to.

In a few moments, you are going to walk back up the staircase. When you reach the top you will be completely awake. When you reach the top of the stairs you will feel refreshed and alert. The closer you get to the top of the staircase, the more awake you will feel... 1... 2... 3... 4... 5... You are beginning to awaken... 6... 7... 8... 9... 10... You are beginning to awaken... 11... 12... 13... 14... 15... You are beginning to awaken... 16... 17... 18... 19... 20... You are almost awake... 21... 22... 23... 24... 25... Open your eyes... You are completely awake... You feel renewed and refreshed... Now take a deep refreshing breath, an awakening breath... You feel clear and alert...

You are very relaxed and calm. You are very relaxed and calm… You feel yourself sinking further and further, heavier and heavier, into a deeply relaxed state. You are almost at the bottom of the staircase. You notice how restful you feel in this relaxed state, you notice how relaxed you feel in your shoulders… arms… legs… feet and toes. You are completely relaxed. Recall your goal and repeat it to yourself, envisioning yourself at that goal.

You are going to descend the last five steps. When you reach the bottom of the staircase, you will feel completely relaxed and calm… 4… 3… 2… 1… You are at the bottom of the stairs. You feel completely relaxed and calm. You are in a very deep state of relaxation. You continue to feel completely relaxed… Let your mind drift… Notice how relaxed you feel… Notice how wonderful you feel having reached your goal. Thank yourself for reaching the goal.

[pause for about three minutes]

It is time now to say goodbye to this relaxed state. Know that you can always return here. You can imagine yourself descending the staircase whenever you feel the need to become relaxed and to reach your goal. This place of relaxation and reaching your goals is your own special place. You can return to this place whenever you want to.

In a few moments, you are going to walk back up the staircase. When you reach the top you will be completely awake. When you reach the top of the stairs you will feel refreshed and alert. The closer you get to the top of the staircase, the more awake you will feel… 1… 2… 3… 4… 5… You are beginning to awaken… 6… 7… 8… 9… 10… You are beginning to awaken… 11… 12… 13… 14… 15… You are beginning to awaken… 16… 17… 18… 19… 20… You are almost awake… 21… 22… 23… 24… 25… Open your eyes… You are completely awake… You feel renewed and refreshed… Now take a deep refreshing breath, an awakening breath… You feel clear and alert…

Chapter Six
Creative Visualization

Creative visualization is a great therapeutic tool to help clients decrease their stress levels by using their imagination. Creative visualization transports participants to a calm and beautiful place. It has been used effectively to treat the following disorders:

- headaches
- muscle spasms
- chronic pain
- generalized and situation specific anxiety
- cancer
- phobias
- heart conditions

The benefits of using creative imagination include:

- Changes brain and tissue chemistry by inducing the relaxation response
- Reduces tension of voluntary and involuntary muscles
- Induces positive changes in attitude and mood
- Stimulates the body's self-healing abilities

At the Department of Psychiatry at Mount Sinai Hospital in Toronto, Ontario, guided imagery was used as a treatment modality for bulimia nervosa. Bulimia has been described as involving impairment in affect regulation and in self-soothing. A model of guided imagery therapy suggests that imagery therapy has multiple levels of actions and can assist these individuals in the regulation of affect by providing as external source of soothing and also enhancing self-soothing (Esplen & Garfinkel, 1998).

In a study conducted at the Department of Pathology at the Oregon Health and Science University in Portland, Oregon, women who were in treatment for Stage I or II breast cancer took part in an eight-week imagery training program. The researchers found that the hypnotic guided imagery did cause some transient changes in well-being and immune parameters (Bakke, Purtzer & Newton, 2002).

Guided imagery was also used to increase diabetes self-care at the Professional Program in Nursing at the University of Wisconsin in Green Bay, Wisconsin. An imagery script was developed and used to aid diabetic clients in maintaining their diabetic regimen. Participating in this cognitive experience indicated that the motivation script used with them by healthcare practitioners was effective. The major treatment areas were blood testing, regular exercise, weight management, and consumption of a restricted lifetime diet (Wichowski & Kubsch, 1999).

Implementation Concerns

Decrease outside stimulus during this activity, and conduct this group in a clinic or conference room if possible. Dim the lights or use lamps with 25- or 40-watt bulbs. Turn off the television and overhead lighting.

If you decide to use background music, choose instrumental tapes or CDs rather than music with lyrics. If planning to use a guided imagery lesson plan which takes place in a natural setting (e.g., forest, beach, lake), choose a tape or CD with corresponding sounds. These tapes and CDs are available at most music and New Age stores.

Explain to clients that you are going to guide them through a visualization which uses natural settings to help them decrease their stress level. For clients with adequate cognitive abilities, ask them to use the Stress Meter before and after the activity to determine whether they have experienced a reduction in stress. Heart rate monitoring can also be utilized.

When conducting a guided imagination group, explain to clients that they will be utilizing their senses (e.g., touch, sound, smell, sight).

For best results a short stretch and breathing exercise prior to starting the guided imagination exercise will relax your clients.

Be sure to pause for at least 10 to 15 seconds when three dots (…) appear in the script and 30 to 45 seconds between paragraphs or logical pausing points. If you feel more comfortable, tape the scripts prior to the session to allow yourself time to make changes to the script if applicable or to add your own thoughts/ideas.

Consider photocopying the creative visualization scripts for clients and encourage them to try to do the exercises on their own. For best results, recommend that they use this technique three times a day, particularly when waking up and just before going to bed.

Special Considerations

This exercise is not recommended for people who are actively hallucinating. Clients will need to be able to sit still for about a half hour, therefore guided imagery exercises are not recommended for agitated clients, or limit the length of the exercise to a much shorter time.

Some of the imageries imply that the client is physically able to perform certain activities. Therefore, if you believe that the client will be disturbed by the concept of performing a task which he or she is no longer able to do, edit that portion of the exercise.

Recommended Resources

Shakti, G. (2002). *Creative visualization: Use the power of your imagination to create what you want in your life*. Novato, CA: New World Library.

Shakti, G. and Allen, M. (2002). *Creative visualization* [audiotape]. Novato, CA: New World Library.

References

Bakke, A.C., Purtzer, M.Z., and Newton, P. (2002). The effect of hypnotic-guided imagery on psychological well-being and immune function in patients with prior breast cancer. *Journal of Psychosomatic Research, 53*(6), 1131–1137.

Esplen, M.J. and Garfinkel, P.E. (1998). *Journal of Psychotherapy Practice and Research, 7*(2), 102–118.

Wichowski, H.C. and Kubsch, S.M. (1999). Increasing diabetic self-care through guided imagery. *Complementary Therapies in Nursing and Midwifery, 5*(6), 159–163.

Guided Imagery Scenario 1
The Forest

Close your eyes… Imagine that you have arrived at a forest. It is very beautiful. Take a moment to look at the trees…

Notice how the wind rustles through the leaves of the trees. Listen to the wind… Take a moment to breathe in and smell the forest. It smells like fresh pine…

You look up at the sky and it is a perfect color blue. Billowing clouds move across the sky. Find a cloud and watch it as it glides through the sky… A bird flies above. Focus your attention on its flight. You feel hope…

It sings to another bird. Listen to the bird chirping…

You find a pine cone that has fallen to the ground. You pick it up and notice its intricate design…

You touch it. It feels prickly and a little sticky, but it's so beautiful…

Bring it to your nose and breathe in the smell of pine…

Continue on into the forest. You arrive at a meadow filled with flowers. Take a moment to look at the colors of the flowers… Blue, yellow, lilac, red, orange, pink, green, white… You are filled with a sense of peace.

As you travel deeper into the forest, you arrive at a lake. The water glistens in the sun. The sky is reflected in the lake. You notice a cloud mirrored in the lake. You watch it as it floats by… You see a couple on a small rowboat as they row it to shore. You watch them as the boat glides through the water. When they arrive at the shore, they offer the boat to you. You row the boat to the middle of the lake. You place the oars down and lie in the boat. It drifts in the water…

Take a moment and imagine that you have closed your eyes. You can hear the wind… You can smell the pines…

Imagine that you have opened your eyes. Look up at the sky. Watch a cloud…

You place your hand in the water. It is cold but it feels so refreshing. You find yourself smiling… You row back to shore…

It's time now to leave the forest. You follow the path out the forest, past the meadow. You look again at the colorful flowers. You remind yourself that the image of the flowers will remain with you long after you leave the forest.

In a minute I will be asking you to open your eyes. Say goodbye to the forest. The trees sway in the wind… You know that even when the trees are no longer in your sight, they will remain in your memory… A bird chirps. The bird is saying goodbye, but you know you will be back to hear another bird sing…

It's time now to leave the forest. You have had such a lovely time in the forest. I'm going to count backwards, from ten. When you're ready, open your eyes. 10… 9… 8… 7… 6… 5… 4… 3… 2… 1…

Now open your eyes.

Guided Imagery Scenario 2
The Beach

Close your eyes. Imagine that you have arrived at the beach. You look out at the sea. The horizon seems limitless. You find a place on the beach and place a beach blanket on the sand. You settle down on the blanket and look out again toward the sea…

You watch the waves. They're mesmerizing. You are lost in the moment of the endless ebb and flow of the waves…

Listen to the waves…

Listen to the waves…

Watch and listen to the waves…

You breathe in deeply and smell the ocean air…

You gather a fistful of sand in your hand and feel its fine texture. Then making a small sifter out of your hand, you let go of the sand a little bit at a time. The sand trickles…

You look out again toward the ocean and see swimmers in the water. They body surf, as they navigate the waves… Watch them…

You hear them laugh with great glee…

You watch the sailboats in the ocean. They drift along the horizon. You pick a sailboat on which to focus your attention and you watch it as it sails along…

You hear a sea gull above and you watch it as it swoops down into the water…

Now focus your attention on two small children building a sandcastle. It's quite intricate. They've built a castle with lots of walls and turrets. You watch them as they continue to build the castle…

You walk to the edge of the water and allow the sea water to circle your feet. The water is cold, but it is refreshing. You stand there thinking how wonderful it feels to be at the beach. The water swirls around your feet…

You decide to look for seashells. You find a beautiful seashell and pick it up. It is made of many colors. Look at it closely…

You imagine all the places this seashell has traveled to end up in your hands. You bring the seashell to your ear and you can hear the roar of the sea… You put the seashell in your pocket. You plan to take it home to remind you of your great day at the beach.

You return to your blanket and lie down. Imagine that you are closing your eyes. You can feel the heat of the sun on your body. It feels comforting…

You lie on the beach and you are at peace. Your mind is completely focused on the moment. The sea is endless but it represents all of life's possibilities. Think of your own desires and hopes and remember that they are within your reach…

Soon it will be time to leave the beach… In a moment I will be asking you to open your eyes. It's time to say goodbye to the beach. You sit up and look out toward the sea. You breathe in the sea air. You focus your attention again on the ebb and flow of the water. It's time now to leave the beach. You have had such a lovely time at the beach. I'm going to count backwards, from ten. When you're ready, open your eyes. 10… 9… 8… 7… 6… 5… 4… 3… 2… 1…

Now open your eyes.

Guided Imagery Scenario 3
Your Home

Close your eyes. You are sitting on the couch, watching TV. It's been a long day and you just want to relax. The program, however, is quite violent and you decide that it's making you kind of jittery. You turn off the television. Take in the silence… Breathe in… Hold your breath… Now breathe out. You put on some soft music.

Listen to the melody… Now get comfortable. Roll your head back and forth, slowly… Listen again to the sound of the music.

Light a candle. Watch as the flame flickers.… Make a wish… Think about the wish and will it to become true. Continue to watch the candle…

You feel so relaxed. You decide to take a bath. Imagine taking the candle and entering your bathroom. Turn on the water in your bathtub. Pour some bubble bath into the tub. You watch as the water rises. The fragrance of the bubble bath is quite sweet. Breathe it in…

Once the bathtub is full, slowly get into it. Feel the water swirling around you… Feel the comfort of the heat of the water… Relax… Let your mind drift… You breathe in slowly… Breathe out… Breathe in… Breathe out. You take a washcloth and lather it with soap. You clean your body, slowly rubbing your body… Place the washcloth on your face and close your eyes. You feel a million miles away. You are completely relaxed… Breathe in and the smell the bubble bath again. Remove the washcloth. Imagine that you open your eyes again and look at the candle flickering. You remember the wish you made before and you wish it again… Hold on to that wish…

You're ready to get out of the bathtub. Slowly rise from the tub and pull out the plug. Find a warm, fluffy towel and dry yourself fully. Notice how the towel feels as it envelops your body… You feel so safe and warm…

It's time now for bed. You take the candle and place it on your nightstand. Find your night clothes. Put them on… Now it's time to get into bed. Fold back the blanket and sheets and get into your bed. Notice how the sheets feel against your body. Breathe in… Breathe out… It's time now to go to sleep. Blow out your candle… Sweet dreams…

Pretend it's the next morning and it's time to awaken. You have had such a restful night. I'm going to count backwards, from ten. When you're ready, wake up. 10… 9… 8… 7… 6… 5… 4… 3… 2… 1… Now begin to wake up.

Chapter Seven
Aromatherapy

Aromatherapy is the therapeutic use of aromatic oils extracted from plants. Essential oils are extracted from a plant's flower, leaves, stalk, bark, rind, or roots. The essential oils are mixed with other oil, alcohol, or lotion and then applied to the skin, sprayed in the air, or inhaled. Essential oils are often used in candles and incense. Massage therapists have used essential oils to enhance massage experiences. Many products are available for use while bathing.

Theoretically, the plant oils produce fragrances which stimulate the odor-sensing nerves in the nose. In turn, impulses that control memory and emotion are sent to the brain. Depending on the type of oils used, the results can be either stimulating or calming. Essential oils are thought to interact with the body's hormones and enzymes. Aromatherapy has been used in the treatment of:

- burns
- infections
- depression
- insomnia
- high blood pressure
- stress

Proponents of aromatherapy believe that the benefits of aromatherapy include:

- Changes in blood pressure
- Stimulates the body's glands to produce pain-fighting substances
- Increases relaxation
- Increases stimulation
- Lessens fatigue
- Stimulates the immune system
- Decreases anxiety

At the Wolfson Research Centre at Newcastle General Hospital, Institute for Ageing and Health, Newcastle Upon Tyne, United Kingdom, aromatherapy was used as an effective treatment for the management of agitation in severe dementia. In a controlled study, researchers used the essential oil of *Melissa officinalis* (lemon balm) combined with a base lotion and applied to the patients' faces and arms twice a day by the staff. Researchers found that the aromatherapy with essential oil is a safe and effective treatment for clinically significant agitation in people with severe dementia, with additional benefits for key quality-of-life parameters (Ballard, O'Brien, Reichelt & Perry, 2002).

Aromatherapy was used with hospice patients to decrease pain, anxiety, and depression at the Department of Nursing at the University of Nevada in Las Vegas. This study measured the responses of 17 cancer hospice patients to humidified essential oil aromatherapy. Vital signs as well as levels of pain, anxiety, depression, and a sense of well-being were measured. Results reflected an improvement in vital signs, depression, and a sense of well-being (Louis & Kowalski, 2002).

Furthermore, Australian wildflower essences were used effectively at nine Perth hospitals as a complementary therapy practice for stress and pain management (Balinski, 1998).

Implementation Concerns

Essential oils should be used as an adjunct to a program and not as a primary therapeutic tool. For best results, use the essential oils in a vaporizer, or in candles or incense (if the facility allows use of either candles or incense). Another way to use the essential oils is to add a few drops to a handkerchief or apply several drops directly to the client's wrist, temples, neck, or shoulders.

Aromatherapy can be used individually or in a group setting. Decrease outside stimulus during this activity, and conduct this group in a clinic or conference room if possible. Dim the lights or use lamps with 25-

or 40-watt bulbs. Turn off the television and overhead lighting.

If you decide to use background music, choose instrumental tapes or CDs rather than music with lyrics. These tapes and CDs are available at most music and New Age stores.

For clients with adequate cognitive abilities, ask them to use the Stress Meter before and after the activity to determine whether they have experienced a reduction in stress. For best results, a short stretch and breathing exercise prior to starting the aromatherapy activity will help to relax clients.

Special Considerations

Research is limited about the benefits of aromatherapy and there are several contraindications. Essential oils should not be used with people who suffer from asthma or skin allergies. Use of essential oils is *not* recommended for pregnant women or young children. Do not place the oils near the eyes or mouth as they can cause irritation. The oils should never be swallowed as the are dangerous if taken internally. If using handkerchiefs, prepare individual hankerchiefs for each participant.

Implementation

The essential oils known for their calming properties include:

- German chamomile (*Matricaria chamomilla*)
- Rose (genus *Rosa*)
- Lavender (genus *Lavandula*)
- Jasmine (*Jasminum officinale*)
- Neroli oil (*Citrus aurantium*)

Applications

Smell

After completing a short stretching exercise, place several drops of one of the essential oils on the client's wrist. Suggest that they breathe in the scent of the oil for several seconds. Ask clients to close their eyes and allow their sense of smell to take in the aroma of the oils. Follow with several deep breaths.

End with a discussion period which includes highlighting the benefits inherent in using the oils.

Hand Massage

Place samples of essential oils in small containers or cups. Distribute the samples of an essential oil to the clients. The handout may be distributed at this time as well. Instruct the clients to place several drops of the essential oil on the palm of their right hand. Show them how to use their left thumb to follow the contours of their right hand with stroking movements and circular motions. Now suggest to the clients to bring their left thumb down to massage their right wrist. Then, when ready, work their left thumb back up the hand and massage each finger.

After several minutes, instruct the clients to switch hands (i.e., use their right thumb to massage their left hand). After they have completed the hand massage, allow the clients several moments of silence.

End with a discussion regarding their feelings after finishing the hand massage.

Vaporizer

Prior to beginning the group, prepare the vaporizer by adding several drops of essential oil into the water of the vaporizer. Dim the lights and put on some soft music. Gather your clients and begin the group. Explain that they will be sitting quietly and using their sense of smell to relax them. It is okay to use a relaxation tape or soft background music along with the aromatherapy. Give your clients a 20-minute aromatherapy "mini-vacation." End with discussion.

Recommended Reading

Davis, P. (1999). *Aromatherapy.* Essex, UK: C.W. Daniel Co. Ltd.

Lawless, J. (1995). *The illustrated encyclopedia of essential oils: The complete guide of oils in aromatherapy and herbalism.* London, UK: Element Books.

References

Balinski, A.A. (1998). Use of Western Australian flower essences in the management of pain and stress in the hospital setting. *Complementary Therapies in Nursing & Midwifery, 4*(4), 111–117.

Ballard, C.G., O'Brien, J.T., Reichelt, K., and Perry, E.K. (2002). Aromatherapy as a safe and effective treatment for the management of agitation in severe dementia: The results of a double-blind, placebo-controlled trial with *Melissa. Journal of Clinical Psychiatry, 63*(7), 553–558.

Louis, M. and Kowalski, S.D. (2002). Use of aromatherapy with hospice patients to decrease pain, anxiety, and depression and to promote an increased sense of well-being. *Journal of Hospice and Palliative Care, 19*(6), 381–386.

Hand Massage Handout

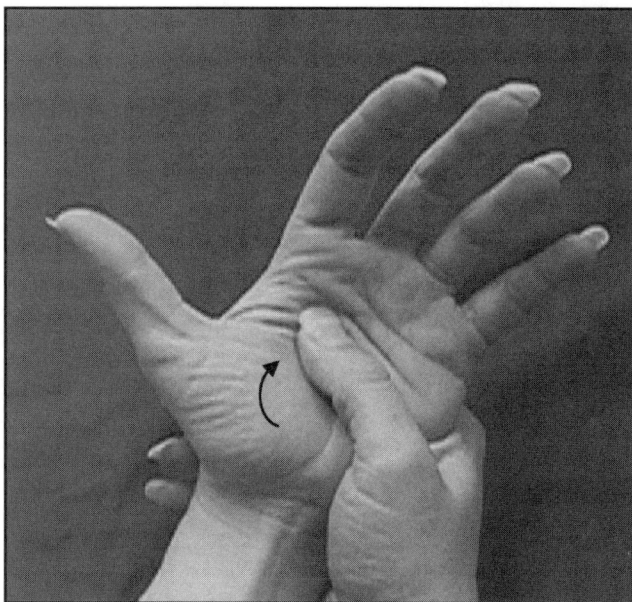

(1) Place several drops of essential oil in the palm of your left hand. With your right thumb follow the contours of your right hand with stroking movements. Use the thumb to stroke palm in a circular motion (Illustration #1).

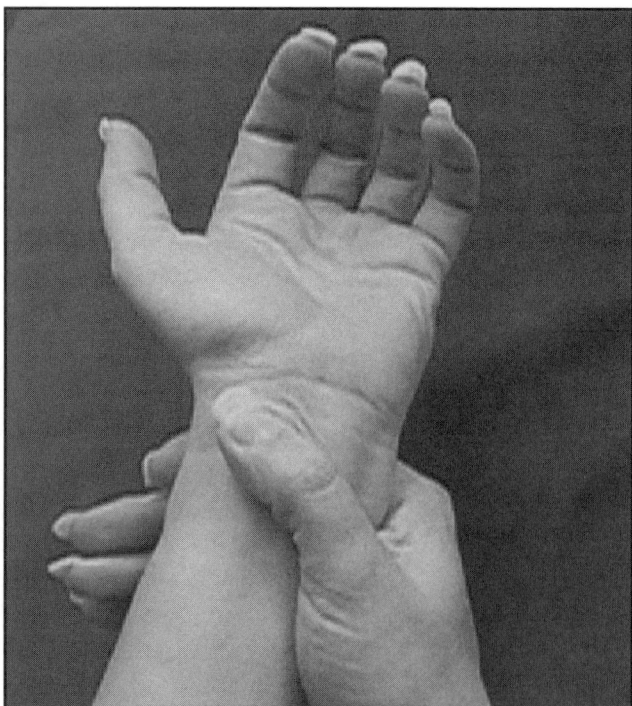

(3) Now gently and slowly squeeze each finger with your thumb and forefinger (Illustration #3).

(4) Change hands, using your left thumb to massage your right hand.

(5) After completing the hand massage, allow yourself several moments of silence.

(2) Bring thumb down to the wrist and repeat the stroking movement in a clockwise fashion. (Illustration #2).

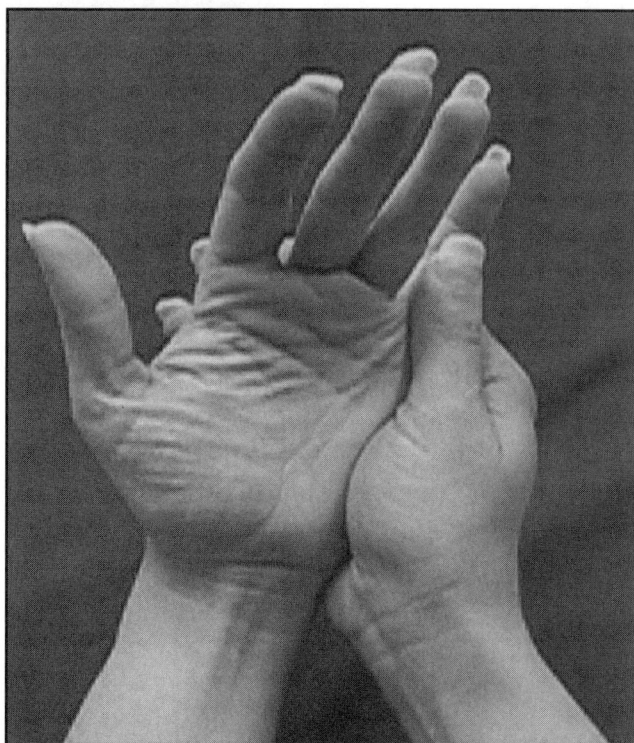

Chapter Eight
Acupressure

The oriental medical practice of acupuncture and acupressure has been used to treat disease for thousands of years. Acupuncture uses tiny needles while acupressure uses the hands to stimulate certain points of the body.

From a theoretical standpoint, the human body encloses an ongoing flow of bioenergy (life-force) called *chi*. Energy flows along specific pathways called *meridians* and controls the functioning of all of the organs. Along the meridians are a large number of controlling nerve endings, called *acupoints*. There are about 365 acupoints along the meridians in which *chi* is concentrated and enters and leaves the body. If you are healthy, energy flow is in balance. This is not the case when you are sick. However, by stimulating the acupoints in unhealthy individuals balance can be restored.

While the practice of acupuncture and acupressure has been a long-standing way of treating illness in the Eastern countries, recently it has become more popular in the Western countries.

Acupressure involves the use of finger and thumb pressure to stimulate the acupoints. It has been used to treat the following conditions:

- headaches
- insomnia
- anxiety
- depression
- menopause
- back problems
- allergies
- stomach problems
- stress

Benefits of using acupressure include:

- Reduces symptoms
- Balances of the body's energy flow
- Reduces stress

In a research project conducted at the Department of Anesthesiology at the Faculty of Health Sciences in Linkoping, Sweden, pressure on 15 classical acupoints decreased postoperative pain (Felhender & Lisander, 1999).

Acupressure was also used successfully in a study at the Department of Nursing at the National Taipei Nursing College in Taiwan. Eighty-four elderly people suffering from disturbed sleep took part in the study which confirmed that acupressure was an effective treatment in improving quality of sleep (Chen, Lin, Wu & Lin, 1999).

Furthermore, acupressure was determined to be a beneficial adjunct treatment in a pulmonary rehabilitation program at the School of Nursing, Chang Gung College of Medicine and Technology in Taiwan (Maa, Gauthier & Turner, 1997).

Implementation Concerns

Using acupressure in therapeutic recreation programs is recommended only as an adjunct to the medical treatment the client is receiving at the agency or clinic. Most states have laws prohibiting the use of acupressure unless you are a licensed Chinese medical practitioner. If a client wants to receive a more extensive treatment, they will need to be referred to a clinic licensed by the state.

Decrease outside stimulus during this activity, and conduct this group in a clinic or conference room if possible. Dim the lights or use lamps with 25- or 40-watt bulbs. Turn off the television and overhead lighting.

If you decide to use background music, choose instrumental tapes or CDs rather than music with lyrics. These tapes and CDs are available at most music and New Age stores.

For clients with adequate cognitive abilities, ask them to use the Stress Meter before and after the activity to determine whether they have experienced a reduction in stress. For best results, a short stretch and breathing exercise prior to starting the acupressure exercise will help to relax clients.

Special Considerations

Acupressure should *not* be used:

- during pregnancy
- for people with heart conditions
- if the acupressure point is located under a mole, wart, varicose vein, abrasion, bruise, or cut
- before or 20 minutes after heavy exercise
- before or 20 minutes after consuming a large meal
- before or 20 minutes after bathing or showering

Implementation

Explain to the clients that they will be using their fingers to stimulate certain acupoints in their bodies which will help them relieve stress. There are several points which are indicated for stress reduction. For best results, instruct clients to move from one point to another in a clockwise manner.

Once you have identified the acupoint to work on, ask the clients to take one or two of their fingertips and press down on the point. Tell the clients to increase pressure on the acupoint slowly and comfortably. Caution clients that if they begin to feel any pain, they need to release some of the pressure. The clients should be able to feel a faint pulse beneath the acupoint. This can take as little as three or up to ten minutes. When the clients are ready to move to the next acupoint, suggest that they release the pressure from the current acupoint very gradually. There is no right or wrong amount of pressure. Each client will have a different reaction to this exercise.

Recommended Readings

Cerney, J.V. (1999). *Acupuncture without needles: Do-it-yourself acupressure—The simple at-home treatment for lasting relief of pain.* Paramus, NJ: Prentice Hall.

References

Boyd, K.T. (2002). Finding the acupoints. Retrieved October 25, 2002, from http://www.geocities.com/jrh_iii/acupressure

Chen, M.L., Lin, L.C., Wu, S.C., and Lin, J.G. (1999). The effectiveness of acupressure in improving the quality of sleep of institutionalized residents. *Journals of Gerontology: Series A, Biological Sciences and Medical Sciences, 54*(8), M389–394.

Felhendler, D. and Lisander, B. (1999). Effects of noninvasive stimulation of acupoints on the cardiovascular system. *Complementary Therapies in Medicine, 7*(4), 231–234.

Maa, S.H., Gauthier, D., and Turner, M. (1997). Acupressure as an adjunct to a pulmonary rehabilitation program. *Journal of Cardiopulmonary Rehabilitation, 17*(4), 268–276.

How to Use Acupoints

By using your hands to stimulate certain acupoints in your body, you will be able to relieve stress. There are several points which are especially helpful for stress reduction. Take some time to look at the examples and determine which acupoints you would like to try. For best results, move from one point to another in a clockwise manner.

Take one or two of your fingertips and press down on the first acupoint. Begin to increase the pressure on the acupoint, slowly and comfortably. If you begin to feel any pain, release some of the pressure. After a couple of minutes, you should be able to feel a faint pulse beneath the acupoint. This can take as little as three minutes or up to ten minutes. Sit quietly and feel the pulse. When you are ready to move to the next acupoint, release the pressure from the current acupoint very gradually, if you have any questions about the process, be sure to ask a healthcare professional about your concerns.

Acupoints for Anxiety

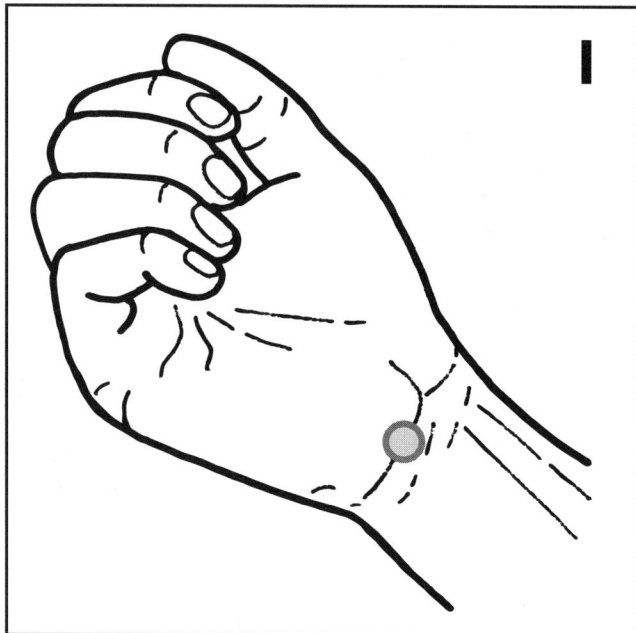

This point is on the largest crease of the inner wrist, on a line with the little finger.

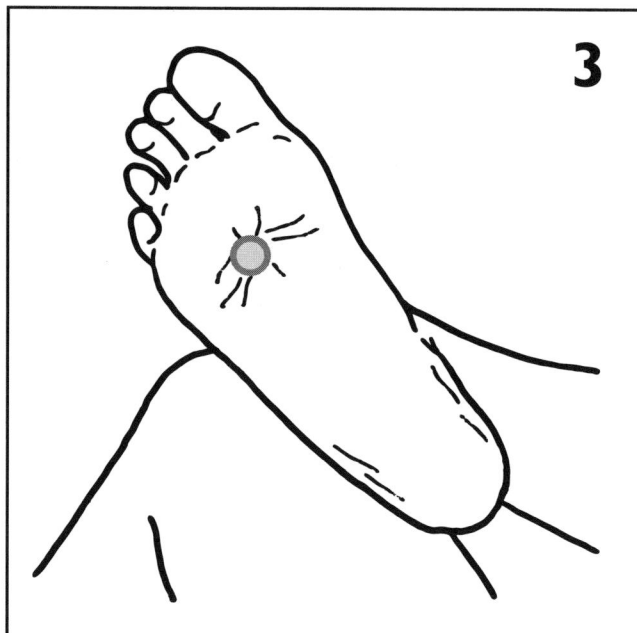

This point is in the middle of the sole of the foot, just behind the ball.

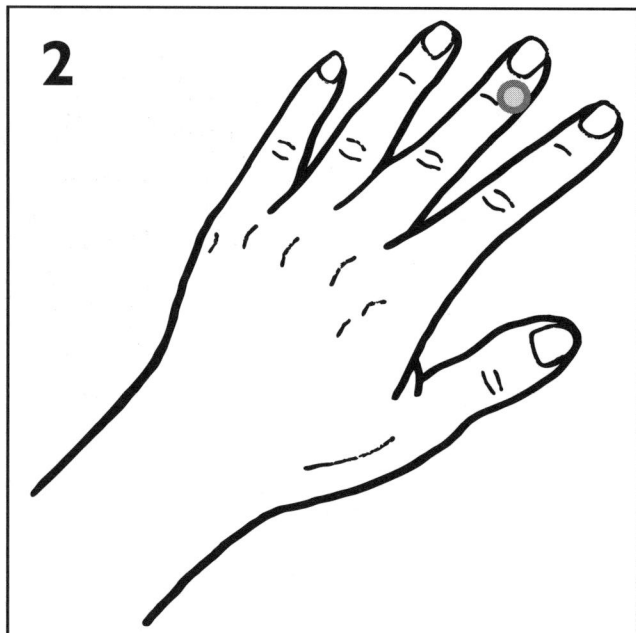

This point is on the middle finger, just above the nail on the side closest to the thumb.

Acupoints for Insomnia

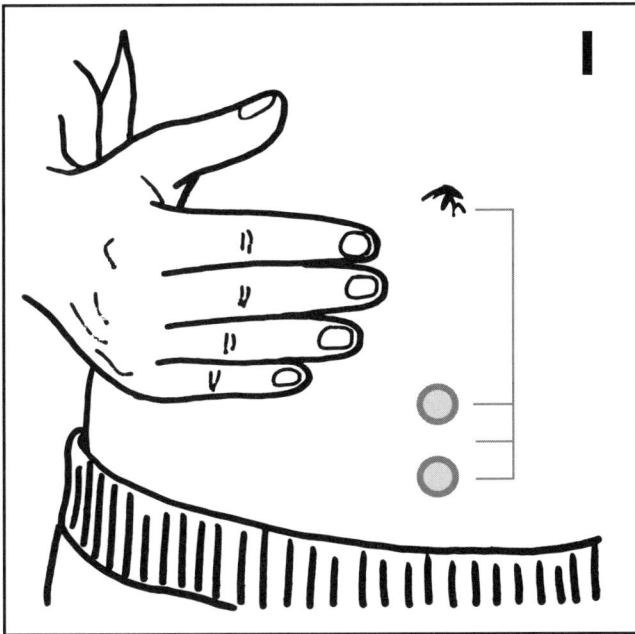

To find this point, measure one hand-width below the navel. Another point with similar effects can be found two thumb widths below this one.

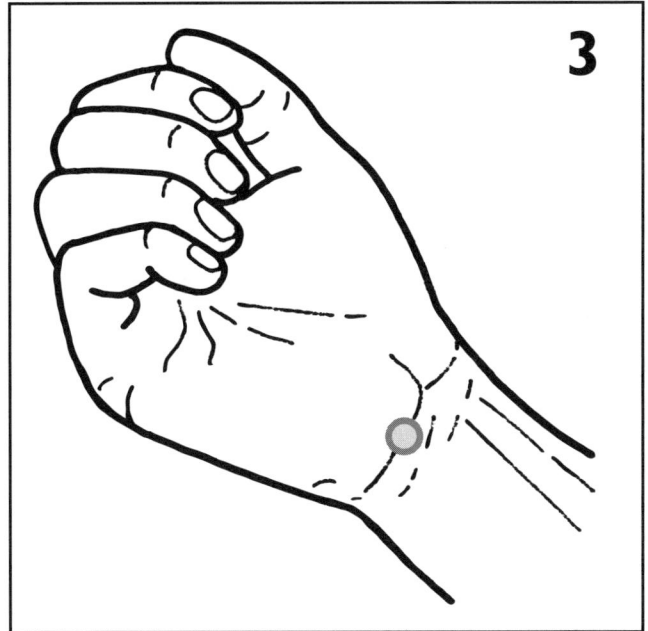

This point is on the largest crease of the inner wrist on a line with the little finger.

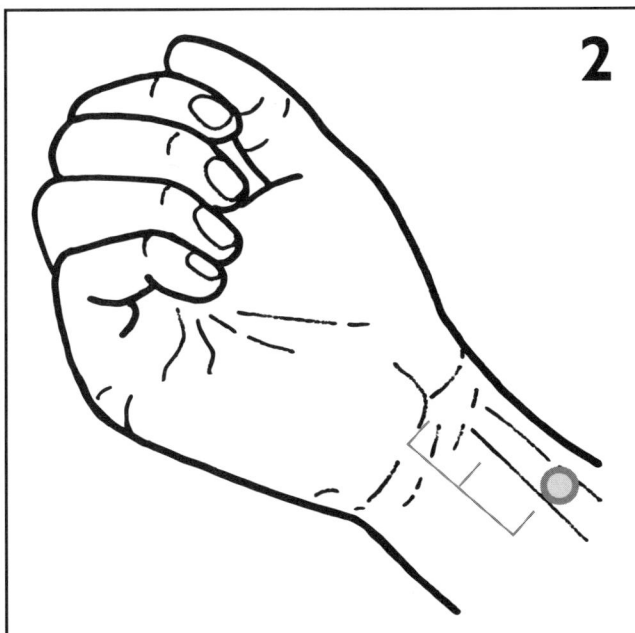

Measure two thumb-widths from the largest crease on the inside wrist. The point falls between the tendons in the middle of the wrist.

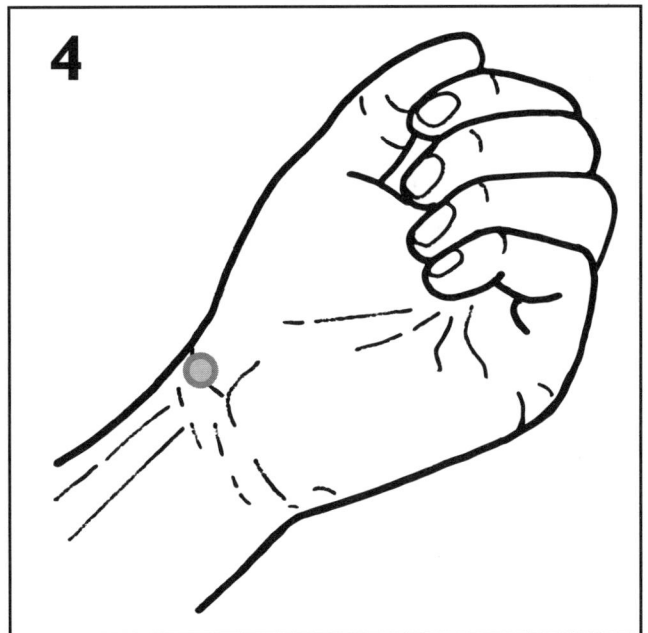

This point is found on the largest crease of the inner wrist on a line with the thumb.

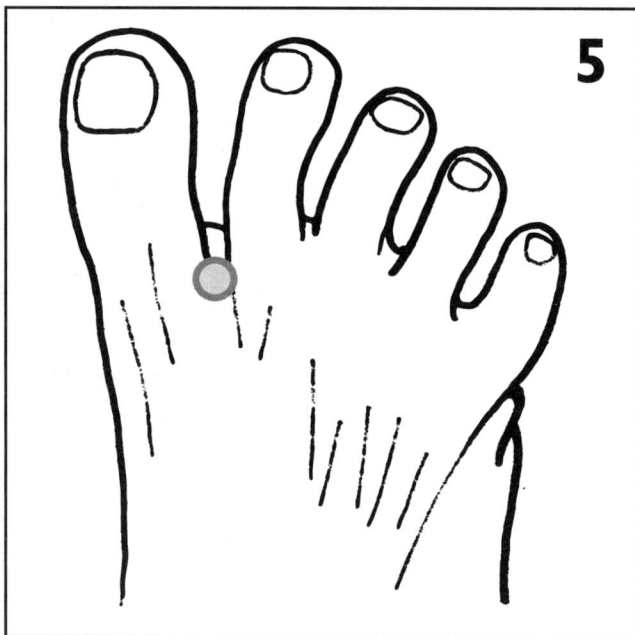

This point is just above where the big toe and the second toe separate on the upper surface of the foot.

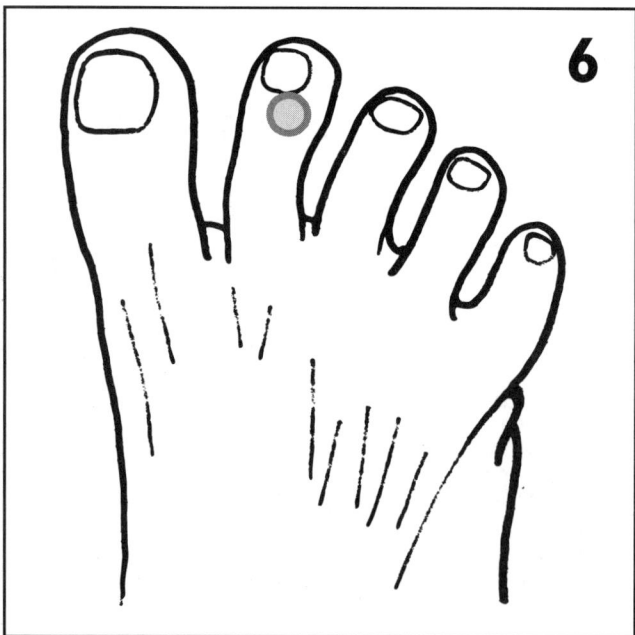

This point is just behind the nail of the second toe on the side opposite the big toe.

Acupoints for Headaches

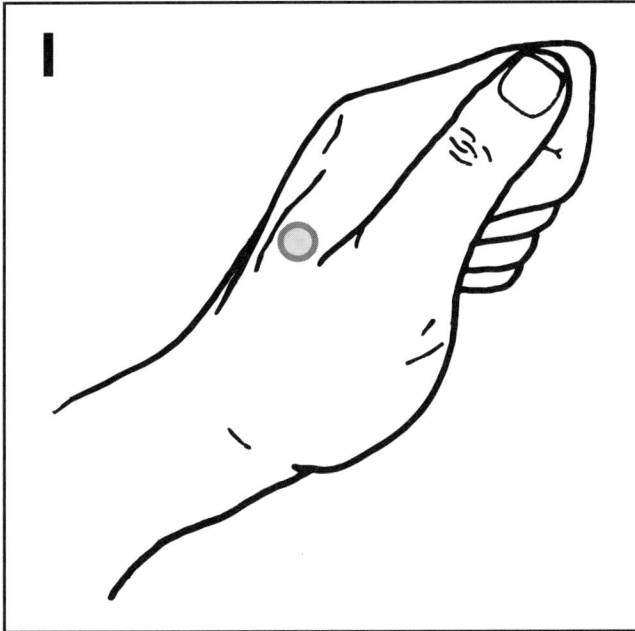

1

This point is good for most problems from the waist up. Squeeze thumb and forefinger together forming a ridge above the thumb. The point is in the middle of that ridge just above the end of the crease formed by thumb and forefinger.

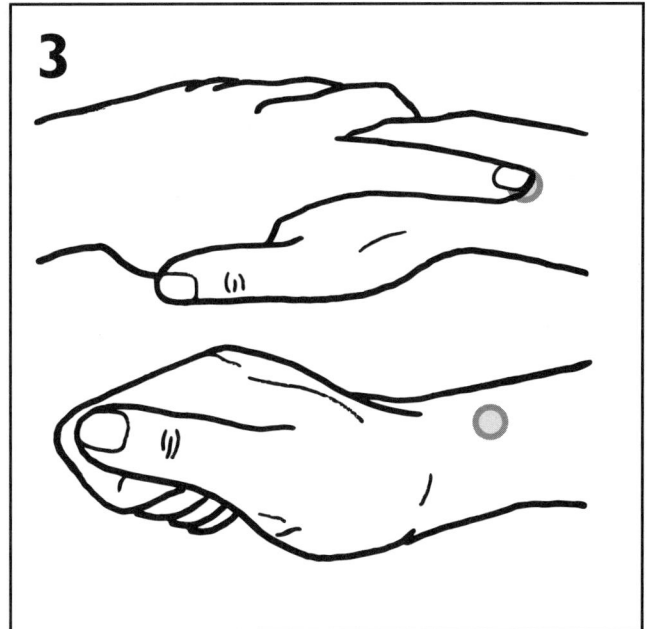

3

Clasp you hands together as in (top), touching your upper wrist with your forefinger. The point is found on a line with the thumb in a small depression (bottom). Remembering the position of the point, unclasp your hands and apply pressure in the proper manner.

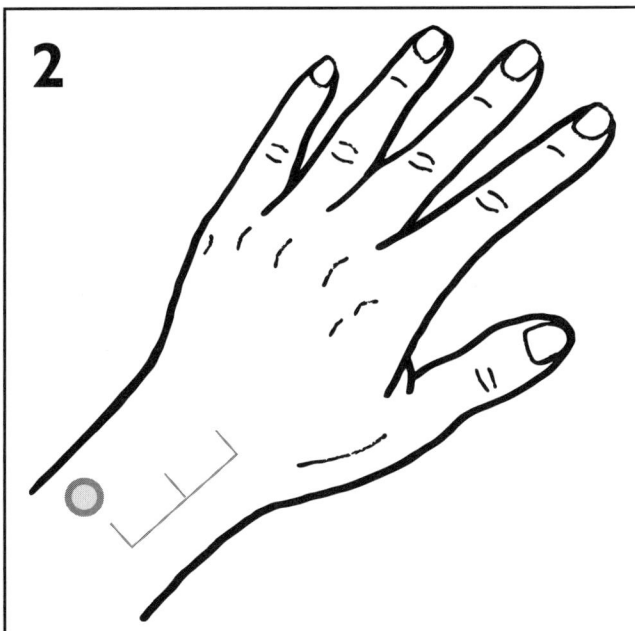

2

This point is two thumb-widths above the outside of the wrist lined up with the middle finger.

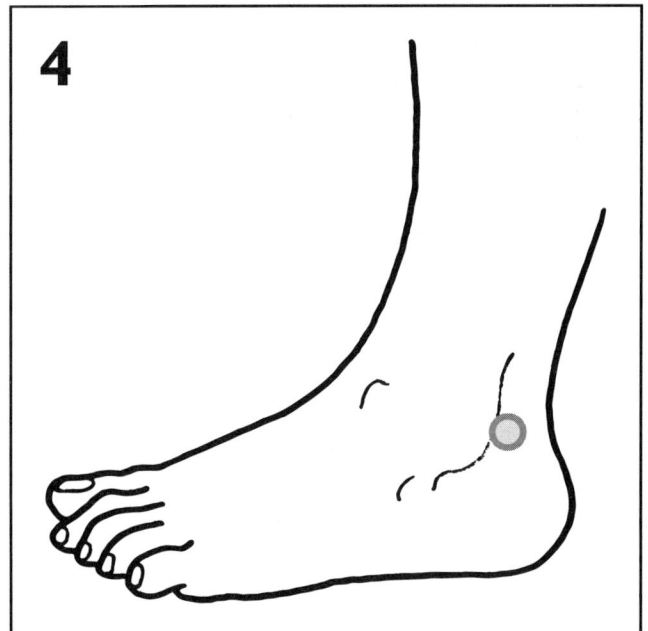

4

This point is in the depression just behind the outer anklebone.

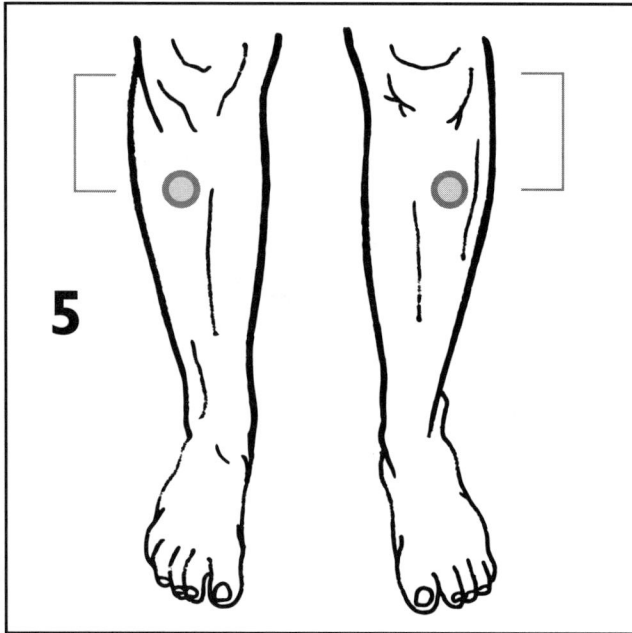

This point is very effective for most problems from the waist down. It is found one hand-width below the bottom edge of the kneecap on the outside in a depression between the shinbone and the leg muscle.

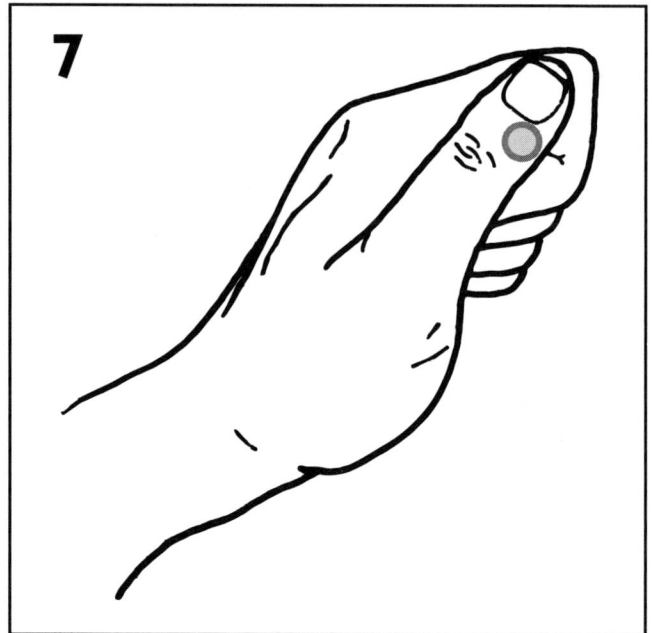

This point is found just behind the thumbnail, on the side opposite the fingers.

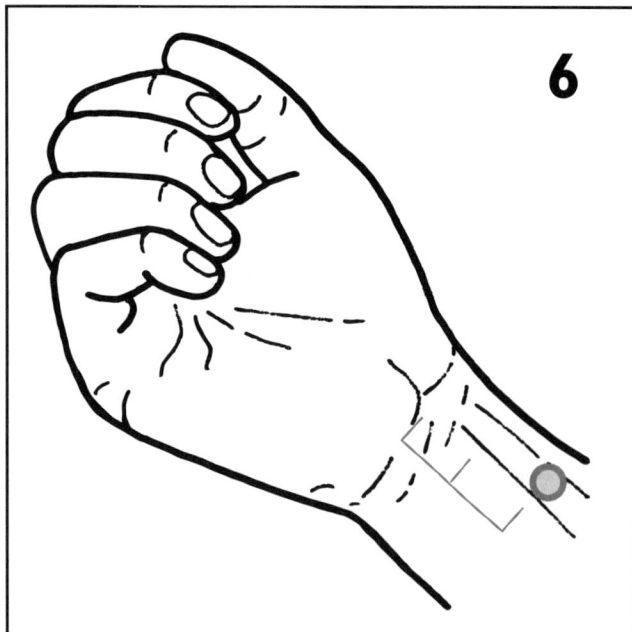

Measure two thumb-widths from the largest crease on the inside wrist. The point falls between the tendons in the middle of the wrist.

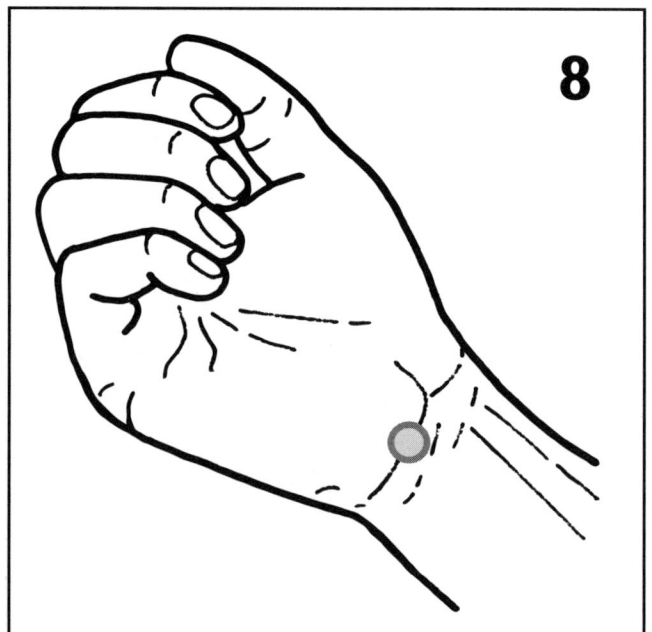

This point is on the largest crease of the inner wrist on a line with the little finger.

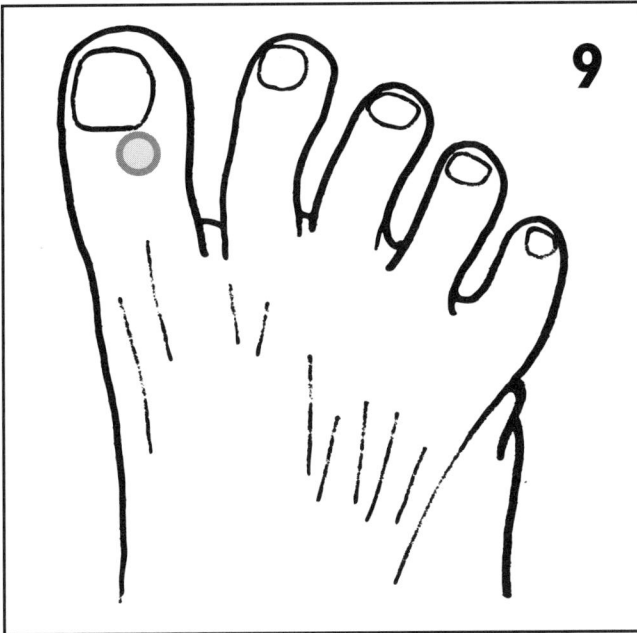

This point is found on the big toe on the side closest to the second toe, just behind and slightly to the side of the nail.

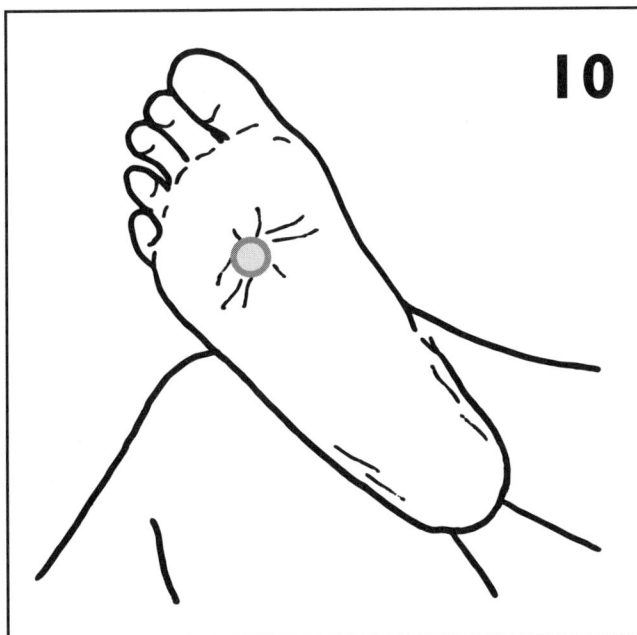

This point is in the middle of the sole of the foot, just behind the ball of the foot.

Chapter Nine
Autogenics

The term *autogenics* comes from the Greek word meaning "generated from within." The purpose of autogenics is to induce the relaxation response by visualizing various sensations in the body, such as heaviness in the neck, shoulders and limbs, warmth in the limbs, a calm heartbeat, relaxed breathing, and coolness in the forehead.

Autogenics have been used to treat the following conditions:

- stress
- migraine headaches
- ulcers
- high blood pressure
- irritable bowel syndrome
- premenstrual syndrome
- eczema
- substance abuse

The benefits of autogenics include:

- Changes the brain and tissue chemistry inducing the relaxation response
- Regulates unwanted tension in voluntary and involuntary muscles
- Improves ability to handle stress
- Reduces anxiety

In a research project at the ARC Cancer Support Centre in Dublin, Ireland, a group of cancer patients took part in an autogenic therapy (AT) program. Each participant completed a Hospital Anxiety and Depression Scale and Profile of Mood States questionnaire before and after a ten-week autogenic therapy course. The results indicated a significant reduction in anxiety, increase in "fighting spirit," an improved sense of coping, and improved sleep as apparent benefits of AT practice (Wright, Courtney & Crowther, 2002).

In a research project performed at the Center for Adaptive Computer Education at the School of Occupational Therapy at the Dalhousie University in Halifax, Nova Scotia, autogenic training was part of a relaxation training program administered to four adults with severe brain injury. Significant improvement was noted as measured by scores of a scale of illness-related dysfunction (Lysaght & Bodenhamer, 1990).

Implementation Concerns

Decrease outside stimulus during this activity, and conduct this group in a clinic or conference room if possible. Dim the lights or use lamps with 25- or 40-watt bulbs. Turn off the television and overhead lighting.

If using background music, choose instrumental tapes or CDs rather than music with lyrics. These tapes and CDs are available at most music and New Age stores.

For clients with adequate cognitive abilities, ask them to use the Stress Meter before and after the activity to determine whether they have experienced a reduction in stress.

For best results a short stretch and breathing exercise prior to starting the autogenic exercise will help clients relax.

Be sure to pause for at least three to five seconds when three dots (…) appear in the script and 10 to 15 seconds between paragraphs or logical pausing points.

Special Considerations

If the client has physical limitations, alter the exercise in order for him or her to have a successful experience. Determine the needed adaptations prior to the exercise.

Recommended Reading

Kermani, K. (1996). *Autogenic training: The effective holistic way to better health*. London, UK: Souvenir Press Ltd.

References

Lysaght, R. and Bodenhamer, E. (1990). The use of relaxation training to enhance functional outcomes in adults with traumatic head injuries. *American Journal of Occupational Therapy, 44*(9), 797–802.

Wright, S., Courtney, U. and Crowther, D. (2002). A quantitative and qualitative pilot study of the perceived benefits of autogenic training for a group of people with cancer. *European Journal of Cancer Care, 11*(2), 122–130.

Autogenics Script

Your right arm is heavy...
Your right arm is heavy...
Your right arm is heavy...
Your right arm is heavy...

Your left arm is heavy...
Your left arm is heavy...
Your left arm is heavy...
Your left arm is heavy...

Both of your arms are heavy...
Both of your arms are heavy...
Both of your arms are heavy...
Both of your arms are heavy...

Your right leg is heavy...
Your right leg is heavy...
Your right leg is heavy...
Your right leg is heavy...

Your left leg is heavy...
Your left leg is heavy...
Your left leg is heavy...
Your left leg is heavy...

Your right arm is warm...
Your right arm is warm...
Your right arm is warm...
Your right arm is warm...

Your left arm is warm...
Your left arm is warm...
Your left arm is warm...
Your left arm is warm...

Both of your arms are warm...
Both of your arms are warm...
Both of your arms are warm...
Both of your arms are warm...

Your right leg is warm...
Your right leg is warm...
Your right leg is warm...
Your right leg is warm...

Your left leg is warm...
Your left leg is warm...
Your left leg is warm...
Your left leg is warm...

Both of your legs are warm...
Both of your legs are warm...
Both of your legs are warm...
Both of your legs are warm...

Your right arm and leg are warm and heavy...
Your right arm and leg are warm and heavy...
Your right arm and leg are warm and heavy...
Your right arm and leg are warm and heavy...

Your left arm and leg are heavy...
Your left arm and leg are heavy...
Your left arm and leg are heavy...
Your left arm and leg are heavy...

Both of your arms and legs are warm and heavy...
Both of your arms and legs are warm and heavy...
Both of your arms and legs are warm and heavy...
Both of your arms and legs are warm and heavy...

Your shoulder and neck are heavy...
Your shoulder and neck are heavy...
Your shoulder and neck are heavy...
Your shoulder and neck are heavy...

Your shoulder and neck are warm...
Your shoulder and neck are warm...
Your shoulder and neck are warm...
Your shoulder and neck are warm...

Your shoulder and neck are heavy and warm...
Your shoulder and neck are heavy and warm...
Your shoulder and neck are heavy and warm...
Your shoulder and neck are heavy and warm...

Your stomach is warm...
Your stomach is warm...
Your stomach is warm...
Your stomach is warm...

Your shoulder and neck are warm...
Your shoulder and neck are warm...
Your shoulder and neck are warm...
Your shoulder and neck are warm...

Your breathing is calm and relaxed...
Your breathing is calm and relaxed...
Your breathing is calm and relaxed...
Your breathing is calm and relaxed...

Your heart is calm and relaxed...
Your heart is calm and relaxed...
Your heart is calm and relaxed...
Your heart is calm and relaxed...

You feel a coolness in your forehead...
You feel a coolness in your forehead...
You feel a coolness in your forehead...
You feel a coolness in your forehead...

Your whole body is calm and relaxed...
Your whole body is calm and relaxed...
Your whole body is calm and relaxed...
Your whole body is calm and relaxed...

Your whole body feels quiet, comfortable and relaxed.

When you open your eyes you will feel refreshed and alert.

Chapter Ten
Music Relaxation Techniques

TRSs have used music as a therapeutic tool for years. Music can be used to enhance the client's physical, psychological, cognitive, and social functioning.

Music has been used to aid in the treatment of the following conditions:

- memory loss in the elderly
- speech problems related to stroke or brain injury trauma
- psychiatric disorders in adults
- children with either medical or psychological problems
- hospice clients
- chronic pain
- residents in long-term care facilities
- at-risk adolescents
- substance abuse
- mothers in labor
- people with learning disabilities
- insomnia

The benefits of using music include:

- Can assist with memory recall
- Provides positive changes in mood and emotional states
- Reduces stress and anxiety
- Increases socialization
- Stimulates both the right and left sides of the brain
- Enhances pain management

Calming music in tandem with hand massage was found to alter the immediate environment of agitated nursing home residents in a study conducted at the University of Massachusetts in Lowell (Remington, 2002).

Music also helped maintain the attention of older adults with cognitive impairment in a research project conducted at the center for Music Research at Florida State University (Gregory, 2002).

Implementation Concerns

Music can be utilized in both individual and group settings. One of the myths regarding music is that the participant needs to have an established musical ability. This is not the case. Anyone can enjoy music.

Fast, rhythmic, loud music can lead to physiological arousal and increases the activity in the automatic nervous system. Conversely, by playing soft music, the automatic nervous system becomes calmer and more relaxed. Pulse rates can be altered by the music's volume and speed. Breathing is also affected by the type of music played. For relaxation purposes, it is best to play music which has less than 60 beats per minutes. Most people have a heart rate around 60–75 beats per minute. Therefore, to induce the relaxation response it is suggested to choose music with a slower beat.

For best results, use music which is familiar to you and your clients. Avoid using too much variety in the music selection. Additionally, lyrics which are sad, such as lyrics which tell about a lost love or are political in nature, may defeat the purpose of the group. Choose instrumentals or songs with a positive world outlook. (See Music Recommendations). Use a prerecorded audiotape or CD for these activities.

Explain to the clients that you are going to play music which will help them decrease their stress level. For best results, a short stretch and breathing exercise prior to starting the exercise will relax your clients.

Be sure to pause for at least 10 to 15 seconds when three dots (…) appear in the scripts and 30 to 45 seconds between paragraphs or logical pausing points.

Special Considerations

Music can be used successfully with most of clients. It is best to play music which is familiar to the clients. Therefore, when working with older adults, use music from their era. Conversely, if you are working with young children, lullabies and children's songs are encouraged.

According to the website activitytherapy.com, relaxation music is good for meal times and toward the end of the day. The website recommends

> to pick pieces that have an even tempo and something soothing without words. If you use the same music every day as part of a routine, this may signal that the day is ending and time to start getting ready for bed.

If a client expresses any discomfort or is unable to follow the directions of the activity due to agitation, then it is recommended that the client not participate in the activity until he or she can be further assessed.

When using the progressive relaxation with music script, this exercise is *not* recommended for people who are actively hallucinating. The progressive relaxation with music script should be used with caution if your client has an illness causing psychotic symptoms as this exercise can lead to an out-of-body state.

Music Recommendations

New Age

New age composers have created many pieces that are appropriate for relaxation. Recommended artists include

- Peter Davidson
- Enya
- Stephen Halpern
- Yanni

Classical

- Ludwig van Beethoven:
  Egmont overture, Symphony no. 3 in E flat major "Eroica" Op. 55, Symphony no. 5 in C minor "Fate" Op. 67, Symphony no. 9 in D minor "Choral" Op. 125, Adagio from Symphony no. 9

- Camille Saint-Saens:
  Symphony no. 3 in C minor "Organ" Op. 78

- Gustav Mahler:
  Symphony no. 1 in G major "Titan"

- Frederick Chopin:
  "Baccarole," Études

- Alfredo Ortiz:
  Harp for Quiet Moment (I, II)

- Franz Peter Schubert:
  Prelude to *Rosamunde, Princess of Cyprus*

- J.S. Bach:
  Two Concertos for Two Pianos, Air for the G String from the Orchestral Suite in D

- Wolfgang Amadeaus Mozart:
  Concerto for Flute and Harp, Concertos for Flute and Orchestra (1, 2)

- George Frideric Handel:
  Harp Concerto (Boston Skyline), Largo from *Xerxes*

- Franz Peter Schubert:
  Prelude to *Rosamunde, Princess of Cyprus*

- Johann Pachelbel:
  Canon in D

- Antonio Vivaldi:
  Flute concertos, *The Four Seasons*

Popular Music

- Norah Jones: *Come Away With Me*
- Nelly Frutado: *Whoa Nelly*
- John Mayer: *Room for Squares*

Classic Rock/Pop

- Peter Gabriel: *So* and *Us*
- Sting: *Nothing Like the Sun*
- The Police: *Synchronicity*
- Simon and Garfunkel: *Parsley, Sage, Rosemary and Thyme*
- Judy Collins: *Best Hits*
- Joni Mitchell: *Ladies of the Canyon*
- Stevie Wonder: *Secret Lives of Plants* and *Songs in the Key of Life*
- John Lennon: *Imagine*
- Miles Davis: *Kind of Blue*

Earlier Performers

- Frank Sinatra
- Judy Garland
- Patsy Cline
- Ray Charles
- Rosemary Clooney

Recommended Reading

Lingerman, H.A. (1995). *The healing energies of music* (New ed.). Wheaton, IL: Quest Books.

References

Gregory, D. (2002). Music listening for maintaining attention of older adults with cognitive impairments. *Journal of Music Therapy, 39*(4), 244–264.

Remington, R. (2002). Calming music and hand massage with agitated elderly. *Nursing Research, 51*(5), 317–323.

Music Relaxation Technique 1
Mind/Body Connection

Sit in a chair or lie on a mat in a comfortable position. Place your palms in the yoga "savansa" relaxation pose in which the palms of the hand are facing up…

Allow the music to embrace you. Gently breathe in and breathe out. Think of yourself as a sponge, absorbing the music through every pore of your body…

Breathe deeply in time to the music. Inhale to the beat, exhale to the beat…

Listen to your heart beating…Begin to let the rate of the music regulate your heartbeat…

Close your eyes and feel the music pulsing gently against your muscles and nerves. Allow your muscles and nerves to relax with each beat…

Focus on the spot in the middle of your forehead known in yoga as the third eye. Feel the music as it touches your third eye…

Allow the music to wash over you, like a wave…

Focus all of your attention on the music. Allow yourself to become completely immersed in the music. If a thought enters your head, say hello to it, then let it go. Let the music be your focus. Become one with the music. Listen to the song. It is peaceful… It is restful… You are at peace… You are completely relaxed… Listen to the music… Let your thoughts go… Listen to the music… You are at peace… You are completely relaxed… All is well…

Take a couple of minutes to continue to relax, without the music. When you are ready, open your eyes.

Music Relaxation Technique 2
Progressive Relaxation With Music

Listen to the music. Allow the music to embrace you. Gently breathe in and breathe out. Think of yourself as a sponge, absorbing the music through every pore of your body…

Breathe deeply in time to the music. Inhale to the beat, exhale to the beat…

Allow the music to wash over you, like a wave… Think of the music as warm and healing…

As you begin, you are going to experience the tension in your feet. Relax your feet. Feel the music gently caressing your feet…

Take a deep breath. Breathe in, hold it, and exhale. You have become more relaxed… You are feeling more comfortable, more relaxed as you continue with this exercise.

Allow the music to travel to your calves. Feel the tension in your calves. Relax your calves. Allow the music to wash over your calves…

Take a deep breath. Breathe in, hold it, and exhale. You have become more relaxed… You are feeling more comfortable, more relaxed as you continue with this exercise.

Now we will be working on your thighs and quadriceps. Feel the tension in your thighs and quadriceps. Let the music sweep across your thighs and quadriceps…

Take a deep breath. Breathe in, hold it, and exhale. You have become more relaxed… You are feeling more comfortable, more relaxed as you continue with this exercise…

Now we will be working on your stomach and lower back. Feel the tension in your stomach and lower back. Allow the music to caress your stomach and lower back…

Take a deep breath. Breathe in, hold it, and exhale. You have become more relaxed… You are feeling more comfortable, more relaxed as you continue with this exercise.

Now we will be working on your chest and back. Feel the tension in your chest and back. Take a deep breath… Allow the music to surround your chest and back…

You have become more relaxed... You are feeling more comfortable, more relaxed as you continue with this exercise.

Now we will be working on your hands. Feel the tension in your hands. Allow the music to wash over your hands...

Take a deep breath. Breathe in, hold it, and exhale. You have become more relaxed... In just a few minutes you are going to feel more comfortable, more relaxed as you continue with this exercise.

Next, we are going to concentrate on the your upper back, shoulders, and neck. Feel the tension in your upper back, shoulders, and neck. Allow the music to caress you...

Take a deep breath. Breathe in, hold it, and exhale. You have become more relaxed... In just a few minutes you are going to feel more comfortable, more relaxed as you continue with this exercise.

Now we will concentrate on your facial muscles. Notice the tension around your mouth, lips, and jaw. Allow the music to wash over your facial muscles...

Inhale. Exhale, Relax. Let it all go... You feel completely relaxed and safe...

Now we are going to concentrate on your eyes. Feel the tension in your eyes. Allow the music to enter your eyes...

Inhale... Exhale... Let go of all of your tension... You are feeling very relaxed and calm...

Focus your attention on your body. Let the music enter your body. Listen to the music... Feel the music...

You are entirely relaxed. You have let go of all of your tension. You feel as if you are floating on a cloud. Begin to notice your breath as you lay quietly. Breathe in, breathe out. Breathe in, breathe out... Let your mind go. Let it go...

Take a couple of minutes to continue to relax, without the music... When you are ready, open your eyes.

Section II
Exercise

This section on exercise provides lesson plans for conducting stretching, yoga, and tai chi. There are two sections to the yoga and tai chi exercises. The first section provides examples of yoga and tai chi exercises which can be used by able-bodied individuals; the succeeding set provides adaptations on the exercises for physically challenged individuals. The benefits of exercise are many. Most doctors recommend a minimum of 45 minutes of exercise at least three times a week. As a TRS, it is important to determine each individual's ability to perform various exercises. This may mean that some clients may need to start at a point less than the recommended 45 minutes three times a week stated above. However, the end result is the same—getting clients to begin to think about moving.

Chapter Eleven
Beginning an Exercise Program

Providing exercise is an important component of any therapeutic recreation program. Depending on the population, therapeutic recreation specialists work to either develop or redevelop their clients' ability to exercise. Exercise is critical for helping individuals lower their stress levels in the following manners:

- When exercising, the body releases endorphins, which help reduce the body's anxiety levels.

- Exercise enhances oxygenation to the blood. The blood is transported to the brain, where it increases a sense of calm and alertness.

- Exercise can decrease blood pressure, lower the heart rate and slow breathing rates—all signs of reduced arousal and stress.

- Exercise reduces blood fat levels and the risks for heart attacks and strokes.

- Exercise may increase life span.

Physical benefits of exercise include developing the body through increasing:

- muscle strength
- muscle endurance
- cardiovascular endurance
- flexibility
- weight reduction

Emotional benefits of exercise include:

- Increases sense of accomplishment
- Increases self-esteem
- Enhances the ability to have fun
- Participating in a constructive use of leisure time
- Increases socialization

Different forms of exercise include:

- *Aerobic exercise* (such as walking, biking, aerobics classes, swimming, and jogging) involves the heart, lungs, and muscles. Aerobic exercise aids in strengthening the heart and blood vessels, and also burns calories.

- *Anaerobic exercise* (such as weight training) is high in intensity, uses energy stored in the muscles, and helps increase muscle strength.

- *Flexibility exercises* (including stretching and bending) are important for improving range of motion in the joints and muscles.

The 1996 *Surgeon General Report on Physical Activity and Health* reported that

Physical activity reduces the risk of premature mortality in general, and of coronary heart disease, hypertension, colon cancer, and diabetes mellitus in particular. Physical activity also improves mental health and is important for the health of muscles, bones, and joints.

According to the research completed by the Surgeon General, more than 60% of American adults are not regularly physically active and 25% of all adults are inactive. Furthermore, this study recommends emphasizing the amount rather than the intensity of physical activity to offer more options from which people can select when incorporating physical activity into their daily lives.

Special Considerations

Consult with the client's physician and obtain a medical clearance for the client. In developing an exercise program for your department, assess each client regarding his or her physical ability and work closely with your healthcare team.

If the client is currently taking medication, it is important to monitor his or her physical exertion throughout the activity. Any client complaining of feeling lightheaded or dizzy should be asked to sit down for the remainder of the activity.

When working with clients who are using wheelchairs, the brakes should be locked and power turned off if the chair is powered. If the brakes are not in good working order, place a sand weight or wheelchock to keep the chair from rolling. If the clients need to have their upper body stabilized during the exercise activity, strapping should be installed before the group begins. The wheelchair seatbelt should also be strapped.

Clients who have sustained a spinal cord injury may have restricted use of their trunk muscles, therefore some twisting exercises may be contraindicated. Spinal cord injured clients may have some thermoregulation impairments, increasing the possibility of overheating during exercise.

When working with a client who has cognitive limitations, exercises should be simplified so that the client understands the directions.

If the client has not been involved in an exercise program prior to treatment, start slowly and increase the amount of exercise gradually.

A brief warmup stretch is recommended prior to any exercise activity. A set of cool down exercises should also be utilized after completion of the exercise activity to decrease the chance of stiffness and sore muscles.

This section includes several worksheets for clients to help them increase their awareness of the full range of exercises and physical activities available to them. It also includes a section on stretching, yoga, and tai chi, all which can be adapted for physically challenged individuals.

Teach clients how to measure their heart rates in conjunction with an exercise program. Two easy methods can be used to check one's pulse rate. One method checks the pulse at the wrist (i.e., radial pulse). The other is at the neck (i.e., carotid pulse).

For a radial pulse check, have the clients use the tips of their index and third fingers. The radial artery can be found on the thumb side of either wrist and lies just a little below the base of the thumb. The pulsing artery can be felt when the fingers are in the right place.

The carotid pulse can be taken in the place just below the jaw and along either side of the windpipe on the throat. Suggest that clients use their first and second fingers and to press gently.

Use a digital watch or the second hand on a face watch and have the clients count their pulse for six seconds then multiply this number by ten.

Recommended Reading

Fisher, P. P. (1995). *More than movement for fit to frail older adults*. Baltimore, MD: Health Professional Publishers.

References

National Center for Chronic Disease Prevention and Health Promotion. (1996). *Physical activity and health: A report from the Surgeon General*. Washington, DC: U.S. Department of Health and Human Services.

Tips for Beginning an Exercise Program

1. **If you haven't exercised for an extended period of time, start slowly.** You may have better results sticking to an exercise program if you start in small increments. Make it your first week's goal to participate in exercise three to four times a day for ten-minute sessions.

2. **Doing housework, gardening, or working on some sort of home improvement activity is also a form of exercise.** You can kill two birds with one stone by working on your home or garden. Your residence will look a lot better and you'll burn calories at the same time.

3. **Schedule time for exercise into your daily routine.** Use a daily calendar to pencil in time for your exercise program. You'll be more likely to stick to the exercise plan if you've made a commitment to it on your calendar.

4. **Keep a record of your exercise program.** Use an activity diary or calendar to keep track of the exercise you have done. It'll help with your motivation.

5. **Be sure to incorporate warmup and cool down stretches into your exercise program.** Many people beginning an exercise program forget to prepare their bodies for exercise. Warmup and cool down stretches are an absolute necessity.

6. **Join a health club, the YMCA, or take exercise classes at your local park or through adult education programs.** Exercise classes abound. Consider all of the recreational resources available in your community.

7. **Adaptive exercise course are also available.** If you are concerned that your physical limitations may inhibit taking an exercise class at the above venues, inquire about adaptive exercise courses at the local YMCA or parks. Many health associations also offer adaptive exercise programs.

8. **Listen to your body.** If you are not feeling well, don't exercise. If you strain a muscle while exercising, consult your physician before starting up again.

9. **Wear appropriate footwear.** Wear shoes and socks which provide the proper amount of support and protection. Most sporting good stores have trained sales staff who can help you choose the right shoe.

10. **Ask a friend to exercise with you.** There's nothing better than having a friend to help you stay on track when beginning an exercise program. You can help motivate each other and it's a great way to spend time together.

11. **Join the Sierra Club or a hiking group.** The Sierra Club and other hiking associations offer all sorts of hikes, both locally and nationally. Some clubs offer international hiking adventures as well. Hiking is a wonderful form of exercise and you'll get to see great sights along the way.

12. **Choose an activity you're physically able to do.** If you have been physically idle for an extended period of time, don't choose an exercise activity which you are not physically capable of doing. Consider walking, swimming, cycling, or other activities you can pursue at your own pace.

Physical Activity Checklist

There are so many enjoyable ways to become physically active. Here's a list of activities to consider:

Fitness

aerobics
jogging
swimming
weight training
yoga
exercise videotape
exercise audiotape

Sports

ice skating
archery
basketball
football
baseball
soccer
handball
racquetball
tennis
volleyball
bowling
golf
Ping Pong (table tennis)
darts

Outdoors

cycling
hiking
downhill skiing
cross-country skiing
water skiing
canoeing
horseback riding

Rollerblading/skating
rock climbing
fishing
boating
scuba diving
snorkeling
sailing
backpacking
hiking
motorcycling
surfing
body surfing
water rafting
mountain climbing

Calorie Values for 30 Minutes of Activity*

Aerobic exercise	250 calories
Basketball	246 calories
Baseball	162 calories
Bowling (nonstop)	234 calories
Cycling (5.5 mph/hr)	174 calories
Dancing (moderate)	144 calories
Football	288 calories
Gardening	126 calories
Golfing	144 calories
Housecleaning	156 calories
Running (5.5 mph/hr)	375 calories
Skiing	336 calories
Stretching	140 calories
Swimming	281 calories
Tai chi	140 calories
Tennis	180 calories
Volleyball	195 calories
Walking (2 mph/hr)	120 calories

*For a person weighing 150 pounds. Calories calculated based on research data from *Medicine in Science and Sports and Exercise: The Official Journal of the American College of Sports Medicine.*

Exercise Log

Month:

	Exercise	Time Started	Time Ended	Total Time	Comments
1					
2					
3					
4					
5					
6					
7					
8					
9					
10					
11					
12					
13					
14					
15					
16					
17					
18					
19					
20					
21					
22					
23					
24					
25					
26					
27					
28					
29					
30					
31					

Chapter Twelve
Stretching

Stretching exercises are recommended as a prelude to many of the mind/body activities provided in this book. Stretching can also be completed as an activity unto itself.

Benefits of stretching include:

- Reduces muscle tension
- Helps improve coordination
- Increases range of motion
- Promotes blood circulation
- Improves muscle and joint flexibility
- Helps develop body awareness

A 2003 study conducted at the Department of Physical Education and Sports Science, Division of Sports, Laboratory of Coaching at the Aristotle University of Thessaloniki in Greece found that junior team handball players who took part in a 20-minute stretch program prior to playing handball experiences significantly increases range in all of their lower joint and trunk flexion.

Furthermore, a 2003 literature search conducted at the Department of Public Health at the School of Medicine at Wakayama Medical School in Japan found that back-stretching exercises reduced the risk of vertebral fractures.

Implementation Concerns

Decrease outside stimulus during this activity, and conduct this group in a clinic or conference room if possible. Dim the lights or use lamps with 25- or 40-watt bulbs. Turn off the television and overhead lighting. Simple stretching exercises can be used bedside or in a wheelchair. Stretching can also be practiced in an outdoor setting.

Loose clothing is recommended. Provide mats for able-bodied clients if possible.

When working with clients who are using wheelchairs, the brakes should be locked and power turned off if the chair is powered. If the brakes are not in good working order, place a sand weight or wheelchock to keep the chair from rolling. If the clients need to have their upper body stabilized during the exercise activity, strapping should be installed before the group begins. The wheelchair seatbelt should also be strapped.

If using background music, choose instrumental tapes or CDs rather than music with lyrics. These tapes and CDs are available at most music and New Age stores.

Explain to clients that you are going to guide them through a series of stretching exercises to help them lower their stress level. For clients with adequate cognitive abilities, ask them to rate their stress levels with the Stress Meter before and after the activity. When teaching clients stretching exercises, remind them to only stretch to the point where they feel a mild tension. Instruct clients *not* to bounce/bob when stretching as this may result in tearing of the connective tissue. Each stretch should be held for 10–30 seconds. For best results, have clients hold the stretch for 10 seconds at first and work up to a 30 second maximum hold time. Breathing should be slow and controlled.

Special Considerations

Clients should be medically cleared for participation in stretching exercise programs. Be sure to meet with their treatment team to determine whether stretching is an appropriate exercise for the client.

When working with clients who are using wheelchairs, the brakes should be locked and power turned off if the chair is powered. If the brakes are not in good working order, place a sand weight or wheelchock to keep the chair from rolling. If the clients need to have their upper body stabilized during the exercise activity, strapping should be installed before the group begins. The wheelchairs seatbelt should also be strapped.

Be sure to instruct clients to complete the exercises slowly and to not overdo any of the stretches or bounce/bob when stretching as this may result in the tearing of the connective tissue.

Recommended Resources

Anderson, B. (1980). *Stretching*. Bolinas, CA: Shelter Publishing.

Anderson, B. and Aitken, L. (director). *Stretching* [videotape]. Cupertino, CA: Bodytrends Health & Fitness.

References

Yoshimura, N. (2003). Exercise and physical activities for the prevention of osteoporotic fractures: A review of the evidence. *Nippon Eiseigaku Zasshi, 58*(3), 328–337.

Zakas, A., Vergou, A., Grammatikopoulou, M.G., Zakas, N., Sentelidis, T., and Vamvakoudis, S. (2003). The effect of stretching during warming-up on the flexibility of junior handball players. *Journal of Sports Medicine and Physical Fitness, 43*(2), 145–149.

Chair Stretches

(1) Sit in a comfortable position. Back should be straight. Arms to side. Slowly roll your head clockwise in a full circle. Repeat three times. Rotate head counterclockwise three times.

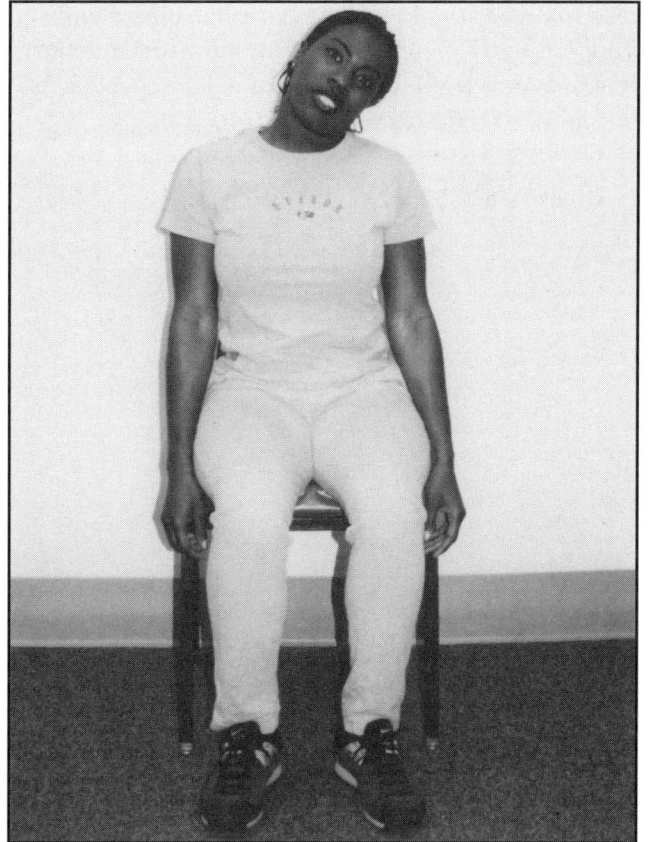

(2) Slowly rotate shoulders forward. Repeat three times. Rotate shoulders backward three times.

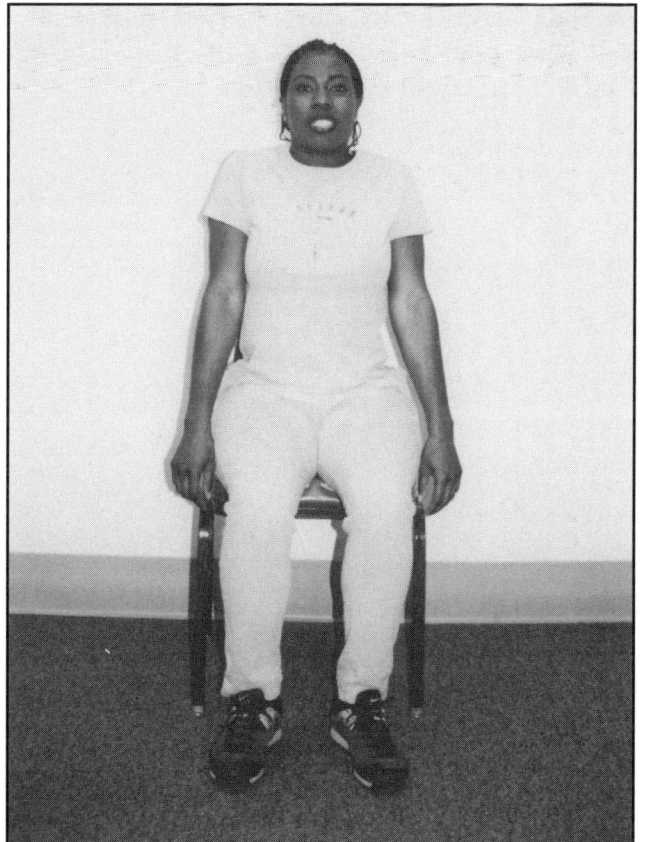

(3) Hold your right arm just above the elbow with your left hand. Gently pull your elbow toward your left shoulder. Hold for 10–30 seconds. Repeat using left arm and right hand. Hold 10–30 seconds.

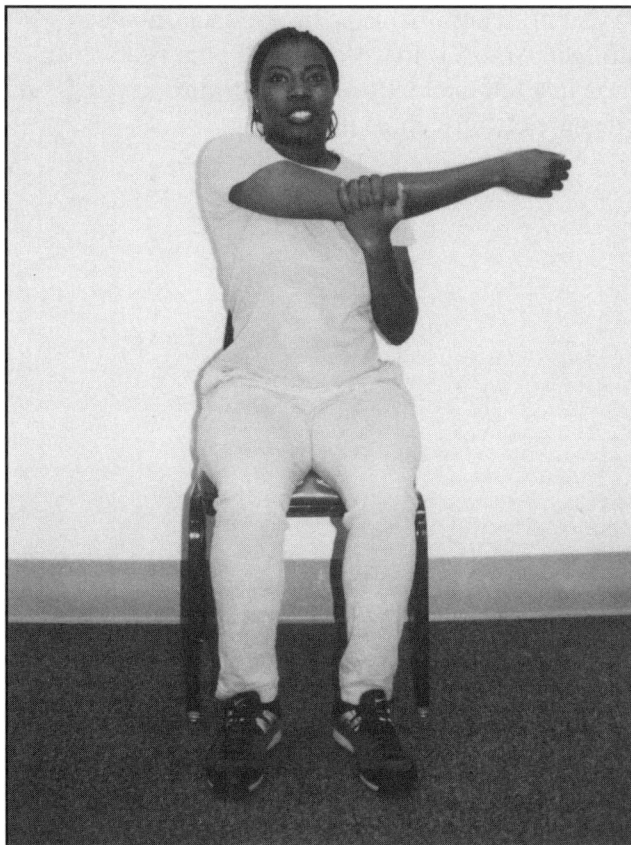

(4) Hold your right elbow with you left hand. Gently pull elbow behind head. Hold for 10–30 seconds. Repeat with left elbow and right hand.

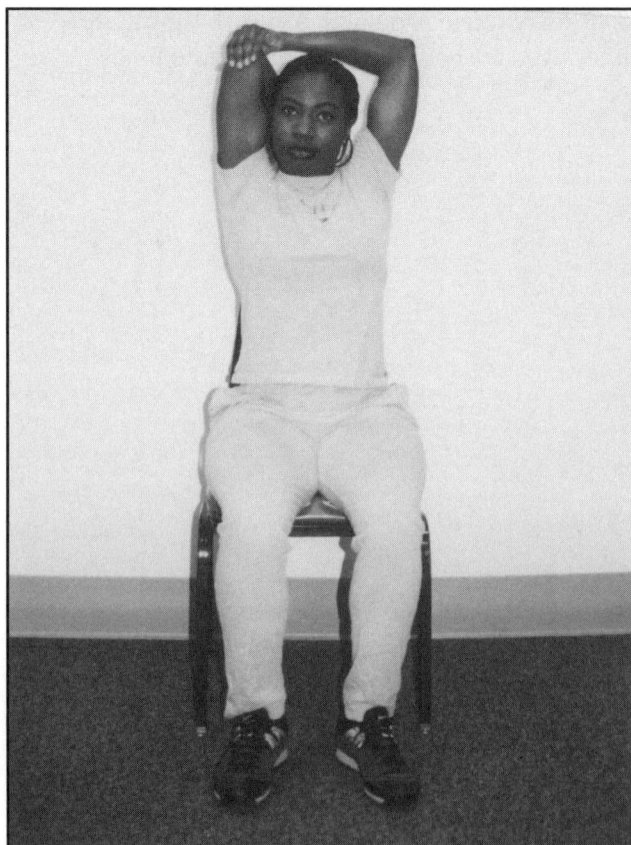

(5) Bend right knee toward chest. Hold leg in place for 10–30 seconds. Repeat with left leg.

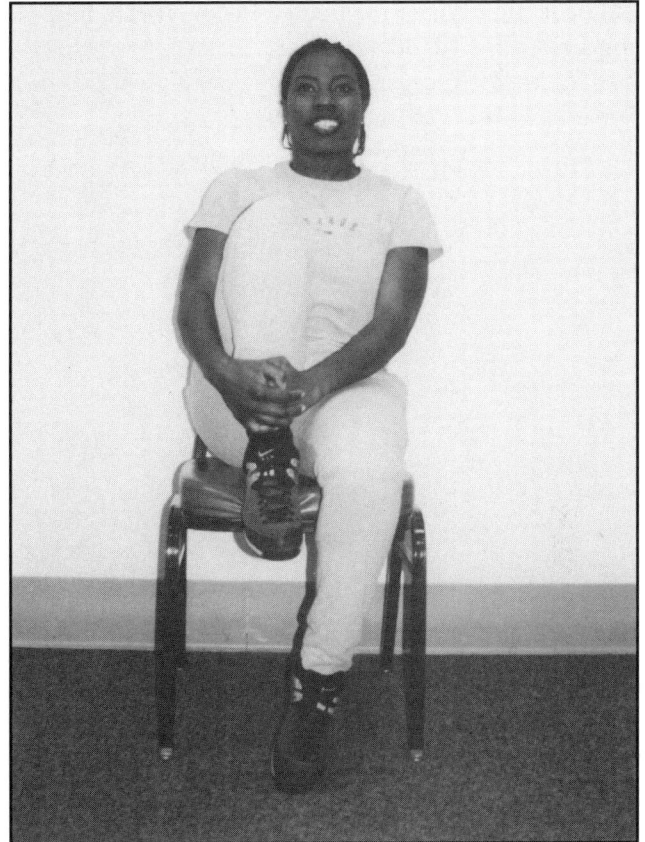

(6) Bring right leg forward, knee straight, slowly rotate foot clockwise three times, then counterclockwise three times. Repeat with left leg.

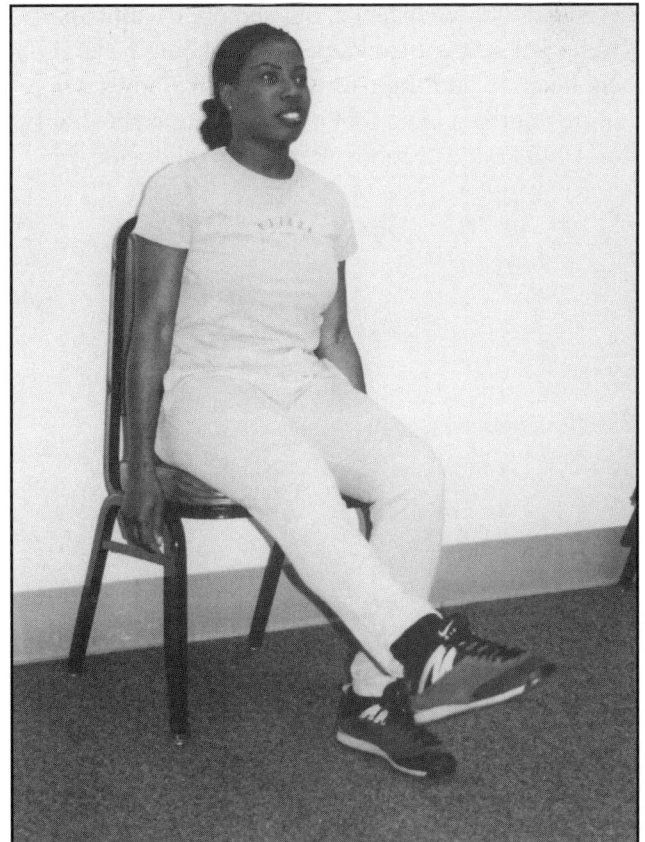

Standing Stretches

(1) Feet slightly apart, extend arms overhead, holding stretch for 10–30 seconds.

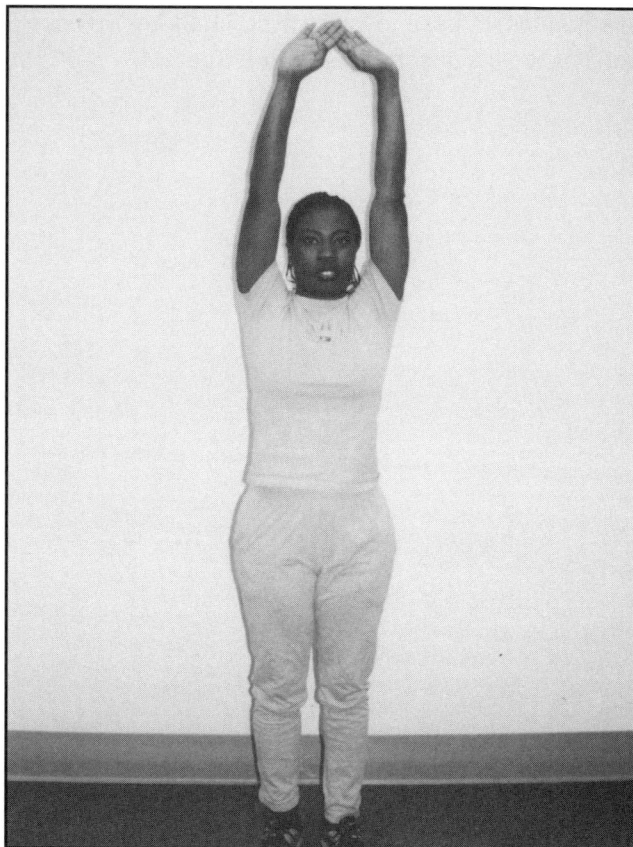

(2) Stand with your feet about shoulder-width apart. Toes point straight forward. Knees should be slightly bent keeping your hips forward. Bend elbows while tuning your head and looking over your right shoulder. Hold 10–30 seconds. Repeat on other side.

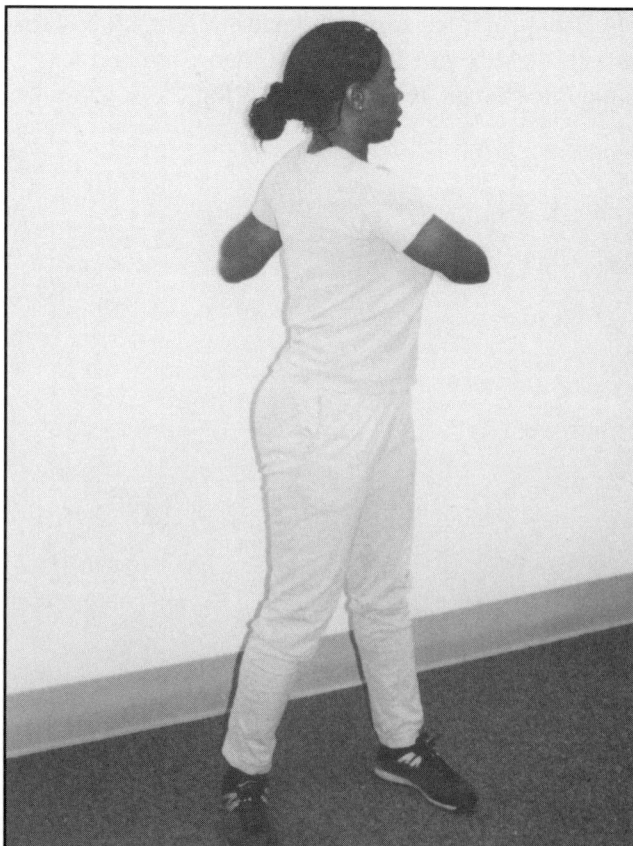

(3) Feet should be shoulder-width apart with toes pointed straight ahead. Knees slightly bent. Slowly bend forward from the hips. Relax neck and arms. Hold for 10–30 seconds.

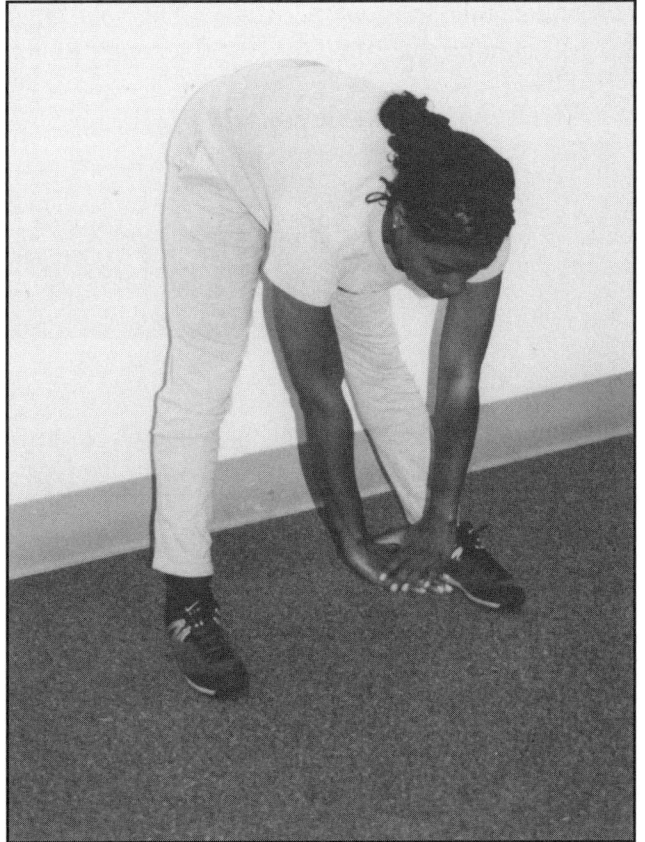

(4) Use a chair or a barre, holding it with your left hand. Hold the top of your right foot with your right hand and gently pull your heel toward your buttocks. Hold for 10–30 seconds. Turn around and repeat on left side.

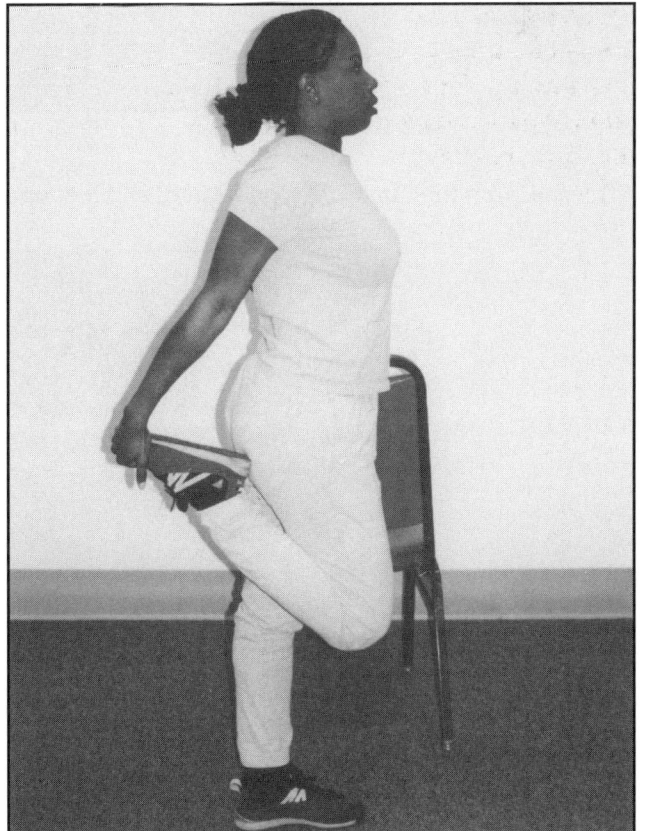

Floor Stretches

(1) Stretch your arms overhead, extending your fingers. Straighten your legs while pointing the toes. Reach as far as is comfortable. Hold for 10–30 seconds. Relax.

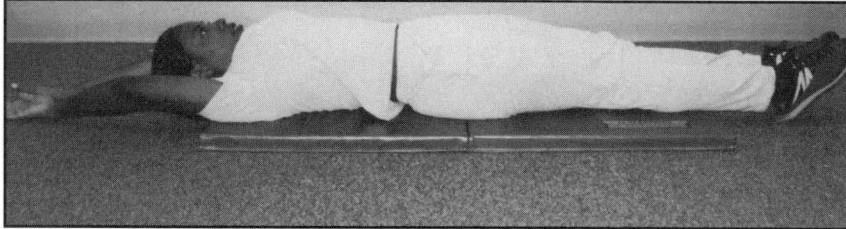

(2) Pull your right leg toward you, keeping your lower back flat. Hold for 10–30 seconds. Repeat with left leg.

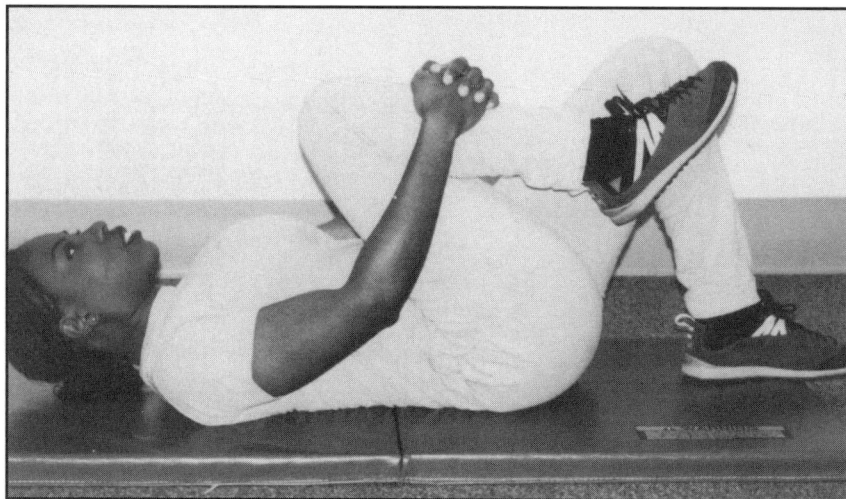

(3) Bend from the hips with legs straight and feet upright, heels close together. Hold for 10–30 seconds.

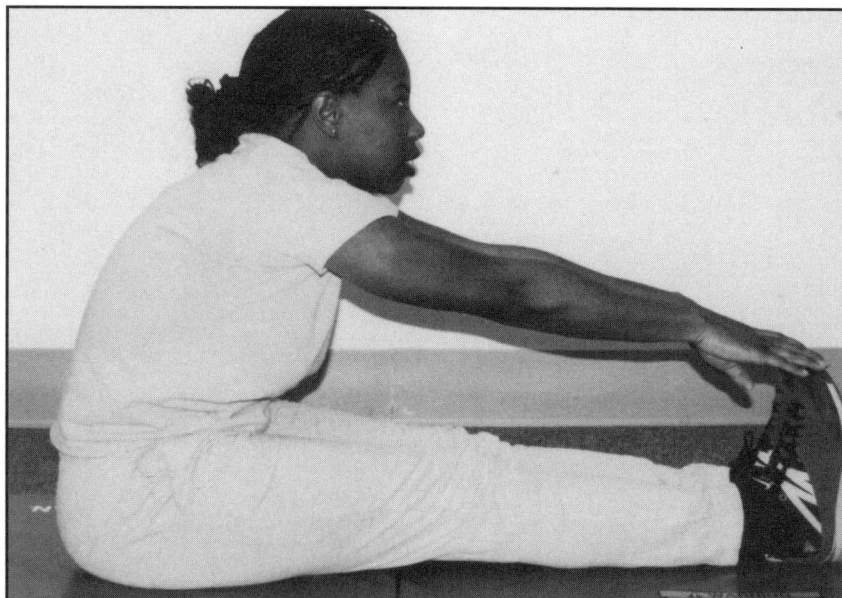

(4) With legs bent under you, reach forward with arms straight. Hold for 10–30 seconds.

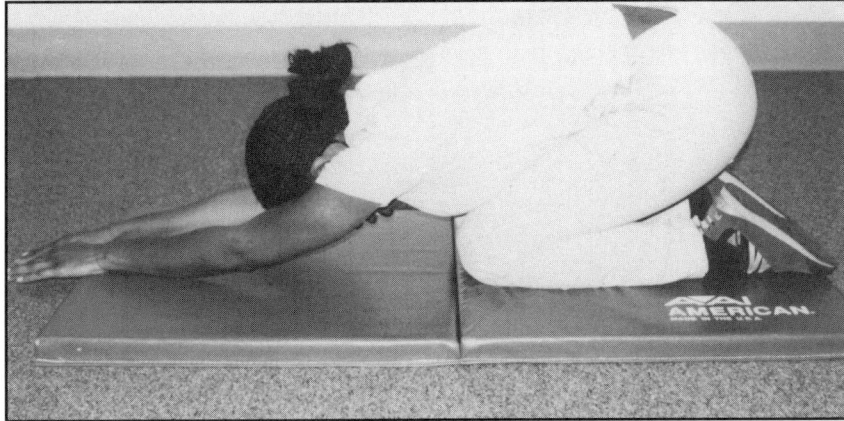

Chapter Thirteen
Yoga

Yoga is one of the oldest forms of exercise. It originated in the East over 6,000 years ago. The term *yoga* comes from the Sanskrit term meaning "union." Yoga assists in developing an individual's mental, physical, and spiritual well-being. It uses *asanas*, a series of postures designed to stretch and strengthen muscles and stimulate nerve centers and organs. The breathing techniques inherent in yoga practice influence the flow of *prana* (i.e., life energy).

Yoga has been used successfully to treat:

- stress
- anxiety
- fatigue
- depression
- headaches
- asthma
- irritable bowel syndrome
- multiple sclerosis
- heart disease
- weight control
- recovery from cancer

Benefits of yoga include:

- Improves circulation
- Regulates blood pressure and blood sugar
- Helps maintain desired body weight
- Increases flexibility and stamina
- Boosts self-confidence
- Promotes a sense of well-being
- Increases oxygenation to cells and muscles
- Strengthens the immune system

A research study conducted at the Bhabha Atomic Research Centre at the Medical Division Mumbai, India, found that yoga asanas play an important role in risk modification for cardiovascular diseases in mild to moderate hypertension (Damodaran, Malathi, Patil, Shah, Suryavansihi & Marathe, 2002).

In another study at the Department of Physiology at the University of Medical Sciences at the GTB Hospital in Shahdara, New Delhi, India, a group of Type-II diabetics took part in a 40-day yoga program. The researchers felt that these yoga practices might be interacting with various, somato-neuro-endocrine mechanisms to have therapeutic effects. Their findings indicated better glycemic control and pulmonary functions for the participants (Malhotra, Singh, Singh, Gupta, Sharma, Madhu & Tandon, 2002).

Implementation Concerns

Decrease outside stimulus during this activity, and conduct this group in a clinic or conference room if possible. Dim the lights or use lamps with 25- or 40-watt bulbs. Turn off the television and overhead lighting. Simple yoga exercises can be used bedside or in a wheelchair. Yoga can be practiced in an outdoor setting as well.

Loose clothing is recommended. Provide mats for able-bodied clients if possible.

If using background music, choose instrumental tapes or CDs rather than music with lyrics. Tapes and CDs are available at most music and New Age stores.

Explain to clients that you are going to guide them through a series of yoga exercises to help them lower their stress level. For clients with adequate cognitive abilities, ask them to use the Stress Meter before and after the activity to determine whether they have experienced a reduction in stress. Heart rates may also be monitored.

Special Considerations

Consult the client's physician and treatment team prior to the client beginning a yoga program.

These exercises should be performed gradually and slowly to develop the body's tolerance to increased energy and cleansing activity. Initial exposure to yoga should not exceed twenty minutes.

Yoga should be practiced several hours before or after eating. Yoga is not recommended after meals.

When working with clients who are using wheelchairs, the brakes should be locked and power turned off if the chair is powered. If the brakes are not in good working order, place a sand weight or wheelchock to keep the chair from rolling. If the clients need to have their upper body stabilized during the exercise activity, strapping should be installed before the group begins. The wheelchair seatbelt should also be strapped.

Caution clients to be aware of any discomfort or dizziness. If they report these symptoms, they may be "pushing" it and will need the stop the exercise for the day. Any exercise which lowers the head below the heart brings an extra supply of blood to the head and may cause dizziness. Consult with your client's physician or review the client's chart to determine whether any medications the client is taking may also cause dizziness during exercise.

Breathing is a very important component of yoga. Remind clients to become aware of their breathing throughout the session. Movements which contract the body or involve bending forward should be accompanied with an exhalation. When your client is either stretching or opening the body, they should be instructed to inhale.

You may want to teach clients the movements first and then add the breathing component since some clients may find the instructions too difficult when concentrating on both the movement and breathing elements at one time.

Recommended Resources

Alberg, M. (1993). *The yoga workbook for seniors.* Sandpoint, ID: The Moon in The Pearl.

Christensen, A. (1999). *The American Yoga Association's easy does it yoga: The safe, gentle way to health and well-being.* New York, NY: Hunt Publishers.

Dworkis, S. (1997). *Recovery yoga: A practical guide for chronically ill, injured and postoperative people.* New York, NY: Three Rivers Press.

Lasater, J. (1995). *Relax and renew: Restful yoga for stressful times.* Berkeley, CA: Rodwell Press.

Videotapes/DVDs

Lundeen, C. (1998). *Kripalu yoga: Gentle with Carolyn Lundeen (Sudha)* [videotape]. Lenox, MA: Wellspring Media.

Periodicals

The Yoga Journal [magazine]. Berkeley, CA: John B. Abbott Publishers.

References

Damodaran, A., Malathi, A., Patil, N., Shah, N., Suryavansihi, and Marathe, S. (2002). Therapeutic potential of yoga practices in modifying cardiovascular risk profile in middle aged men and women. *Journal of the Association of Physicians of India, 50*(5), 633–640.

Malhotra, V. Singh, S., Singh, K.P., Gupta, P., Sharma, S.B., Madhu, S.V., and Tandon, O.P. (2002). Study of yoga asanas in assessment of pulmonary function in NIDDM patients. *Indian Journal of Physiology and Pharmacology, 46*(3), 313–320.

Malhotra, V., Singh, S., Tandon, O.P., Madhu, S.V., Prasad, A., and Sharma, S.B. (2002). Effect of yoga asanas on nerve conduction in Type 2 diabetes. *Indian Journal of Physiology and Pharmacology, 46*(3), 298–306.

Yoga Exercises I
Yoga Poses

(1) Tadasana-Mountain Pose

Stand straight, toes together, heels slightly apart. Weight should be evenly distributed between toes and heels. Tuck tailbone under. Shoulder blades should be back and down, opening the heart. Flex quadriceps, turning inner thighs inward. Arms at side with palms facing forward, fingers spread wide. Chin parallel to the ground. Crown of head faces up. Hold for five breaths.

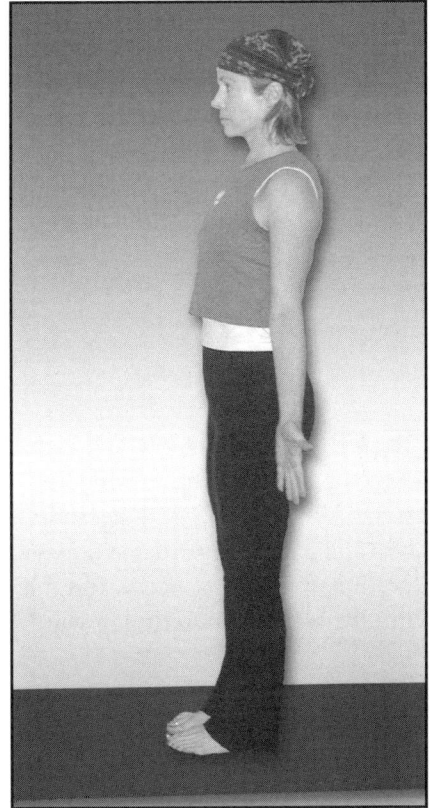

(2) Standing Back Bend

Stand straight, toes together, heels sightly apart. Weight should be evenly distributed between toes and heels. As you inhale, raise arms straight overhead, palms together. Arms should be in line with your ears. Palms are pressed together. Arch chest. Look up toward palms. Hold for one breath.

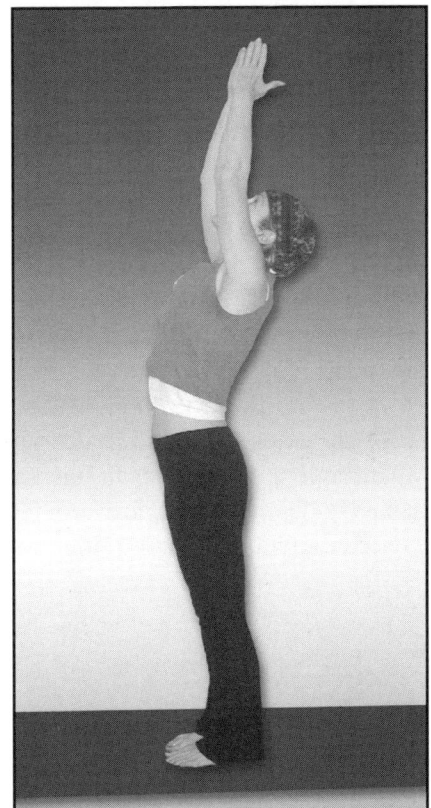

(3a) Forward Bend—Half-Uttanasana

Exhale as you head down from the previous pose. Toes are together. Legs straight or knees slightly bent if uncomfortable. Weight should be on front of the feet. Back should be parallel to the ground. Buttocks and head should be in line with each other. Arms are "airplaned" out to the side also in line with the shoulders. Fingers are spread wide. Head should be tilted forward with the neck long. Eyes face down toward ground. Imagine the crown of the head in a straight line to the other side of the room. One line of energy from the sacral area to crown of the head.

(3b) Uttanasana—Forward Bend

At the end of the exhale, bring feet together with weight on the front of the feet. Knees are slightly bent. Bring arms and hands forward and down to floor or place them on your shins as far as comfortable. Chest faces thighs with the tailbone pointing upward. Take five breaths.

(4) Lunge

Inhale. Move right leg forward, thighs should be parallel to floor. Right knee is at 90° angle to floor. Knee should be directly in line with the ankle. Left knee, shin, and top of left foot on floor. Pelvic area and hips should drop down toward floor. Tailbone should be tucked under. Arms are extended to the sky/ceiling. Palms face each other, fingers wide. Arms in line with the ears. Chin is tucked under. Eyes look forward. Hold. If comfortable, eyes can look up at hands. Hold for five breaths.

(5) Lunge

Inhale. Left leg forward, thighs should be parallel to the floor. Left knee is at a 90° angle to the floor. Knee should be directly in line with the ankle. Right knee, shin, and top of left foot on floor. Pelvic area and hips should drop down toward floor. Tailbone should be tucked under. Arms extended to the sky/ceiling. Palms face each other, fingers wide. Arms are in line with the ears. Chin is tucked under. Eyes look forward. Hold. If comfortable, eyes can look up at hands. Hold for five breaths.

(6) Plank Position

Inhale. Hands to the floor directly under shoulders. Body should be one line of energy from heels all the way to the crown of the head. Don't let the hips sink. Use abdominal muscles to keep midsection of body in line with the torso. Bring the right leg back, then left, putting both feet hip distance apart and raising the knees off the floor. Arms are straight, palms are placed wide on the mat shoulder-width apart, fingers spread out. Weight should be evenly distributed between feet and arms. Weight should be on the balls of the feet with heels extended backwards.

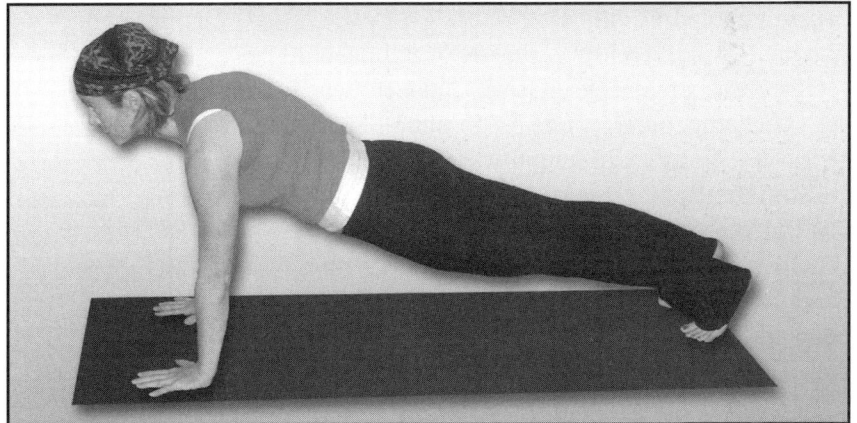

(7) Transition to Cobra

Exhale. Bend knees so that they are touching the mat. Weight should be on the balls of the feet. Tailbone straight up in the air. Arms bent with hands under shoulders on mat—shoulders are back and down. Chin rests on mat. Eyes look straight forward.

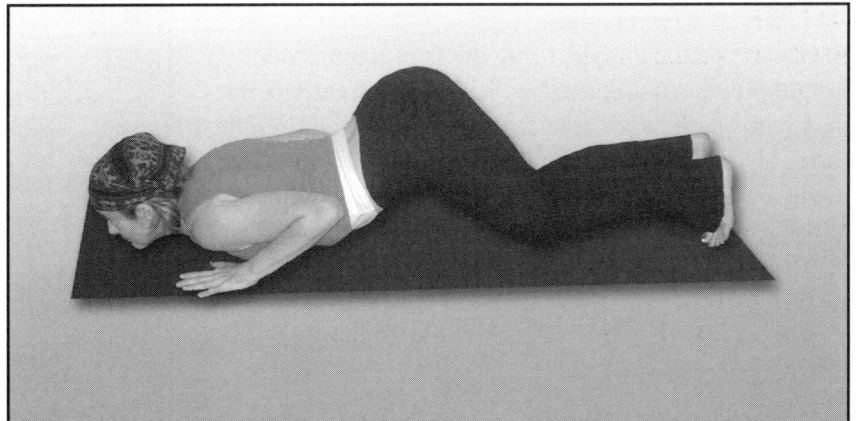

(8) Cobra Pose

Inhale. Lift chest up. Roll shoulders up and backward opening and broadening the chest area. Hands are directly under shoulders, fingers spread wide with equal weight distributed between the hands. Toes and pelvis should be pressing into ground. The only part of the body off ground is the upper torso. Do not lift torso area higher than is comfortable for the lower back. If the lower back is tight, lower the chest until comfortable. Hold for three breaths.

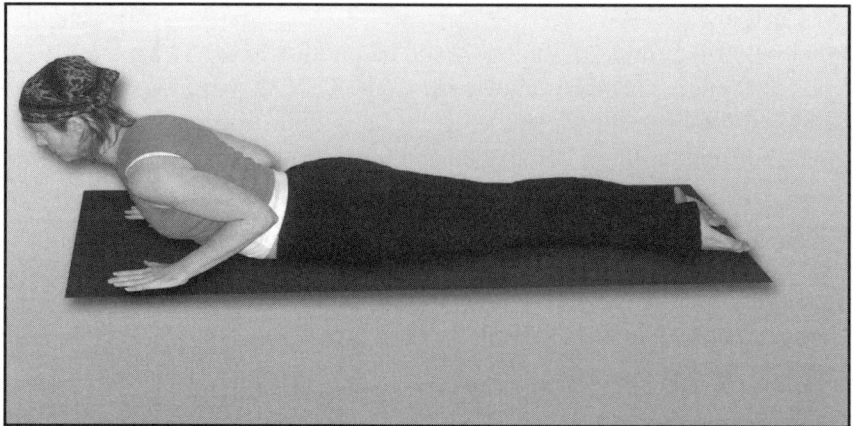

(9) Downward Facing Dog

Exhale. Raise the body as shown. Weight should be equally distributed between hands and feet. Legs straight with heels touching ground (if possible), bend knees if necessary. Tailbone lifts up toward sky/ceiling. Arms are straight. Rotate triceps inward toward each other; quadricep muscles should be equally engaged. Body should form a V-shape, one line of energy running up from the feet to the tailbone, and another from the tail-bone all the way to the hands. Eyes should look at the feet. Turn the toes in toward each other slightly.

(11) Repeat Uttanasana

At the end of the exhale, bring the feet together with weight on the front of the feet. Knees are slightly bent. Bring arms and hands forward and down to the floor or shins, as far as is comfortable. Palms are facing back with fingers opened wide. Chest faces thighs with the tailbone pointing upward. Take five breaths.

(12) Repeat Standing Back Bend

Inhale. Stand straight, toes together, heels slightly apart. Weight should be evenly distributed between toes and heels. Tuck tailbone under. Shoulder blades should be back and down, opening the heart. Pull up on quadriceps, turning thighs inward. Arms are at side with palms facing forward, fingers spread wide. Chin is parallel to the grounds. Crown of head faces up. Hold for five breaths.

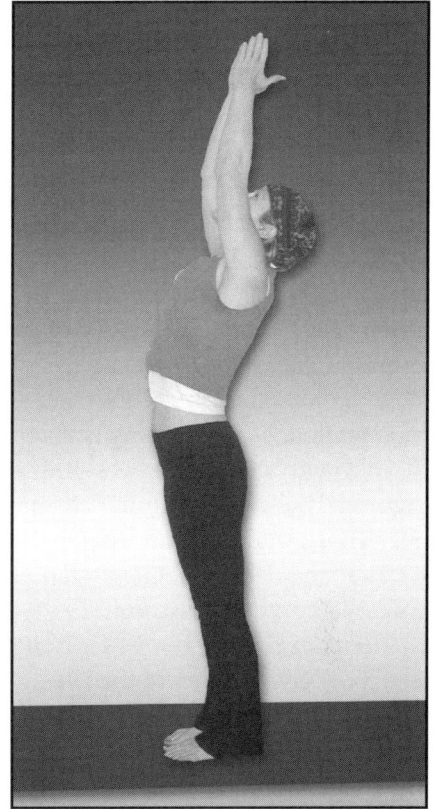

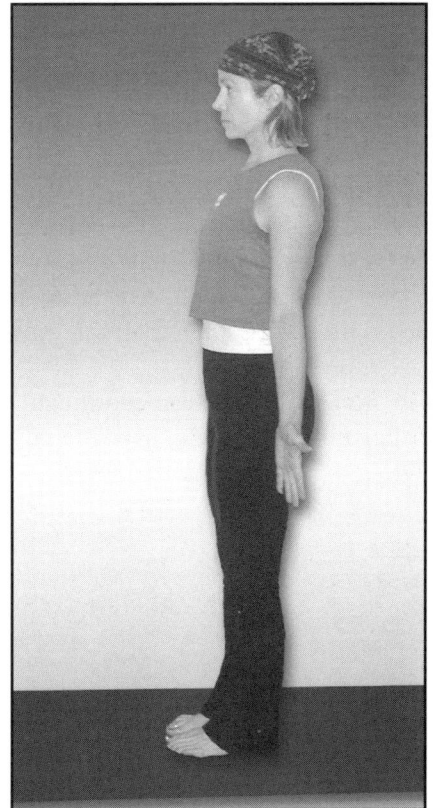

(13) Repeat Tadasana-Mountain Pose

Stand straight with toes together and heels slightly apart. Weight should be evenly distributed between toes and heels. Tuck tailbone under. Shoulder blades should be back and down, opening the heart. Flex quadriceps, turning inner thighs inward. Arms at side with palms facing forward, fingers spread wide. Chin parallel to the ground. Crown of head faces up. Hold for five breaths.

Yoga Exercises II
Seated Yoga Poses

(1) Eye Exercise

Sit in a comfortable position with a straight spine and shoulders back. Head should be well-centered. Palms up. Inhale through nose. Exhale through nose. Do not move head. Visualize the face of a clock in front of your eyes. Bring eyes to the twelve on the clock. Very slowly, move the eyes clockwise, as the eyes touch each number. Repeat, going counterclockwise. Repeat twice. Gently close your eyes. Rub your palms together vigorously and do "palming" by cupping your palms over your eyes. Let your eyes bathe you in healing warmth and darkness. Gently tap your fingers above your eyebrows. Release your fingertips.

Benefits of eye exercises: Strengthens eye muscles and brings circulation to the eyes.

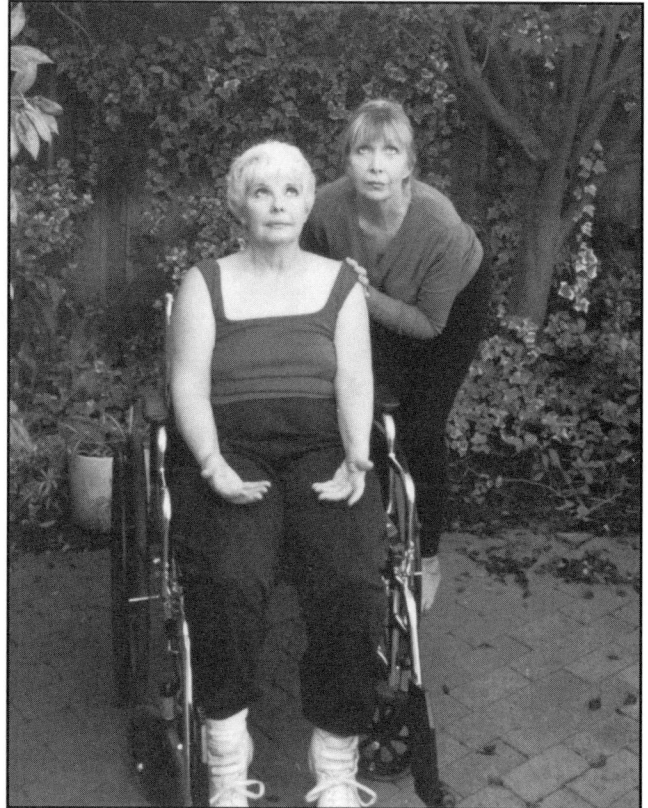

(2) Cross-Training

While inhaling through the nose, raise your right arm and left leg—hold. Exhale and slowly release and lower limbs. Now while inhaling, raise your left arm and right leg—hold. Exhale and slowly release. Repeat two more times.

Benefits: Improved coordination, concentration, balancing of the body, opposite polarities.

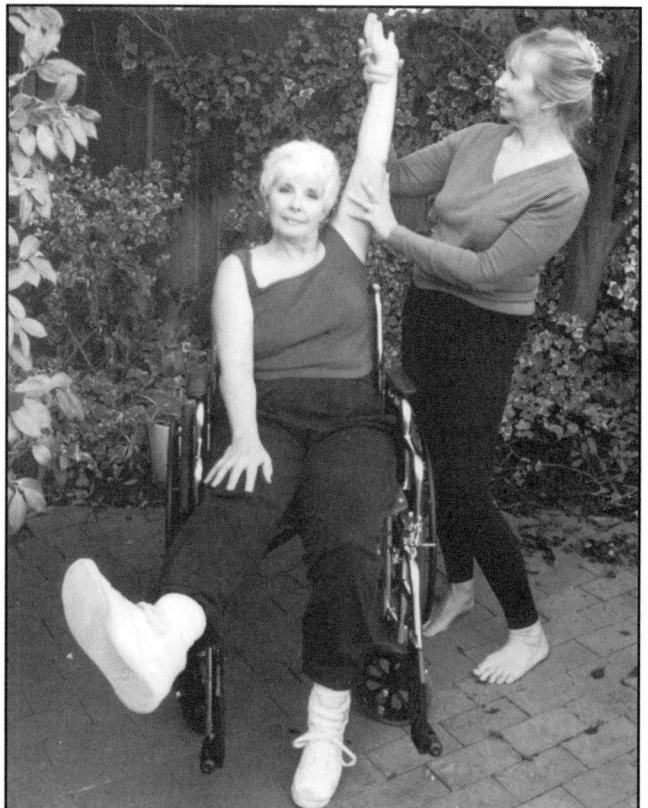

(3) Leg Raises

Slowly inhale. Raise right leg up, stretch the knee as much as you can without straining (do it slowly, but not lazily). Flex and point toes. Push heel out, inhale, drop heel down, exhale, release. Repeat twice on both sides.

Benefits: Improves cardiovascular functioning; stretches knees, back, and hamstrings; and improves flexibility.

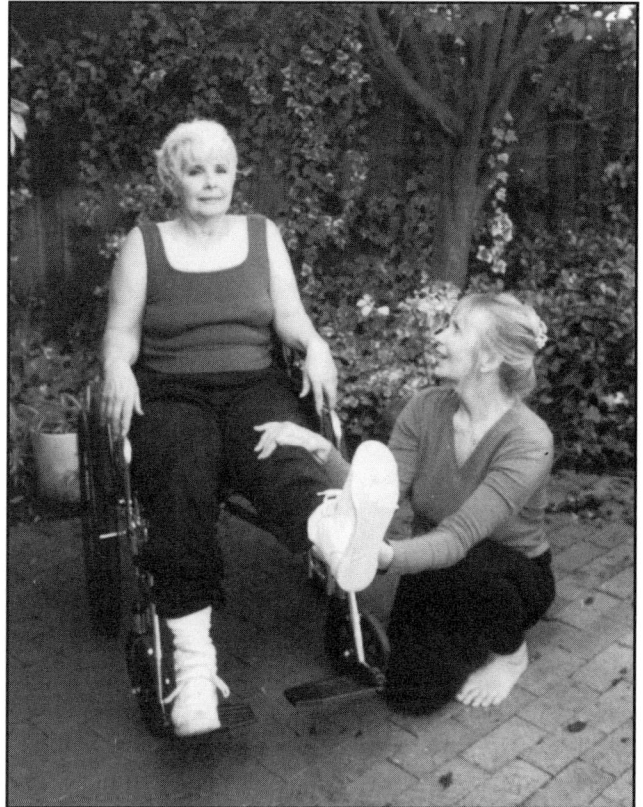

(4) Forward Bending

Inhale. Arms up. Bring your head and arms down comfortably while exhaling.

Benefits: Massages internal organs, stimulates digestion, increases oxygen to the brain, tones spine and lower back, and is a good abdominal workout.

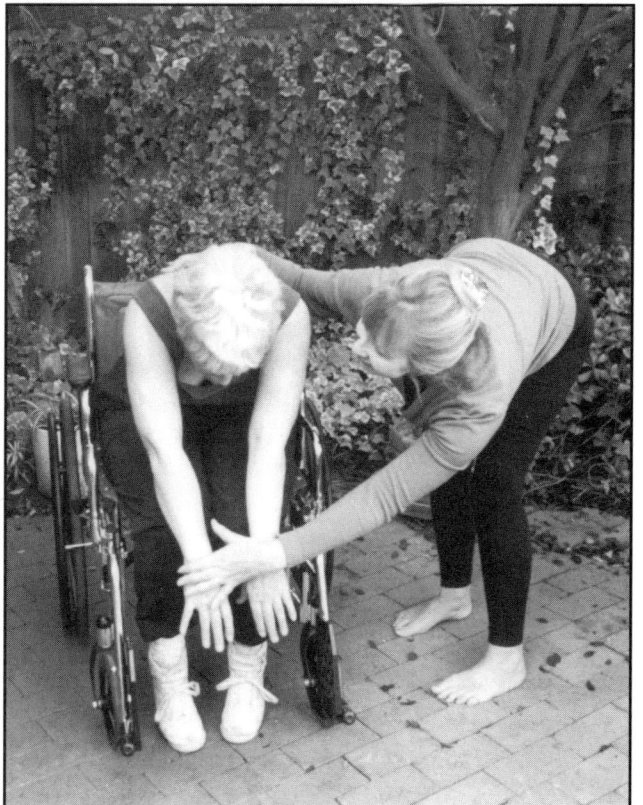

(5) Sideways Stretch

Inhale, arms over head. Exhale, slowly bend to your right side. Inhale, bring your arms back to the middle. Exhale, bring your arms down your left side. Repeat twice.

Benefits: Stretches arms and sides, and improves range of motion and flexibility.

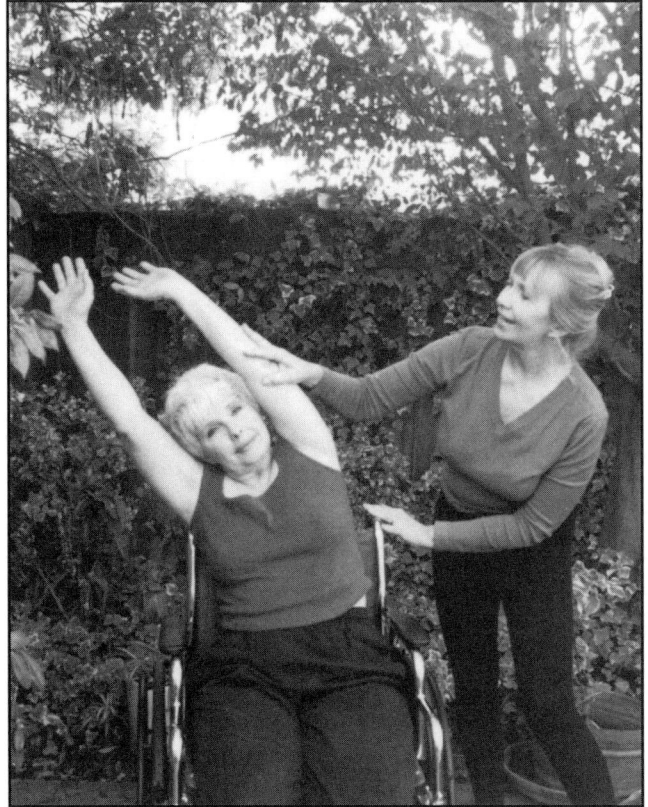

(6) Ankle Rolls

Straighten spine, inhale. Exhale, cross right leg over left leg. Slowly roll ankle six times each way. Repeat on other side.

Benefits: Improves circulation to the feet and prevents swelling.

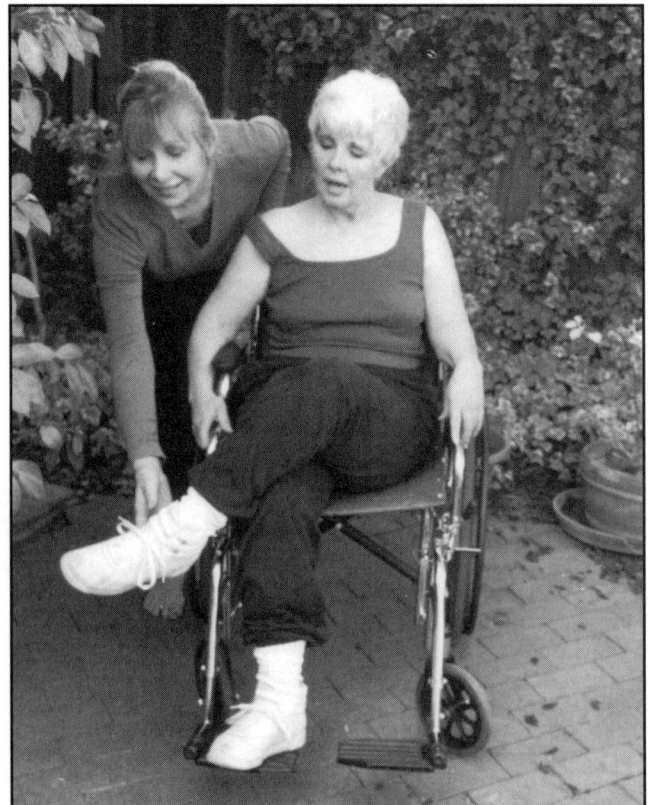

(7) Half Spinal Twist

Sit up straight. Inhale, then exhale while crossing right leg over left leg. Extend arms in front of you, exhale. Twist gently to the left. Rotate the spine while looking over shoulder. Hold for as long as is comfortable. Breathe deeply. Keep face relaxed. Exhale slowly as you unwind to the center. Repeat on other side. Repeat exercise twice.

Benefits: Stimulates the root of the spinal nerves, increases the suppleness of the spine, and increases flexibility.

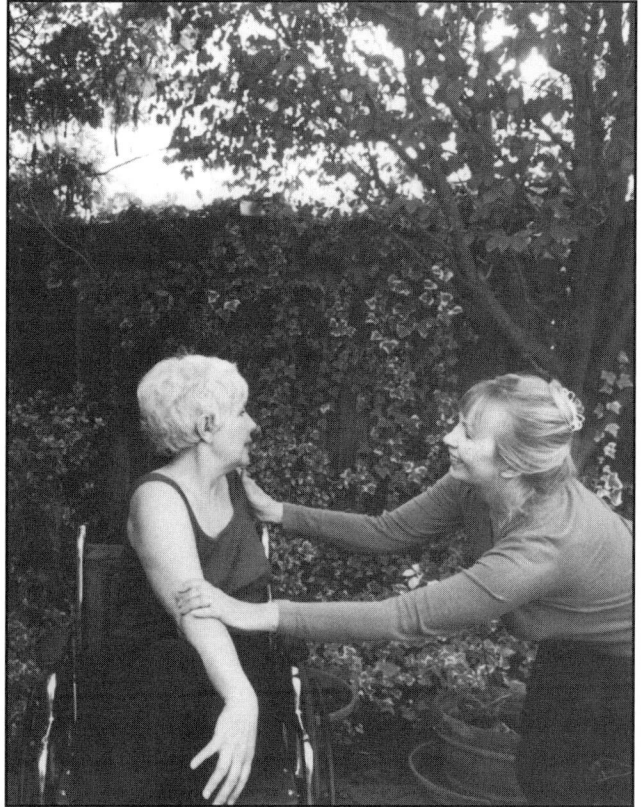

(8) Rotator Cuff

Sit up straight. Inhale. Extend right are over chest, bend elbow and press arm upward. Twist and hold. Inhale and exhale. Repeat on other side.

Benefits: Improves flexibility of joints, improves range of motion, and relaxes the rotator cuff.

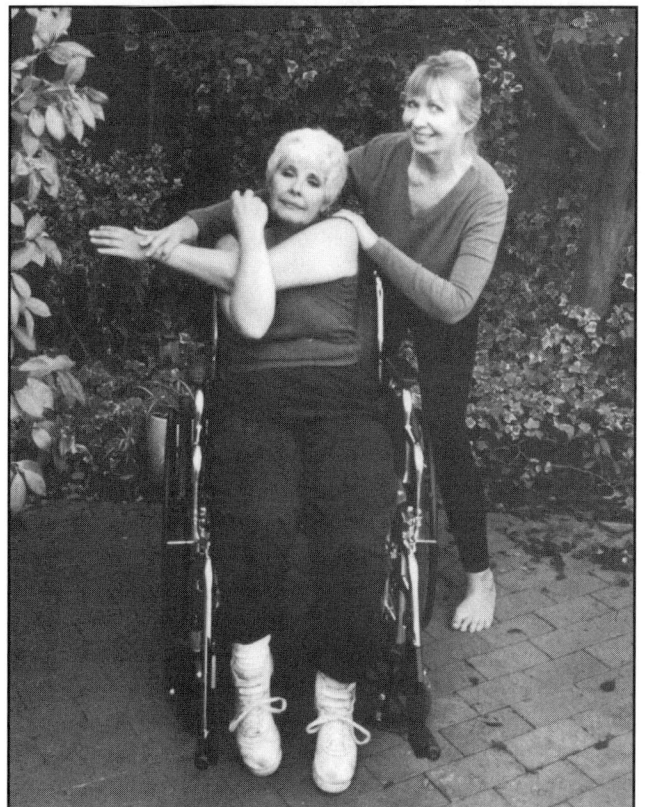

(9) Namaste—Universal Greeting ("saluting my higher self")

Inhale. Bring palms together invoking peace and relaxation. Exhale to let go of stress and tension. Repeat six times. Feel how peaceful and calm your body, mind, and breathing has become.

Benefits: Provides a sense of well-being and serenity, and connects you with your higher self.

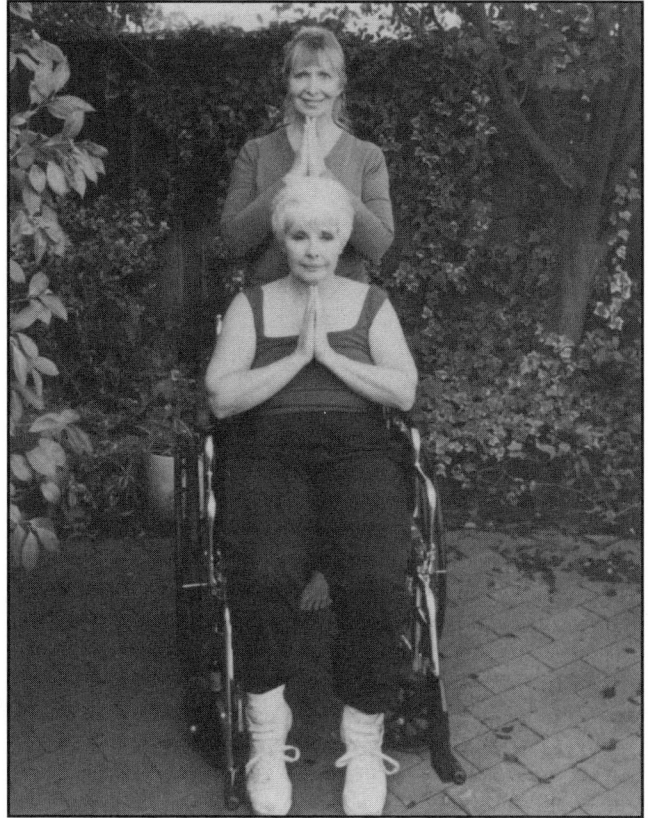

Chapter Fourteen
Tai Chi

Tai chi originated in China over 400 years ago. Tai chi is an exercise form which combines the mind, body, and spirit by synchronizing movement, dance, breathing and meditation. It is a "relaxed process with slow and meditative movement performed while the mind remains always alert to the spatial relationship between the body and its surroundings" (Quarta, 2001).

Tai chi is based on the Taoist philosophy of yin and yang. "Tai is generally interpreted to mean big, huge, grand, immense, or supreme. Chi is interpreted as energy, vitality, and breath" (Crider & Klinger, 2001).

Tai chi has been used successfully in the treatment of:

- stress
- anxiety
- fatigue
- depression
- headaches
- multiple sclerosis
- heart disease
- at-risk adolescents
- children
- older adults

Benefits of tai chi include:

- Regulates blood pressure and blood sugar
- Helps maintain desired body weight
- Increases flexibility and stamina
- Boosts self-confidence
- Promotes a feeling of well-being
- Increases oxygenation to cells and muscles
- Strengthens immune system

A 2001 study conducted at the Department of Sports Science and Physical Education at the Chinese University of Hong Kong Department of Orthopedics and Traumatology found that tai chi exercise had beneficial effects on the cardiorespiratory and musculoskeletal functions, posture control capacity and reduction of falls in the elderly (Li, Hong & Chan, 2001).

Furthermore, the Department of Physical Medicine and Rehabilitation at the National Taiwan University Hospital in Taipei found that tai chi could be prescribed as an alternative program for selected patients with cardiovascular, orthopedic, and neurological diseases (Lan, Lai & Chen, 2002).

Implementation Concerns

Decrease outside stimulus during this activity, and conduct this group in a clinic or conference room if possible. Dim the lights or use lamps with 25- or 40-watt bulbs. Turn off the television and overhead lighting. Simple tai chi exercises can be used bedside or in a wheelchair. Tai chi can also be practiced in an outdoor setting. Loose clothing is recommended.

When working with clients who are using wheelchairs, the brakes should be locked and power turned off if the chair is powered. If the brakes are not in good working order, place a sand weight or wheelchock to keep the chair from rolling. If the clients need to have their upper body stabilized during the exercise activity, strapping should be installed before the group begins. The wheelchair seatbelt should also be strapped.

If using background music, choose instrumental tapes or CDs rather than music with lyrics. These tapes and CDs are available at most music and New Age stores.

Explain to clients that you are going to guide them through a series of tai chi exercises to help them lower their stress level. For clients with adequate cognitive abilities, ask them to use the Stress Meter before and after the activity to determine whether they have experienced a reduction in stress.

Teach clients how to measure their heart rates in conjunction with an exercise program. Two easy methods can be used to check one's pulse rate. One method checks the pulse at the wrist (i.e., radial pulse). The other is at the neck (i.e., carotid pulse).

For a radial pulse check, have the clients use the tips of their index and third fingers. The radial artery can be found on the thumb side of either wrist and lies just a little below the base of the thumb. The pulsing artery can be felt when the fingers are in the right place.

The carotid pulse can be taken in the place just below the jaw and along either side of the windpipe on the throat. Suggest that clients use their first and second fingers and to press gently.

Use a digital watch or the second hand on a face watch and have the clients count their pulse for six seconds then multiply this number by ten.

Special Considerations

Consult the client's physician and treatment team prior to the client beginning a tai chi program.

Tai chi exercises should be performed gradually and slowly to develop the body's tolerance to increased energy and cleansing activity. Initial exposure to tai chi should not exceed twenty minutes.

Caution clients to be aware of any discomfort or dizziness. If they report these symptoms, they may be "pushing" it and will need the stop the exercise for the day. Any exercise which lowers the head below the heart brings an extra supply of blood to the head and may cause dizziness. Consult the client's physician or review the client's chart to determine whether any medications the client is taking may also cause dizziness during exercise.

Breathing is a very important component of tai chi. Remind the clients to become aware of their breathing throughout the session. Movements which contract the body or involve bending forward should be accompanied with an exhalation. When the client is stretching or opening the body, they should be instructed to inhale.

Teach the clients the movements first, then add the breathing component since some clients may find the instructions too difficult when having to concentrate on both the movement and breathing elements at one time.

Tai chi is based on Five Principles. When practicing the exercises, remind your clients to:

1. Relax while bending the knees on the exhale "sinking" or "emptying the chest."

2. Shift weight from side to side.

3. Turn the waist.

4. Keep the spine straight.

5. Use "beautiful lady's wrists" so that energy flows out through the fingertips.

Recommended Resources

Crider, D.A. and Klinger, W.R. (2001). *Stretch your mind and body: Tai chi as an adaptive activity.* State College, PA: Venture Publishing, Inc.

Quarta, C. (2003). *Tai chi in a chair: Easy 15-minute routine for beginners.* New York, NY: Fine Communications.

Videotapes/DVDs

Klein, B. (2000). *Spirit breathing workout for body, mind and spirit: Beginner level.* Sound Beach, NY: Artistic Video.

Dunn, T. (1999). *Tai chi for health: Yang short form.* Santa Monica, CA: Healing Arts.

References

Lan, C., Lai, J.S., and Chen, S.Y. (2002). Tai chi chuan: An ancient wisdom on exercise and health promotion. *Sports Medicine, 32*(4), 217–224.

Li, J.X., Hong, Y., and Chan, K.M. (2001). Tai chi: Physiological characteristics and beneficial effects on health. *British Journal of Sports Medicine, 35*(3), 148–156.

Tai Chi Exercise I

(1) Breathe using the diaphragm and the lower abdomen. Place your left thumb touching your navel and resting the palm against the abdomen. Cover your left hand with your right hand and feel the lower abdomen rising and falling.

    Continue to breathe deeply and slowly while you clear your mind of the everyday static and chatter.

(2) Stand with feet apart about shoulder's-width apart. Feet are parallel, knees sightly bent. Arms hang loosely at sides. Breathe deeply and relax.

    Using the waist, twist from right to left and back again. Feel like a rag doll by letting your arms swing as a result of the waist moving from side to side. Repeat 20 times.

(3) Stand with feet wider (about a shoulder's-width and a half). Continues twisting from the waist while bending the knees slightly deeper and begin shifting weight from one leg to the other. Repeat 20 times.

(4) Wu Chi Position
Feet are parallel, shoulder's-width apart, knees are bent (directly over ankles). Hips are open, shoulders directly over hips, arms crossed in front of heart area of chest right over left and crossed at wrists. Elbows are relaxed and pointing downward (45° away from the body). Begin by holding this pose for 15 seconds. Increase hold time with practice.

(5) Slide the hands open as if hugging a tree or holding a ball. Breathe evenly and deeply. Begin by holding this pose for 15 seconds. Increase hold time with practice.

In these two positions (i.e., 4 and 5), feel yourself sinking and connecting to the earth. The breathing will circulate and open up the chi (i.e., energy) in the body.

As you straighten your knees, bring your arms to rest at your sides, but not touching the body.

(6) Bend the knees (i.e., sinking) while exhaling. Bring arm up in front of the body, past your face and overhead, then allow arms to travel out to each side and down (inscribing the outside of the ball).

    Begin the movement again. Do this continuously—slowly, not rushed—coordinate the movement with the breath. The exhale and sinking begin when the hands are above the head and start their path downward. The inhale begins when the sinking is complete and the arms begin their path upward. Keep in mind that all of the movement is generated from the waist (i.e., center) area. Repeat at least 10 times.

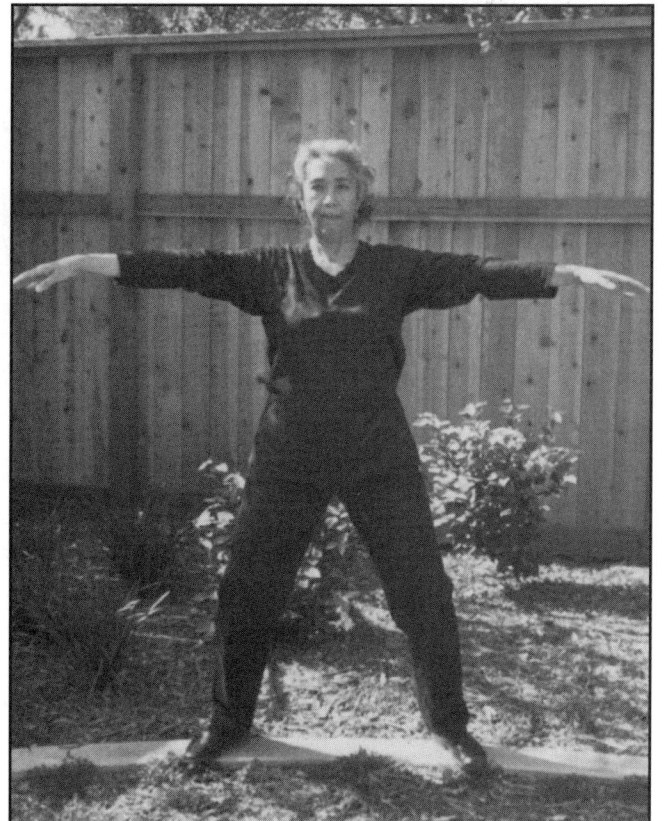

Circling

This exercise contains all of the poses and movement of the tai chi form. It is an excellent warmup exercise and stress reliever. It is done on both sides of the body. Imagine rolling a ball in front of you, shifting the weight and alternating full (i.e., active) and empty (i.e., passive) sides of the body as you roll the ball of energy, circulating the energy.

Begin with feet at shoulder's-width apart. Knees are slightly bent. Shift your weight to the right leg and step forward with the left leg about two feet. Shift your weight to the left leg. Knee is bent and directly over the ankle. Pivot the heel of the right foot to provide a comfortable support. Shift weight so it is evenly distributed over both legs.

Shift the weight to the back leg and bring the right arm back and up. As you turn the waist and begin shifting the weight to the left (i.e., front) leg, let the right arm drop in an arc and up. This is the time when the energy is passive/empty as it conscribes the lower arc. As you turn the waist and shift to the back leg, the arm rolls the ball across the chest and the arm extends ready to empty itself again. When the arm is rolling, the energy across the chest is active/full. Do this several times to warm up the right. Then in this same stance, warm up the left arm.

Begin with the weight shifted to the front leg with the left arm extended forward. As you turn the waist and shift the weight, the left arm drops as does the lower arc to the back and rolls the energy across the chest/body to the front as the arm extends. Repeat several times.

Now while turning the waist and shifting the weight, the arms work in tandem, rolling the energy across the body; rolling the ball, the active part of the body is full, while the passive side is coming up to take over the rolling ball of energy so it does not drop.

Come back to the neutral stance and do the other side.

Shift the weight to the left side and step forward with the right, about two feet.

Work the left arm and the right arm.

Begin turning the waist and shifting the weight while rolling the ball across your body. This is "circling." Imagine that as you circle, it is although you are sitting on a stool with wheels and you are rolling back and forth, turning the waist and shifting the weight.

Always complete your workout. Drop your arms, turn your waist, and shift the weight to bring your feet to the original position of shoulder's-width apart. Bring your arms up and hug the tree. Close your eyes. Breathe easily. Then take three deep breaths. Open your eyes.

Throughout the day, remind yourself to breathe deeply and center yourself in the moment.

Tai Chi Exercises II (Seated)

(1) In a sitting position, take your hands and place them at the nape of your neck. Bend forward while taking five deep breaths.

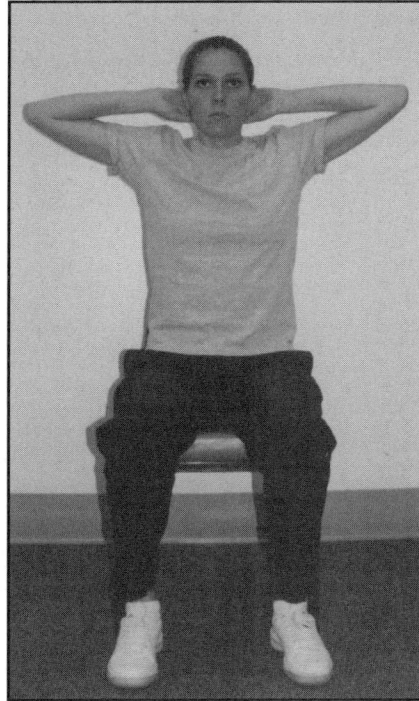

(2) Place your left palm on lower abdomen and place right palm over left palm. Inhale deeply through your nose, exhale through your mouth. Repeat five times.

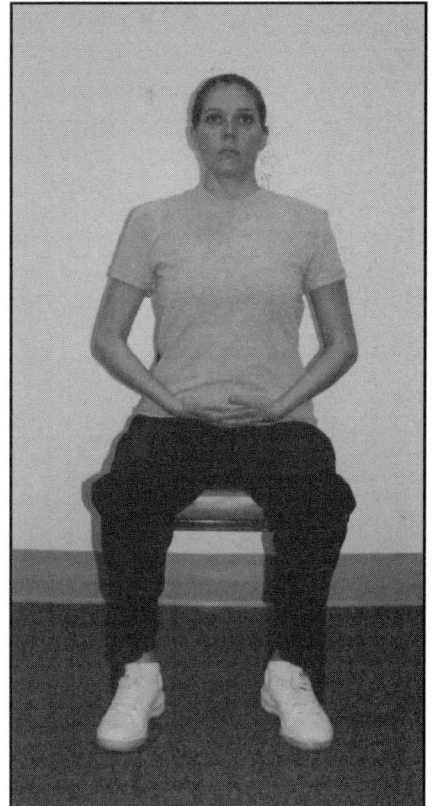

　　Then switch palms, placing your right palm on your lower abdomen and your left palm over your right palm. Breathe in deeply through your nose, exhale through your mouth. Repeat five times.

(3) Raise left hand, fingers pointing up while right palm is placed on ground. Eyes may follow raised hand. Take deep breaths through nose. Exhale through your mouth. Repeat breathing five times. Switch hands and repeat breathing five times.

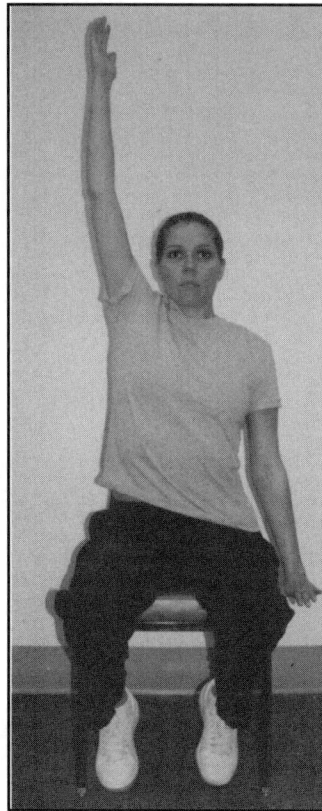

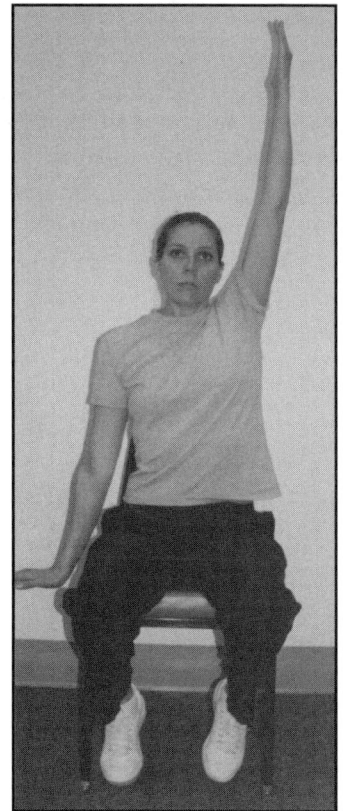

(4) Place palms on left knee as you lower your head, taking five deep breaths through your nose and exhaling through your mouth. Circle head clockwise and move to right knee. The place palms on right knee, lower head and deep breaths five times.

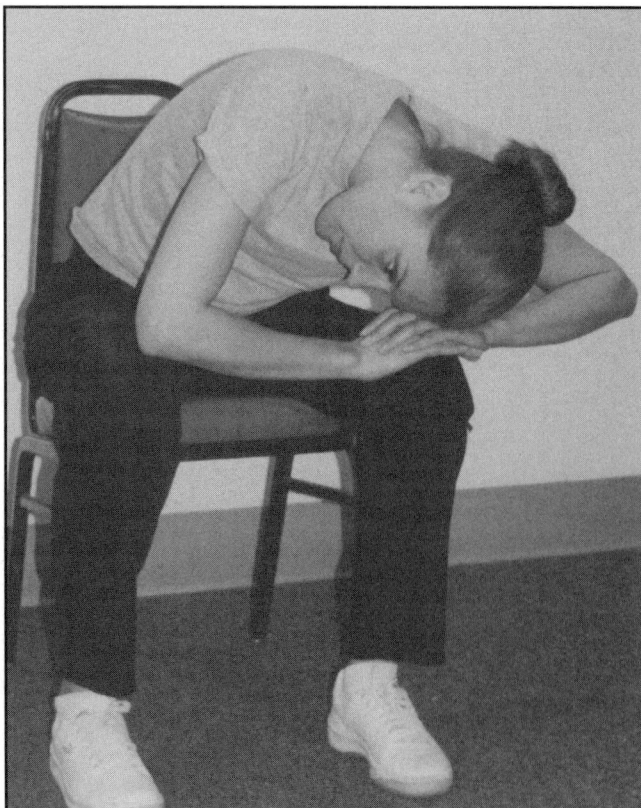

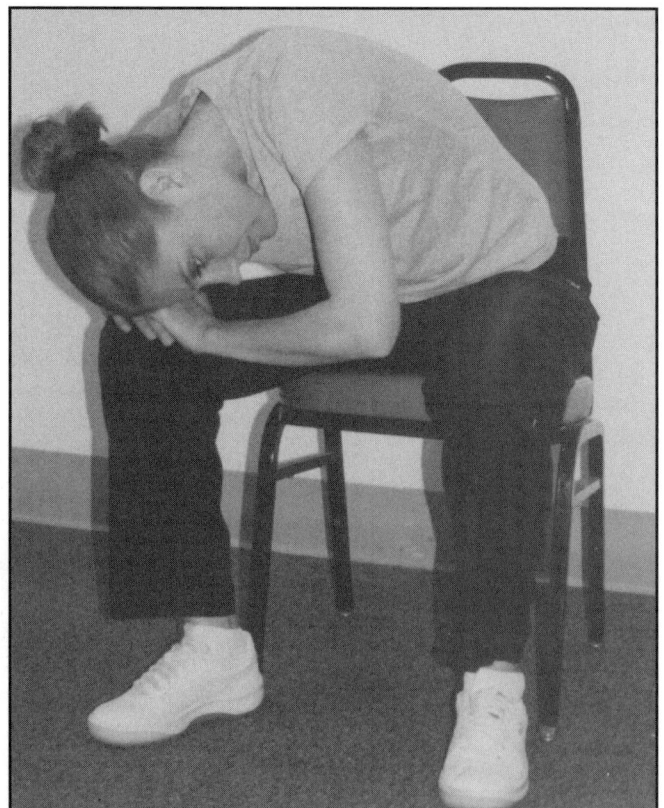

(5) Place hand on left part of chest, fingers interlocked. Move hands in five clockwise circles, taking a deep breath as you make each circle. Then starting from the right part of the chest, move hands in five counterclockwise circles.

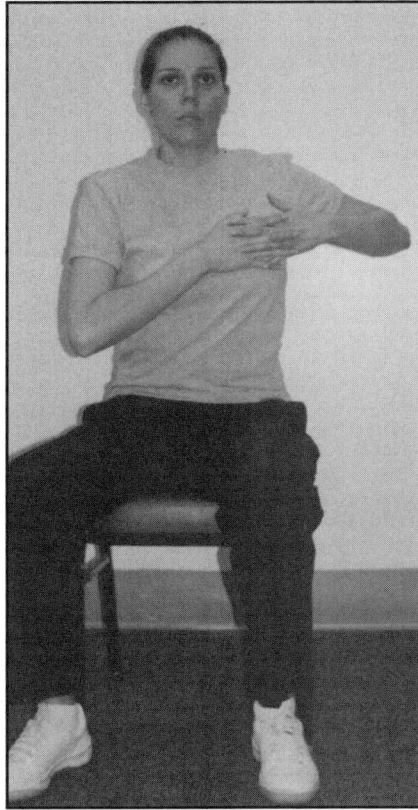

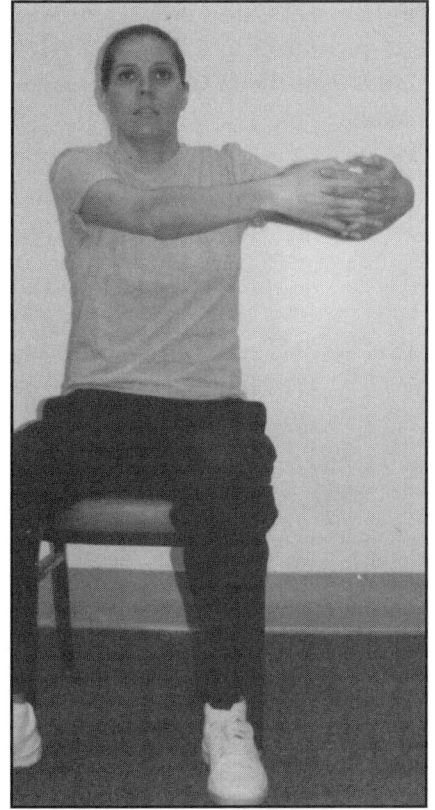

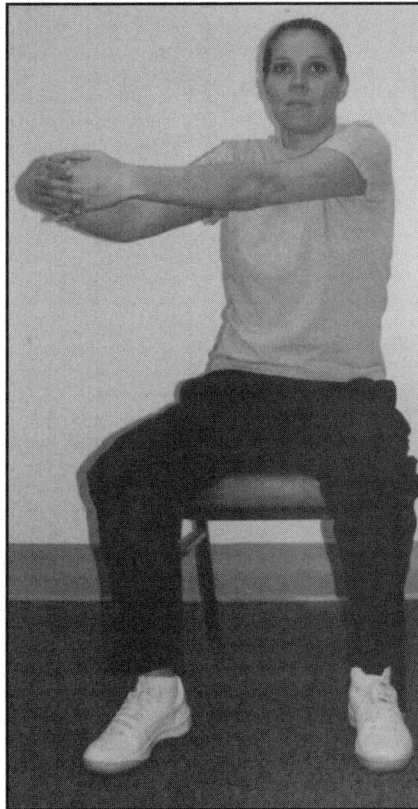

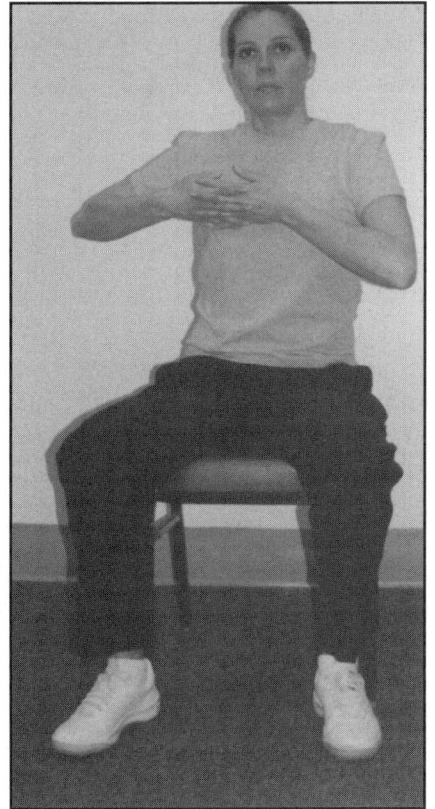

(6) Interlock hands and place them at nape of neck. Sway trunk from side to side while taking five deep breaths.

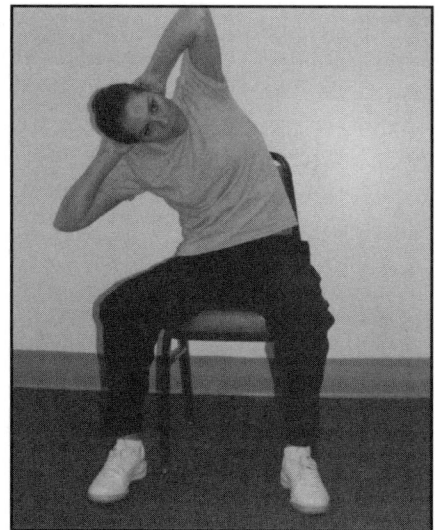

(7) With interlocked fingers, move hands to left and right while lowering head over knees as you take five deep breaths.

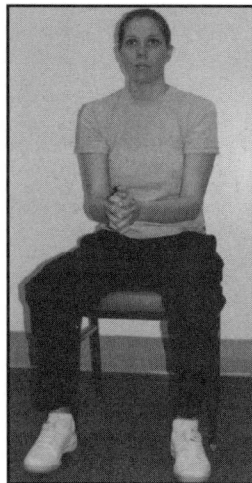

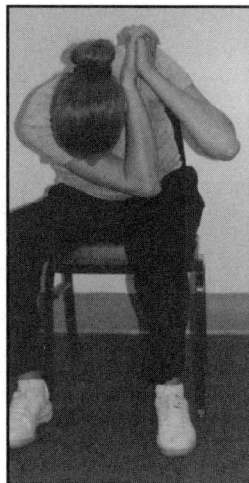

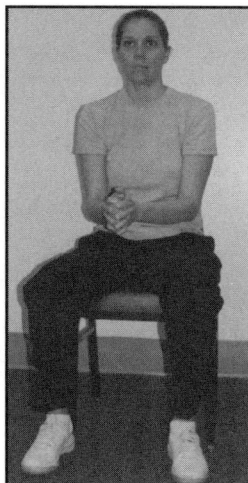

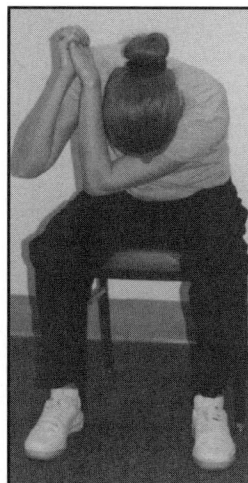

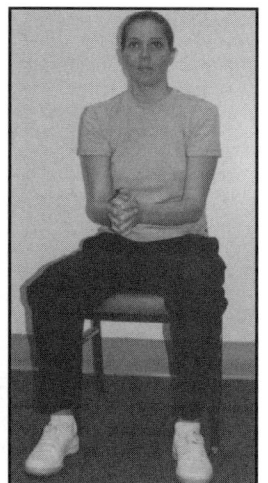

(8) Raise both hands overhead five times, each time with a shrug of the shoulders while breathing deeply.

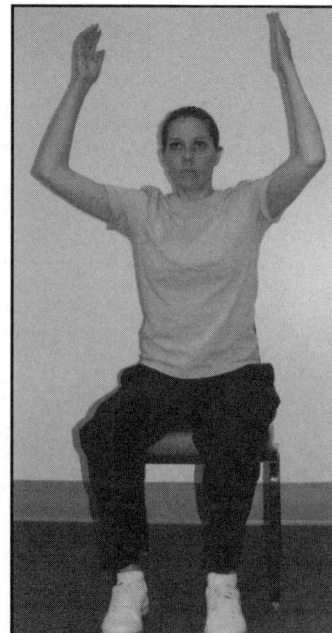

(9) Raise right arm sideways and bend left arm at elbow as if in the act of drawing a bow while taking a deep breath. Alternate with left hand sideways and right arm drawing the bow while taking deep breaths. Repeat five times (ten draws).

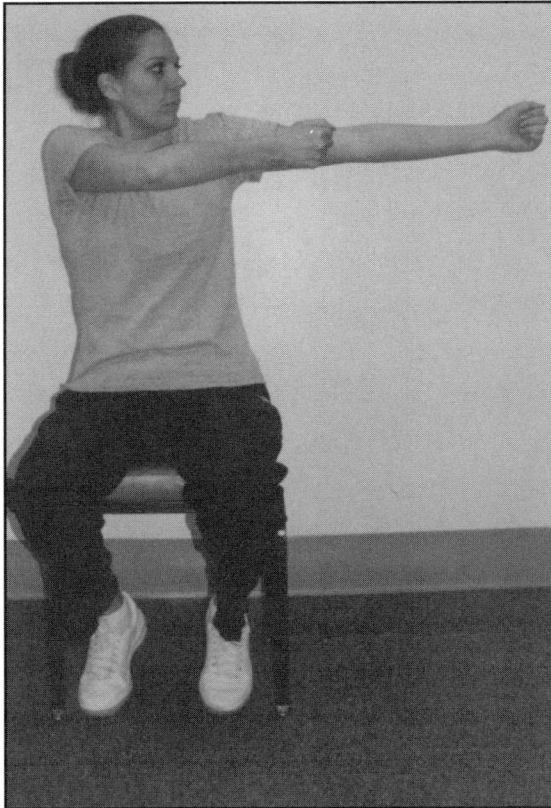

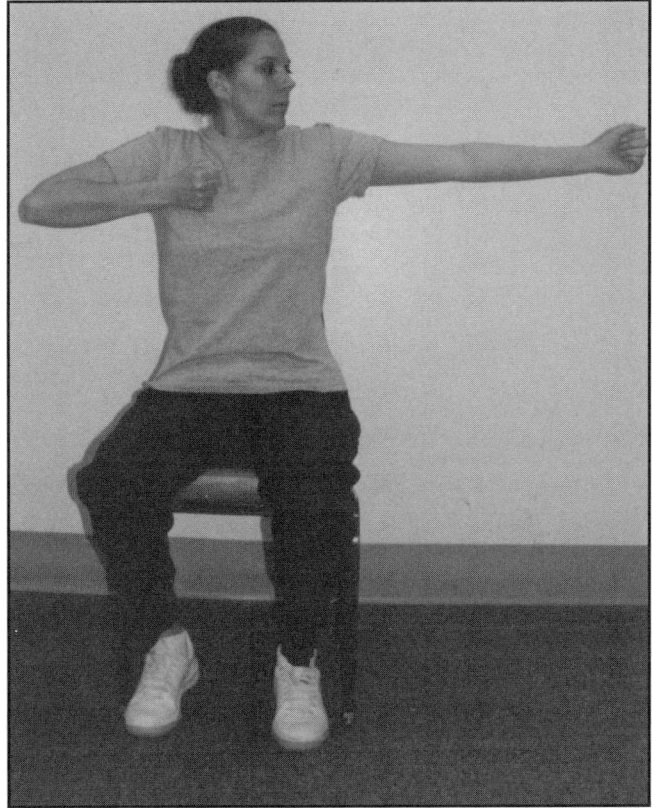

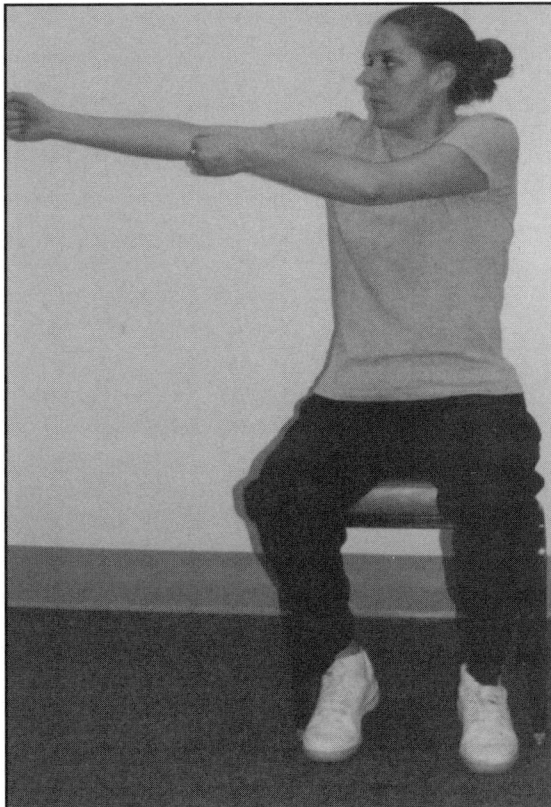

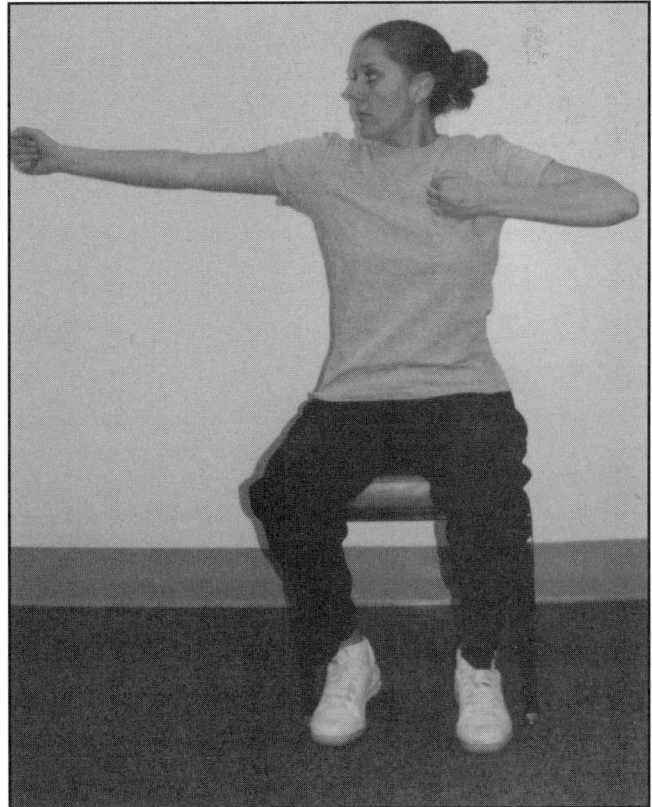

Section III
Wellness

The beginning of this section provides an overview of wellness and the importance of incorporating quality of life issues into a therapeutic recreation stress management program. This section will provide your client with information regarding coping and wellness issues.

In any stress management program, it is important to provide a wellness component to help the client evaluate his or her general lifestyle to determine whether it either aides or abates a general sense of well-being. Determine whether the client is getting sufficient exercise, is eating healthfully, sleeps well, and has an adequate social support network. Also of importance is working with the client on his or her nicotine and alcohol and/or drug intake.

The following chapters have been provided:

- Steps Toward Wellness
- Coping Skills
- Social Support Networks
- Smoking Cessation
- Alcohol and Drug Abuse
- Nutrition
- Sleep Hygiene

Therapeutic recreation specialists often work closely with their clients to help them develop improved coping skills. The coping chapter provides several worksheets on positive and negative coping skills, tips for coping, and problem-solving techniques.

The chapter on social support networks will allow the client the opportunity to determine whether a support group may be of assistance to him or her as an adjunct to treatment. Barbra Streisand sang "People who need people are the luckiest people in the world." The importance of social support is critical in the recovery process.

The chapter on smoking cessation provides a number of tips for quitting smoking. Smoking is a health hazard which can cause cancer, lung disease, heart disease, and hypertension.

In the chapter on alcohol and drug abuse, the client will have a chance to explore his or her using habits and determine the necessary changes to be made. Research has shown that alcohol and drug abuse can either cause or exacerbate medical and psychological conditions such as liver disease, stroke, depression, and anxiety. Furthermore, alcohol related accidents can result in physical injuries or death.

The chapter on nutrition provides worksheets for the clients which will allow them to evaluate their food intake and make the necessary changes for optimal health. The old adage "you are what you eat" has an important message. This chapter will help clients to become aware of the types of food they eat. Watching sugar and salt intake, becoming aware of food additives and caloric intake can help prolong an individual's life and aid in general health. This chapter has two sets of worksheets: The first set provides information for the client with full cognition; a subsequent selection of worksheets are for those clients with some cognitive limitations.

The sleep hygiene chapter offers a variety of tips and includes a Sleep Diary for clients. It has two separate sets of worksheets, again taking into account the client's cognitive abilities. Getting a good night's sleep is critical for a client's general sense of well-being. Insomnia is a symptom rather than an illness. When treating insomnia, have the client look at his or her current sleeping habits and provide information on how to change the behaviors which interfere with good sleep.

Chapter Fifteen
Steps Toward Wellness

In an effort to provide in integrative approach toward health, it is important for therapeutic recreation specialists to provide information on the concepts of wellness. While your clients may have conditions which compromises their health, if clients are able to learn wellness skills which will assist them in their ability to take care of themselves, they can anticipate an improved quality of life.

By providing clients with the opportunity to learn about wellness, the TRS can assist them in making lifestyle changes that will improve their health. Clients who do not understand the concept of wellness may:

- Continue to make unhealthy lifestyle choices
- Experience an increase in somatic symptoms
- Suffer from poor self-esteem
- Feel as if they have little to no control over their lives.

By teaching wellness concepts, clients are more able to:

- Experience a decrease in their stress-related symptoms
- Fell an increased sense of control over their lives
- To make other important changes in their lives
- Experience a sense of accomplishment
- Express feelings of hope.

A 1999 study conducted by Sadur, Moline, Costa, Michalik, Mendiowitz, Roller, Watson, Swain, Selby, and Javorski at the Kaiser Permanente's Pleasanton, California, Center, found that adults with diabetes who attended a wellness program showed improvement in their glycemic control, self-efficacy, and expressed satisfaction about their participation in the program.

One hundred eleven older adults took part in a wellness program in a 2001 study conducted by the School of Nursing at Middle Tennessee State University in Murfreesboro, Tennessee. As a result of the wellness program, the respondents reported greater psychological comfort and a more confident feeling concerning their ability to maintain an independent lifestyle.

Implication Concerns

The materials in this section can be used in either an individual or group setting. Clients with cognitive limitations may need one-to-one assistance to complete the paperwork.

It should be noted that as a treatment team member, the therapeutic recreation specialist should work closely with the interdisciplinary team regarding the client's participation in wellness activities. Should your client need assistance which is beyond the scope of a therapeutic recreation specialist's practice, referral to the client's physician is necessary.

Recommended Reading

Benson, B. and Stuart, E.M. (1993). *The wellness book: The comprehensive guide to maintaining health and treatment stress-related illness*. New York: Simon & Schuster.

References

Campbell, J. and Aday, R.H. (2001). Benefits of using a nurse-managed wellness program. A senior center model. Using community-based sites for older adult intervention and self-care activities may promote an ability to maintain an independent lifestyle. *Journal of Gerontological Nursing, 27*(3), 34–43.

Sadur, C.N., Moline, N., Costa, M., Michalik, D., Mendlowitz, D., Roller, S., Watson, R., Swain, B.E., Selby, J.V., and Javorski, W.C. (1999). Diabetes management in a health maintenance organization. Efficacy of care management using cluster visits. *Diabetes Care, 22*(12), 2011–2017.

Steps Toward Wellness

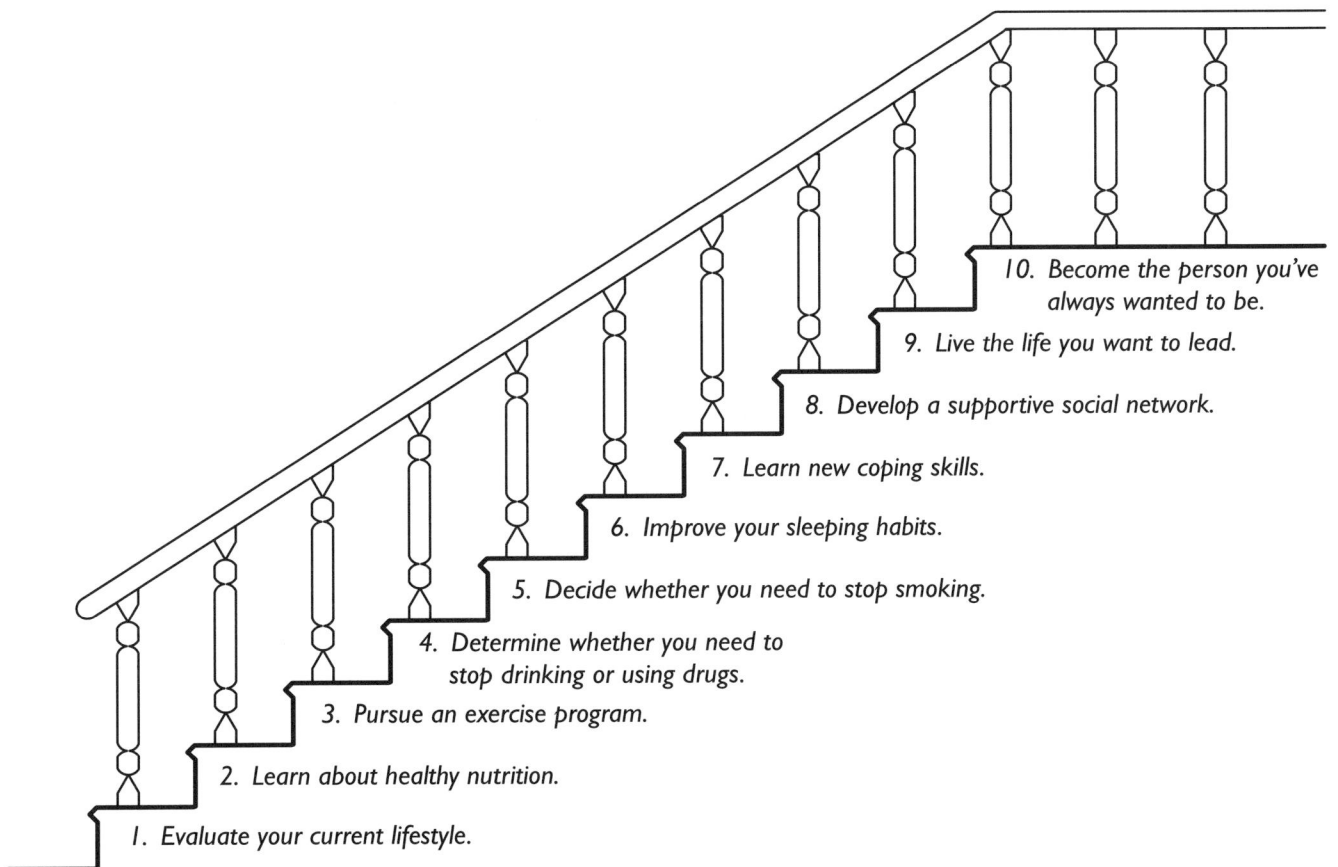

10. Become the person you've always wanted to be.

9. Live the life you want to lead.

8. Develop a supportive social network.

7. Learn new coping skills.

6. Improve your sleeping habits.

5. Decide whether you need to stop smoking.

4. Determine whether you need to stop drinking or using drugs.

3. Pursue an exercise program.

2. Learn about healthy nutrition.

1. Evaluate your current lifestyle.

The Wellness Checklist

Do you need to make some lifestyle changes? Chances are, you do. A number of lifestyle changes will help you feel a whole lot better. Improving your health is often about making a variety of changes, most of which are within your reach. First and foremost, you need to evaluate your current lifestyle.

Check off the items which pertain to your current situation:

❏ I have a health problem and my doctor has suggested I make some lifestyle changes.

❏ I smoke more than five cigarettes a day.

❏ I drink more than I would like to or have been told by my doctor that I need to stop drinking because of a health problem.

❏ I have a problem with drugs.

❏ I am overweight.

❏ I have been told by my doctor that I must change my eating habits.

❏ I do not exercise.

❏ I have insomnia.

❏ I would like to meet other people who have similar problems in order to get some support for my issues.

❏ I would like to feel a whole lot better than I do.

It is important to prioritize the changes you would like to make. One of the mistakes that many people make is that they try to make too many changes at the same time. Now that you have completed this checklist, write down the three items which concern you the most:

1. _____

2. _____

3. _____

It's a good idea to "reward" yourself for making positive changes. Check off a reward you would like to give yourself:

❏ Get a massage

❏ Get a haircut

❏ Get a manicure

❏ Go to a play

❏ Go to a concert

❏ Buy a new outfit

❏ Go to a sports event

❏ Buy a book

❏ Buy a video, CD, or DVD

❏ Take a walk on the beach

❏ Call a friend

❏ Go on a hike

❏ Go on a picnic

❏ Learn a new recreational activity

❏ Have a romantic evening with a special someone

❏ Other _____

The next step is to give yourself a timeline for starting your wellness program. Try to give yourself some time between each lifestyle change you would like to make.

Write down your #1 response: _____

Write down today's date: _____

Now write down the date you would like to begin working on this issue: _____

Write down a reward you will give yourself on your starting date: _____

_____

Your signature   CTRS signature

Congratulations. You have made the first step toward wellness!

Write down your #2 response: _____

Write down today's date: _____

Now write down the date you would like to begin working on this issue: _____

Write down a reward you will give yourself on your starting date: _____

_____

Your signature   CTRS signature

Congratulations. You have made the second step toward wellness!

Write down your #3 response: _____

Write down today's date: _____

Now write down the date you would like to begin working on this issue: _____

Write down a reward you will give yourself on your starting date: _____

_____

Your signature   CTRS signature

Congratulations. You have made the third step toward wellness!

Weekly Wellness Chart

		Monday	Tuesday	Wednesday	Thursday	Friday	Saturday	Sunday
Mood	Excellent 5 4 Good 3 2 Poor 1							
Sleep	Excellent 5 4 Good 3 2 Poor 1							
Nutrition	Excellent 5 4 Good 3 2 Poor 1							
Physical Activity	Excellent 5 4 Good 3 2 Poor 1							
Relationships	Excellent 5 4 Good 3 2 Poor 1							

Comments: _____

_____

_____

_____

_____

_____

_____

_____

Chapter Sixteen
Coping Skills

Therapeutic recreation specialists need to take into account their client's current mental states. Many clients are going through a very hard time and it is easy for them to have negative thoughts and feelings about what is happening to them. It is human nature to catastrophize events. Our client's brains interpret the changes happening in their environment and body, and this can result in triggering their stress response which drives their bodies into the "emergency zone" of fight or flight.

Teaching coping skills and using cognitive behavioral therapy, is an important component of any therapeutic recreation program. Clients who are not able to cope with their stressors may experience:

- Increased muscle tension
- Increased fatigue
- Increased depression
- Compromised immune system
- Headaches
- Stomach problems
- Hypertension

By teaching coping skills, clients are more able to put their life situations into perspective. This can result in:

- Decreased stress-related symptoms
- A sense of control over one's environment
- Increased self-esteem

Cognitive behavioral therapy was used successfully to treat bronchial asthma at the Department of Clinical Psychology at NIMHANS, Bangalore, using behavioral techniques, cognitive restructuring, and cognitive coping skills (Grover, Kumaraiah, Prasadrao & D'souza, 2002).

In a study at the Exercise Physiology and Nutrition Laboratory at University of Massachusetts in Worcester, it was found that participants enrolled in an exercise program displayed an improvement in mood and self-esteem when there was a cognitive component to the training program (Brown, Wang, Ward, Ebbeling, Fortlage, Puleo, Benson & Rippe, 1995).

This was also found to be the case when cognitive behavioral therapy was used in a pain management program at the INPUT Pain Management Unit at St. Thomas Hospital in London. The study determined that cognitive behavioral treatment can be of value in improving day-to-day functioning and quality of life of patients with chronic pain for who conventional medical treatments have apparently failed (Williams et al., 1993).

Special Considerations

The materials in this section can be used in either an individual or group setting. Clients with cognitive limitations may need one-to-one assistance to complete the forms. The Problem Solving II handout has been specifically written for clients with limited cognition.

Recommended Reading

Burns, D. (1980). *Feeling good—The new mood therapy*. New York, NY: Avon Books.

Ellis, A. and Harper, R.A. (1998). *A guide to rational living*. North Hollywood, CA: Wilshire Book Co.

References

Brown, D.R., Wang, Y., Ward, A., Ebbeling, C.B., Fortlage, L., Puleo, E., Benson, H., and Rippe, J.M. (1995). Chronic psychological effects of exercise and exercise plus cognitive strategies. *Medicine and Science in Sports and Exercise, 27*(5), 765–775.

Grover, N., Kumaraiah, V., Prasadrao, P.S., and D'souza, G. (2002). Cognitive behavioural intervention in bronchial asthma. *Journal of the Association of Physicians of India, 50,* 896–900.

Williams, A.C., Nicholas, M.K., Richardson, P.H., Pither, C.E., Justins, D.M., Chamberlain, J.H., Harding, V.R., Ralphs, J.A., Jones, S.C., Dieudonne, I. et al. (1993). Evaluation of a cognitive behavioural programme for rehabilitating patients with chronic pain. *British Journal of General Practice, 43*(377), 513–518.

Tips For Coping

Life is not always easy. Sometimes you have control over the situations which happen to you and sometimes you don't. The important thing is to learn how to cope with the events in your life as best as you can. Here are some tips for coping:

- Remind yourself of the amount of change that has recently happened to you and give yourself a pat on the back for getting the treatment you needed.

- Try to stay in touch with your feelings. It's okay to feel a full range of emotions. Don't try to stuff your feelings. Talk to someone you trust.

- Make the necessary adjustments your need to make.

- Don't make any rash decisions if your are in a current crisis. Try to spend some time of the decisions you are making right now.

- Pace yourself. Don't try to make too many changes at the same time. Prioritize the changes you need to make, then systematically begin to make them.

- Be kind to yourself. You may feel overwhelmed with the stresses in your life, but remember to be good to yourself and by all means, don't blame yourself for whatever is happening in your life.

- Make a list of your accomplishments. Even though you may feel as if nothing is going right at the moment, remind yourself of your achievements.

- Be sure to pursue some of the stress management activities you learned while in treatment.

- Try to learn from the changes you have had to make.

- Remember the Serenity Prayer:
  "Grant me the serenity to accept the things I cannot change, the courage to change the things I can, and the wisdom to know the difference."

Coping Skills

Are you the kind of person who chooses positive or negative coping skills when confronted with a problem? Maybe you do a little bit of both. Here's a list to help you see how you "cope:"

Negative Coping Skills

When I get stressed out I:

- ❑ Smoke cigarettes
- ❑ Have trouble sleeping
- ❑ Eat too much or not at all
- ❑ Get irritable
- ❑ Withdraw emotionally
- ❑ Drink alcohol or use drugs
- ❑ Ignore the problem and hope it goes away
- ❑ Worry all the time
- ❑ Don't exercise

Positive Coping Skills

When I get stressed out I:

- ❑ Seek out family and friends for support
- ❑ Exercise
- ❑ Take some time to relax
- ❑ Do some deep breathing exercises
- ❑ Read
- ❑ Meditate
- ❑ Talk about my feelings
- ❑ Take some time off from work or responsibilities
- ❑ Daydream
- ❑ Try to maintain a healthy diet
- ❑ Try to maintain a sense of humor
- ❑ Try to make the necessary changes to decrease the stress I'm experiencing

Now that you have had a chance to see how you cope, did you find you used positive or negative coping strategies to help you? The problem with using negative coping skills is that you will eventually feel worse. It's not always easy to choose positive coping strategies, but you will feel a whole lot better.

Write down three positive coping skills you would like to pursue:

1. _____

2. _____

3. _____

Cognitive Distortions

Below are ten examples of cognitive distortions people tend to make about various life situations. Check off the type of thinking you have often experienced:

❒ I often think in all-or-nothing categories. I view things in either black-or-white.

❒ I often overgeneralize. I view a single negative event as meaning that everything will turn out badly.

❒ I dwell on the negative. I can't stop feeling badly about a situation. I can't think of anything else once I begin dwelling on something bad that happened to me.

❒ I have difficulty thinking about positive experiences. If someone compliments me or if I have had a good day, I tell myself, "It doesn't count."

❒ I jump to conclusions. I make a negative interpretation even when there are no definite facts supporting the conclusion.

❒ I tend to catastrophize situations. I always look for the worst-case scenario.

❒ I let my negative emotions consume me. I figure that if I am feeling so badly, there's nothing I can do to make me feel better.

❒ I use a lot of "shoulds" in my life.

❒ I tend to label situations. It's hard for me to back off on my point of view once I have decided on the situation as being positive or negative.

❒ I tend to over personalize what's going on around me. I consider myself to be of blame even when I know that's not really the case.

Take a moment and look at the cognitive distortions which you have checked off. Write down the three distortions which you most often use. After doing so, write in an alternative way of thinking.

Cognitive Distortion #1 : _____
Alternative thought process for Cognitive Distortion #1:

Cognitive Distortion #2 : _____
Alternative thought process for Cognitive Distortion #2:

Cognitive Distortion #3 : _____
Alternative thought process for Cognitive Distortion #3:

Out With the Negative Thoughts—In With the Positive

The following exercise will help you with reconstructing your thoughts so that you can let go off some of the negative thoughts you have about a certain situation. Take a moment to decide on a situation you would like to change:

Situation you would like to change:

What is you stress level regarding this situation: (10 equals extreme stress, 0 equals no stress at all): _____

What is the worst-case scenario?

How are you feeling or thinking when you envision this worst-case scenario?

When you feel this way, what is your usual response?

Now, take the same situation and think of the best-case scenario?

What can you do to help this situation become a best-case scenario?

What is your stress level when you envisioned a best-case scenario outcome? (10 equals extreme stress, 0 equals no stress at all): _____

How are you feeling now?

Problem-Solving Techniques I

Many people tend to get stuck when they are dealing with a problem. The problem consumes their thinking and they have a difficult time thinking about anything else. Sometimes, there seems to be no solutions at all. Learning how to solve problems takes practice.

1. Isolate the problem. Don't overgeneralize the problem to think that it means the problem defines your entire worldview. What is the problem you are facing and how does it effect your thinking?

2. If you have had a similar situation in the past, what helped you resolve it before?

3. If you can't come up with a solution, ask people in the group to help you solve the problem.

4. Some problems do not have solutions, and you may have to live with the problem whether you want to or not. Sometimes, you need to put the problem aside and become involved in an activity which will allow you to let it go for a period of time. Write down several recreational activities you can pursue in order to give you some time away from your problem.

Problem-Solving Techniques II

Wouldn't it be nice if we lived in a problem-free world? Unfortunately, with living comes a certain amount of problems. The good news is that some problems have solutions. Below is a list of problems you may be encountering and some solutions which you may want to consider.

❏ I have health problems.
Solutions:
___ Discuss with you doctor the problem(s) you are experiencing.
___ Become your own advocate. Learn more about your health through books, articles, the Internet, and lectures.
___ Determine whether you can change your diet to help you get better.
___ Join a support group to help you feel more comfortable about your health problem.
___ Contact an local, national, or international association which addresses the health problem.
___ Speak to your family and friends about your health concerns.

❏ I have money problems.
Solutions:
___ Begin to keep track of the money you spend.
___ Learn more about budgeting.
___ Meet with a financial advisor about your money problems.
___ Take a class on budgeting.
___ Talk to a vocational rehabilitation counselor about getting work.
___ Talk to a job coach about changing jobs.
___ Open a savings account and determine a certain amount of money which you will deposit on a monthly basis. Put that money aside and think of it as your nest egg.

❏ I have relationship problems.
Solutions:
___ Seek out counseling to discuss your relationship problems.
___ Join a relationship support group.
___ Read books and articles about how to improve relationships.
___ Make a list of all the things you would like to have in a relationship.

❏ I spend too much time doing nothing.
Solutions:
___ Speak to a recreation therapist about increasing your recreational and social involvement.
___ Go to your local park and see what kinds of recreational programs are available.
___ Buy your local newspaper and look at the listings of local events.
___ Surf the Internet to locate a listings of local events.
___ Make a contract with yourself that you will try one new activity a week.
___ Call a friend and ask him or her out for coffee.

❏ I feel anxious and depressed.
Solutions:
___ Become involved in a stress management program.
___ Speak to a counselor about your feelings.
___ Join a support group.
___ Become involved in an exercise program.
___ Speak about your feelings with friends and family.
___ Learn yoga.
___ Learn meditation.

After completing this worksheet, do you feel more hopeful? Often we get overwhelmed by our problems and forget to think about solutions. Most problems take some time to resolve themselves, however, by knowing that you can make changes in your life, you can begin to feel a lot better.

Chapter Seventeen
Social Support

One of the roles of therapeutic recreation specialists is to assist clients in developing their social support network during treatment and as part of the discharge planning stage of treatment. Some clients have been socially isolated prior to treatment and may express a desire to develop a social support network. Even clients who have a strong support network of friends and family may still want to seek further support for their current physical or mental condition with people who are in "their same shoes."

Without social support individuals may experience the following:

- Social isolation
- Depression
- A sense of aloneness
- Exacerbation of physical or psychological symptoms
- Increased stress
- Inability to express thoughts or feelings about medical or psychological problem(s)

The benefits of clients having a strong social support network include:

- Increases socialization
- Offers a sense of belonging
- Decreases physical and psychological symptoms
- Increases self-esteem
- Increases feeling of control of their current situation
- Offers a place to express thoughts or feelings about their illness or condition
- Offers the opportunity to impart information pertinent to their illness or condition

In a study conducted at the Department of Clinical Neuroscience, Section of Psychiatry at St. Goran's Hospital, Karolinska Institute, Stockholm, Sweden, a group of bipolar clients were given a one-year follow-up questionnaire to determine their perceived level of social support. The bipolar patients with full inter-episode remission perceived more social support than those who did not achieve full remission (Johnson, Lundstrom, Aberg-Wetedt & Mathe, 2003).

Furthermore, social support was determined to be helpful in decreasing social support in patient with chronic illness in a study completed at the Department of Psychology at the State University of New York at Stony Brook (Symister & Friend, 2003).

Social support can be enhanced through a variety of activities and organizations including:

- support groups
- religious communities
- schools
- parks
- libraries
- the YMCA and YWCA
- singles events
- special interest groups

Implementation Concerns

The worksheets in this section will help clients determine their current social support needs. The worksheets offer information on how to join a support group, provide a list of social activities available in the community, and give tips on improving social skills. These handouts can be used in both individual and group settings. If conducted in a group, encourage a discussion period after the clients have completed the worksheets.

Special Considerations

Clients with limited cognitive abilities may need one-to-one assistance with the worksheets.

Recommended Reading

Bhaerman, S. and McMillan, D. (1986). *Friends & lovers—How to meet the people you want to meet.* Cincinnati, OH: Writer's Digest Books.

Klein, L. (2000). *The support group sourcebook: What they are, how you can find one, and how they can help you.* Hoboken, NJ: Wiley & Sons.

Wuthnow, R. (1996). *Sharing the journey: Support groups and America's new quest for community.* New York, NY: Free Press.

References

Johnson, L., Lundstrom, O., Aberg-Wistedt, A., and Mathe, A.A. (2003). Social support in bipolar disorder: Its relevance to remission and relapse. *Bipolar Disorders, 5*(2), 129–137.

Symister, P. and Friend, R. (2003). The influence of social support and problematic support on optimism and depression in chronic illness: A prospective study evaluating self-esteem as a mediator. *Health Psychology, 22*(2), 123–129.

Tips For Joining a Support Group

You may want to consider joining a support group as an adjunct to your treatment. Support groups can be extremely helpful. They can help you in the following ways:

Mutual Help

In a support group, you will find other people who have the same issues or problems. You will have the opportunity to hear other people talk about their experiences, and you can share yours with them. You will feel as if you are not alone.

Dissemination of Information

One of the benefits of belonging to a support group is to learn from the other members about services, events, and medical information available to you about your condition or health issues.

Support groups are composed of peers. Rather than having a healthcare professional lead support groups, they are run by its members. Members strive to help one another. If professionals are involved (and sometimes they are), they are there for ancillary support.

Volunteers run the groups. Members are the leaders and there are very rarely any monetary fees involved in membership.

You'll be able to give as well as receive. Being able to assist someone else is a wonderful experience and has tremendous therapeutic value.

Support groups can help you stay on track. Support groups can help you with your determination to stay on-track with the lifestyle changes you are trying to make.

Sponsorship

Twelve-step groups such as Alcoholics Anonymous suggest you find a sponsor at their meetings. This is a member who has "been around the block" and can be a role model for you. Most support groups use the same concept. The "old-time" members will seek you out to help you become more comfortable at the meetings.

Buddy systems are in place. Even when you're not at a support group meeting, you will be encouraged to phone or meet with other members so that they can give you additional support when you need it.

Meetings are confidential. One of the primary rules of support groups is to respect and protect the member's privacy. You will be able to speak openly at the meetings.

Bring a Friend

If you are shy and have problems meeting new people, ask a friend to go with you to the first meeting.

Qualities I Like in Myself and Others

Positivity Traits

In Myself

- ❑ Accepting of others
- ❑ Affectionate
- ❑ Good communicator
- ❑ Enthusiastic
- ❑ Good problem solver
- ❑ Independent
- ❑ Perceptive
- ❑ Reliable
- ❑ Good sense of humor
- ❑ Attractive

Qualities I Want in People Around Me

- ❑ Adventurous spirit
- ❑ Caring
- ❑ Creative
- ❑ Good listener
- ❑ Honest
- ❑ Loyal
- ❑ Good attitude
- ❑ Responsible
- ❑ Thoughtful
- ❑ Well-groomed

Take a look at the qualities that are important to you in yourself and in others.

1. What did you learn about yourself after completing this exercise?

2 What did you learn about others?

Tips for Making and Keeping New Friends

It's not always easy meeting new people. If you're shy, it is harder. Even outgoing people can sometimes feel socially awkward. Establishing rapport with another individual takes practice and determination. But it's certainly worth it!

Maintain Eye Contact

Easier said than done, maintaining eye contact is extremely important when making new friends or maintaining current friendships. If you want someone to know you are listening to them, be sure to look into their eyes while conversing.

Respect the Personal Spaces of Others

We all have our own definition of personal space, but it's important to determine when you are standing or sitting too close to someone or vice versa. You can basically tell if you have invaded someone's personal space if they move away from you slightly. In the same way, if you feel as if someone has entered your own private space, it's okay to move to a distance where you feel most comfortable. Shaking hands, a pat on the back, and even a hug (if you ask for one) are all acceptable forms of saying hello, goodbye, or indicating support.

Beware of Overwhelming Someone With Your Issues

Take some time to get to know someone before you confide your deepest thoughts and feelings. It's important to establish emotional boundaries with people. As you get to know someone better, you can begin to really talk about your concerns, but don't try to become best friends overnight.

Learn To Appreciate Differences

While we all like to have friends who have the same interests and share a similar point of view, it's also nice to meet people who act or think differently. Even with friends with similar interests, allow them to have diverse tastes and ideas from yours. No two people are created the same. Respect that.

Pace Your Friendships

When you meet new people and you really like them, don't smother them with too much attention. You should try to find a natural rhythm to the friendship. You can't hurry love, and it's a good idea not to hurry friendships either.

Keep the Topic of Conversation on Neutral Subjects

The basic rule of thumb is to avoid talking about politics, religion, or sex, unless you know someone well. Remain prepared for different points of views. These topics are often emotionally laden.

Try To Be an Active Listener

Don't be the only one talking. Be sure to give everyone the chance to participate in the conversation.

Invite a Friend or Acquaintance To Accompany You to a New Event

If you are shy or feel awkward in social situations, you may feel more comfortable if you ask someone to go with you.

Find Activities You Enjoy

If you are trying to expand your social horizons, choose an activity you enjoy and find out where that activity is taking place in your community.

Join a Support Group

If you are living with a physical or mental condition which has been difficult to deal with, consider joining a support group. You'll feel a lot better about your situation if you get support from other people who understand it. You can locate support groups through your local newspaper, libraries, the Internet, the phone book, and word-of-mouth.

Expanding Your Social Horizons

Are you looking for new activities where you can meet people with similar interests? Check off the activities which interest you:

_____ Sport leagues	_____ Playing cards
_____ Support groups	_____ Scrabble clubs
_____ Church activities	_____ Collecting antiques
_____ Adult education courses	_____ Computer groups or classes
_____ Art classes	_____ College courses
_____ Health clubs	_____ Boating/sailing clubs
_____ Libraries	_____ Golfing
_____ YMCA or YWCA	_____ Ice skating rinks
_____ Drama groups	_____ Pet shows
_____ Choir	_____ Automobile shows
_____ Sierra Club or other hiking groups	_____ Photography classes or clubs
_____ Dance classes	_____ Museums
_____ Language classes	_____ Social or political activism
_____ Biking clubs	_____ Environmental activism
_____ New Age classes or events	_____ Coffeehouses
_____ Writing groups	_____ Comedy clubs
_____ Book clubs	_____ Other _____
_____ Community gardens	

Now that you are aware of so many things to do in your free time, write a time line for pursuing these activities in your community. Give yourself some time between starting new activities. The best way to do this is to try an activity for a period of time. Once you have incorporated it into your schedule, you can decide on another activity. What are your three top choices?

1. _____

2. _____

3. _____

Write down your #1 response: _____

Write down today's date: _____

Now write down the date you would like to begin doing this activity: _____

_____

Your signature   CTRS signature

Congratulations. You are about to expand your social horizons and have a good time doing it!

Write down your #2 response: _____

Write down today's date: _____

Now write down the date you would like to begin doing this activity: _____

_____

Your signature   CTRS signature

Congratulations. You are about to expand your social horizons and have a good time doing it!

_____

Write down your #3 response: _____

Write down today's date: _____

Now write down the date you would like to begin doing this activity: _____

_____

Your signature   CTRS signature

Congratulations. You are about to expand your social horizons and have a good time doing it!

Remember, the best way to locate new activities is through your local newspaper, libraries, the Internet, the phone book, and word-of-mouth.

Chapter Eighteen
Smoking Cessation

One of the most important aspects of a wellness program is to provide information assisting your clients who smoke cigarettes to consider becoming non-smokers. The health hazards associated with smoking are many. Diseases associated with nicotine use include:

- cancer
- emphysema
- heart disease
- high blood pressure
- stroke
- asthma
- general health

Individuals who have successfully stopped smoking report the following positive changes:

- A sense of accomplishment
- Less susceptible to colds and other health problems
- Improved ability to breathe
- Experience less fatigue
- Lower anxiety levels
- Fewer headaches
- Enjoy living in a cleaner environment
- Increased energy levels
- Ability to exercise for longer periods of time
- Decreased worry of friends and family who were concerned about their loved one smoking

According to the 2000 Report of the Surgeon General *Reducing Tobacco Use*, pharmacological treatment of nicotine addiction combined with behavioral support will enable 20–25% of users to remain abstinent at one year post treatment (U.S. Department of Health and Human Services, 2000).

Implementation Concerns

The role of the therapeutic recreation specialist is often that of assisting the client to improve his or her health. For the most part, it is best to refer clients who smoke to a smoking cessation program. These programs are available in most hospitals and other health agencies. For referrals, contact the American Cancer Society at 800-227-2345.

Locate a Smokers Anonymous chapter in your community. This program, based on the twelve-step approach, is available in most communities and is free to the public. The worksheets in this chapter can also be used as a supplement to a smoking cessation program.

Recommended Reading

University of California San Diego Cancer Center. (2001). *The Take Control Guide*. San Diego, CA: Author.

Reference

U.S. Department of Health and Human Services. (2000). *Report of the Surgeon General: Reducing Tobacco Use*. Washington, DC: Author.

Tips for Smoking Cessation

If you are thinking about stopping smoking, you have made a decision which will change your life in so many ways you'll be astounded. You are going to feel one hundred times better in a very short period. Give yourself a pat on the back. Your family and friends are going to be very excited too. Here are some general tips for stopping smoking:

Choose a Stop Smoking Date

For best results, think about a date which has some significance to you such as your birthday, a loved one's birthday, anniversary, or a holiday.

Consult Your Physician

Your doctor can help you with the logistics of stopping smoking, prescribe a quitting aid and monitor your health during the process.

Consider a Quitting Aid

The smoking aids now available include nicotine patches, gum, and medication.

The theory behind nicotine gum and patches is that the amount of nicotine will be decreased over time until your body no longer craves it. This method takes about 4 to 12 weeks. The amount of gum or the strength of the gum is determined by the number of cigarettes you were smoking prior to beginning this regimen. Both patches and gum are available as an over-the-counter item; however, you may want to check with your physician since some insurance companies will pay for them.

The most common medication prescribed as an antismoking aid is an antidepressant called Wellbutrin S-R which is also sold as Zyban. It does not contain nicotine, but can reduce cravings associated with smoking cessation. It will take about 1 to 3 weeks to notice any changes; therefore, begin the medication several weeks before your quit date. Most doctors recommend taking the medication for 7 to 12 weeks.

With all of the smoking aids available, it is recommended that you seek some sort of program which will help you stay on-track.

Anticipate Some Withdrawal Symptoms

These include problems in the following areas:

- cravings
- irritability
- anxiety
- headaches
- fatigue
- hunger
- dizziness
- depression
- difficulty concentrating
- constipation
- cough

Do not be alarmed if you experience any of these symptoms, they will pass. Withdrawal symptoms can last for 2 to 4 weeks. Remind yourself that even though you are feeling bad, you have made a decision which will ultimately result in feeling great. In actuality, your body is adjusting to becoming nicotine-free. These symptoms are a sign that you're making progress.

One week before your quit date, sit down and think about why you want to quit smoking. Check off the reasons you want to stop smoking:

- ❐ I have a health problem and it is made worse by smoking
- ❐ My doctor has suggested I stop smoking.
- ❐ I know I will feel a lot better as a nonsmoker.
- ❐ I have a young child and I don't want my child to be exposed to my smoking.
- ❐ My friends and family members have urged me to stop smoking.
- ❐ My clothes, hair, and home smell like cigarettes.
- ❐ I want to exercise more and would like improved stamina.
- ❐ Other _____

Determine the places which you associate with smoking. Check off the where you would most likely smoke:

- ❐ Home
- ❐ Work
- ❐ While working on my computer
- ❐ In my car
- ❐ While listening to music
- ❐ At a club or bar
- ❐ When drinking
- ❐ During a sporting event
- ❐ While talking on the phone
- ❐ While watching television
- ❐ Other _____

One week before your quit date, sit down and think about why you smoke and when. Check off the emotional triggers which you often find result in your smoking a cigarette:

- ❐ A fight or argument
- ❐ Financial problems
- ❐ Relationship problems
- ❐ Work problems
- ❐ Family issues
- ❐ Boredom
- ❐ Stress
- ❐ Other _____

A number of lifestyle changes will help you once you have decided to stop smoking. Check off the activities you might consider pursuing:

- ❐ Begin an exercise program.
- ❐ Begin a relaxation program such as yoga or deep breathing.
- ❐ Join a support group.
- ❐ Take a long walk.
- ❐ Go to the beach, mountains, or a park.
- ❐ Take a long bath.
- ❐ Treat yourself to a massage or facial.
- ❐ Buy yourself a present.
- ❐ Drink plenty of water.
- ❐ Keep a journal.
- ❐ Ask for support from your friends and family.
- ❐ Other _____

Remember that smoking cessation is a process. You are going to feel a whole lot better, but it may take some time before you feel 100% better. Give yourself a huge pat on the back. By deciding to quit smoking, you have become your own best friend.

Chapter Nineteen
Alcohol and Drug Abuse

In the course of treating clients, you may encounter some patients who either need to become abstinent from alcohol or drugs or who have made the decision to do so to improve their general health. The loss of human life from substance abuse is astounding. While therapeutic recreation specialists may not be solely responsible for providing substance abuse treatment, this chapter will provide tips to share with clients who are considering becoming sober.

Alcohol and substance abuse can either cause or exacerbate the following conditions:

- liver disease
- diabetes
- heart disease
- stroke
- skin disease
- high blood pressure
- depression
- anxiety
- circulation problems
- general health condition

There are many benefits when a person chooses to stop drinking or using substances including:

- Improved health
- Increased self-esteem
- Improved relationships with others
- Improved stamina and ability to exercise
- Improved mood

According to the *Diagnostic and Statistical Manual of Mental Disorders Fourth Edition* (DSM-IV), the essential feature of substance dependence is a cluster of cognitive, behavioral, and psychological symptoms indicating that the individual continues use of the substance despite significant substance-related problems. There is a pattern of repeated self-administration that usually results in tolerance, withdrawal, and compulsive drug-taking behavior.

Implementation Concerns

The role of the therapeutic recreation specialist is often that of assisting the client to improve his or her health. For the most part, it is best to refer clients who abuse substances to a chemical dependency program. These programs are available in most hospitals and other health agencies. You may want to locate an Alcohol Anonymous chapter in the community to use as a referral source for your clients. This program, based on the twelve-step approach, is available in most communities and is free to the public. Another support group, called Rational Recovery, uses a cognitive behavioral approach and has also proven to be effective. The worksheets in this book can be used as a supplement to a substance abuse program.

Special Considerations

If the client has a long history of substance abuse or has become physically addicted to a substance, he or she will need to take part in a medically supervised detoxification program.

Recommended Reading

Johnson, V.E. (1986). *How to help someone who doesn't want help: A step-by-step guide for families and friends of chemically dependent persons.* Minneapolis, MN: John Institute.

Kinney, J. and Leaton, G. (1987). *Loosening the grip— A handbook of alcohol information.* St. Louis, MO: Times Mirror/Mosby.

Tighe, A.A. (1999). *Stop the chaos: How to get control of your life by beating alcohol and drugs.* Center City, MN: Hazelden.

References

American Psychological Association. (1994). *Diagnostic and statistical manual of mental disorders* (4th ed.). Washington, DC: Author.

Tips For Becoming Sober

If you are thinking about quitting alcohol and/or drugs, then you have made a decision which will change your life in so many ways you'll be astounded. You are going to feel one hundred times better and in a very short period. Give yourself a pat on the back. Your family and friends are going to be very excited too. Here are some general tips for quitting alcohol and/or drugs.

Deciding to Get Sober

You have made the determination to quit drinking or using drugs. This is a very important step. In fact, it may be the single most important adjustment you make in your life.

Consult Your Physician

Your doctor can help you with the logistics of how to quit using substances. Your doctor can monitor your health during the process or refer you to a substance abuse program to assist you in your detoxification process and to learn recovery tools.

Join a Recovery Program

Consider joining a twelve-step recovery program such as Alcoholics Anonymous or Narcotics Anonymous. You may even want to inquire about the Rational Recovery program which uses a behavioral modification program to help you get sober. In these groups, you will get a lot of support from other people who are in the process of getting sober or have been sober for a period of time. Most communities have these programs. Consult your telephone book for recovery program phone numbers.

Anticipate Some Withdrawal Symptoms

You may have some problems in the following areas:

- cravings
- irritability
- anxiety
- headaches
- fatigue
- increase or decrease in appetite
- dizziness
- depression
- difficulty concentrating
- constipation

Do not be alarmed if you experience any of these symptoms—they will pass. Withdrawal symptoms can last for 2 to 4 weeks, sometimes even longer. Remind yourself that even though you are feeling badly, you have made a decision which will change your life. In actuality, your body is adjusting to becoming substance free. The symptoms are a sign that you're making progress.

Prior to quitting, sit down and think about why you want to quit using alcohol and/or drugs. Check off the reasons you want to get sober:

❒ I have a health problem and it is made worse by using substances.

❒ My doctor has suggested I stop using substances.

❒ I know I will feel a lot better if I am sober.

❒ I have a child/children and I don't want my child/children to be exposed to my drinking and/or using drugs.

❒ My friends and family members have urged me to stop using substances.

❒ I have missed work because I was hung over.

❒ I have lost a job because I was using substances.

❒ I have had financial problems related to using substances.

❒ Other _____

Determine the places which you associate with using alcohol and/or drugs. Check off the places you would most likely drink or use substances:

❒ Home

❒ In my car

❒ While listening to music

❒ At a club or bar

❒ At parties

❒ During a sporting event

❒ While talking on the phone

❒ At friend's home

❒ Whenever and whereever I can

❒ Other _____

It's a good idea to think about the events in your life which trigger your wanting to use substances to "ease the pain." Check off the emotional triggers which you can relate to:

❒ Fights or arguments

❒ Financial problems

❒ Relationship problems

❒ Work problems

❒ Family issues

❒ Boredom

❒ Stress

❒ Physical pain

❒ Other _____

There are a number of lifestyle changes you can make which will help you in your recovery process. Check off the activities you enjoy or would consider:

❒ Begin an exercise program.

❒ Begin a relaxation program such as yoga or deep breathing.

❒ Join a support group.

❒ Take a long walk.

❒ Go to the beach, mountains, or a park.

❒ Take a long bath.

❒ Treat yourself to a massage or facial.

❒ Buy yourself a present.

❒ Drink plenty of water.

❒ Keep a journal.

❒ Ask for support from your friends and family.

❒ Other _____

Remember that sobriety is a process. You are going to feel a whole lot better, but it may take some time before you feel 100 percent. By deciding to quit using substances, you have made a decision which will change your life in ways you never knew possible. Remember—

"Today is the first day of the rest of your life!"

Chapter Twenty
Nutrition

Nutrition is an important component of a stress reduction program. Eating a healthy diet is a critical component of living well and decreasing stress. Several medical problems are associated with poor nutrition including:

- hypoglycemia
- anemia
- colitis
- diabetes
- skin disease
- eating disorders
- obesity

If the client has experienced any of these health problems, he or she should meet with a physician to determine his or her medical status. You may also want to refer the client to a nutritionist who can work with him or her.

While working with the client on nutritional issues, assess the client for the following problems:

- Weight loss
- Weight gain
- Skipped meals
- Increased use of cigarettes
- Increased intake of coffee or soft drinks
- Increased intake of junk food
- Decrease in exercise
- Decrease or increase of appetite
- Eating meals at odd times

Many nutritional problems can be altered when the client is willing to alter the consumption of sugar, caffeine, alcohol, and nicotine. Stress levels will drop dramatically when the client begins to take the initiative to change his or her eating habits.

In the fifth edition of *Nutrition and Your Health: Dietary Guidelines for Americans* (U.S. Department of Health and Human Services & USDA, 2000), the following guidelines were established:

- Let the Pyramid guide your food choices
- Choose a variety of grains daily, especially whole grains
- Choose a variety of fruits and vegetables daily
- Keep food safe to eat

Furthermore, a 2003 World Health Organization and Food and Agriculture Organization Expert Report on diet and chronic disease found that a diet with less saturated fats, sugar and salt, but with more fruits and vegetables along with physical exercise was needed to counter cardiovascular diseases, cancer, diabetes, and obesity (WHO/FAO, 2003).

Implementation Concerns

Two separate programs are offered in this workbook. The first program (Nutrition Exercise I) should be utilized for clients with full cognition who are able to work independently. The Food Diaries should be photocopied before you begin the nutrition portion of your program.

The second program (Nutrition Exercise II) is for clients who may have some cognitive limitations. The first handout provides a checklist of foods options which follow the USDA Food Pyramid guidelines. To use the Food Collage, you should cut out food choices from magazines and ask your clients to use a glue stick to place the pictures on their "plates" provided for them. For best results, meet with the client either individually or in a group to go over the information and to allow for a question and answer period.

Special Considerations

Eating Disorders

If the client has been diagnosed with an eating disorder such as anorexia, bulimia, obesity, or compulsive overeating, or if you suspect that the client may have an eating disorder, he or she should be referred to the treatment team.

Recommended Resources

Brownell, K.D. (2000). *The learn program for weight management*. Dallas, TX: American Health.

Cash, T.F. (1997). *The body image workbook: An 8-step program for learning to like your looks*. Oakland, CA: New Harbinger Publications.

Clark, N. (1990). *Sports nutrition guidebook: Eating to fuel your active lifestyle*. Champaign, IL: Leisure Press.

Katherine, A. (1991). *Anatomy of a food addition: The brain chemistry of overeating*. Carlsbad, CA: Gurze Books.

U.S. Department of Agriculture/U.S. Department of Health and Human Services. (1996). The food guide pyramid. Retrieved October 15, 2003 from http://www.usda.gov/cnpp/images/FoodPyr..eps

U.S. Department of Health and Human Services and U.S. Department of Agriculture. (2000). *Nutrition and your health: Dietary guidelines for Americans* (5th ed.). Washington, DC: Authors.

Willet, W. (2002). *Eat, drink, and be healthy*. New York, NY: Fireside/Simon and Schuster.

World Health Organization, and Food and Agriculture Organization (WHO/FAO). (2003). WHO/FAO release independent Expert Report on diet and chronic disease. Retrieved March 30, 2004 from http://www.who.int/mediacentre/releases/2003/pr20/en/print.html

Nutrition Exercise I

Nutritional Tips To Help You Stay on Track

1. Drink plenty of water. Most nutritionists suggest eight glasses a day. Drinking water will help in the detoxification process by cleansing your body internally.

2. Don't panic if you slip and have a big piece of cake or pie or whatever you fancy. It happens. If you start "criminalizing" foods, you'll end up craving them more.

3. If you're planning to attend a party where you know there's going to be an abundance of food and you're afraid you'll eat too much, have a healthy snack before you go or offer to bring a nutritious dish with you.

4. Try not to eat just before going to bed. It'll make you feel sluggish in the morning and you might want to skip breakfast which isn't a good idea.

5. "If You Can't Have the Body You Love, Love the One You're With." Don't be too hard on yourself. Take a hot bath. Buy wonderful-smelling body lotions. Get a massage. Love yourself. Nurture your body.

6. If you're going to a party and you're afraid that you'll overeat, take a friend who is also trying to eat nutritiously with you. You can be each other's allies. Bring a healthy dish, such as cut veggies, so you'll have something to eat during the party.

7. Begin an exercise program. If you're eating well and exercising at least three times a week, you are going to feel like a million dollars. Don't be too surprised when your friends and family start telling you that you look wonderful. You do!

8. Try to develop a solid support network. By having people to turn to when you're feeling vulnerable, you'll be less likely to reach for unhealthy foods.

9. Think of alternatives to eating when you're feeling down. Take a short walk. Call a friend. Learn yoga.

10. Remember that making changes in your diet takes time and don't expect perfection. So how about starting at the beginning instead of trying to cross the finish line right away?

11. Caffeine is a drug which is accepted by our society even though we are fully aware of its addictive qualities. Found in coffee, tea, soft drinks and chocolate, caffeine offers a nice little buzz and it's legal.

    The American Medical Association recommends limiting your daily caffeine intake to 200 milligrams a day. That equals about 1 ½ cups of coffee a day. If you don't want to stop drinking coffee completely, then try to taper off the amount you drink. If you are having problems with insomnia, stop all caffeine intake after 4:00 p.m., or even earlier in the day if you can. Try to moderate the amount of chocolate you eat and watch out for caffeinated soft drinks. If you're experiencing any jitteriness, insomnia, or stomach problems, you're probably consuming too much caffeine. Detoxing from caffeine can be difficult. Expect considerable discomfort such as headaches, tremors, and fatigue. Drink plenty of water and switch to herbal teas if you still want something hot to drink.

12. **Sugar:** Here's a staggering statistic—most Americans eat between 100–130 pounds of sugar a year. Yikes! Overconsumption of sugar can cause headaches, irritability, fatigue, and inability to concentrate. Sugar is absolutely not recommended for people with blood sugar abnormalities such as diabetes and hypoglycemia. So here's the bottom line—Watch your sugar intake.

13. **Salt:** Salt should be used carefully. If you have a heart condition or suffer from hypertension, it is particularly important to curtail the amount of salt in your diet. If there's too much salt in the food you eat, your body will retain fluids which makes your heart work harder. The body only needs about 2,400 mg of salt each day—that's about ¼ teaspoon of salt. Watch your salt intake and be sure to read food labels for hidden salt in your food.

14. **Vitamins:** Most people fall short of getting all the nutrients they need in their diet. Vitamin supplements, therefore, act as an insurance policy against nutritional deficiencies.

The Food Guide Pyramid

The most sensible way to get and stay healthy is to follow the USDA Food Pyramid. It gives you a guideline for the proper types and amounts of food you should eat every day including:

- grains
- protein
- dairy
- vegetables and fruits
- a limited quantity of foods containing fat, cholesterol, sugar, and salt.

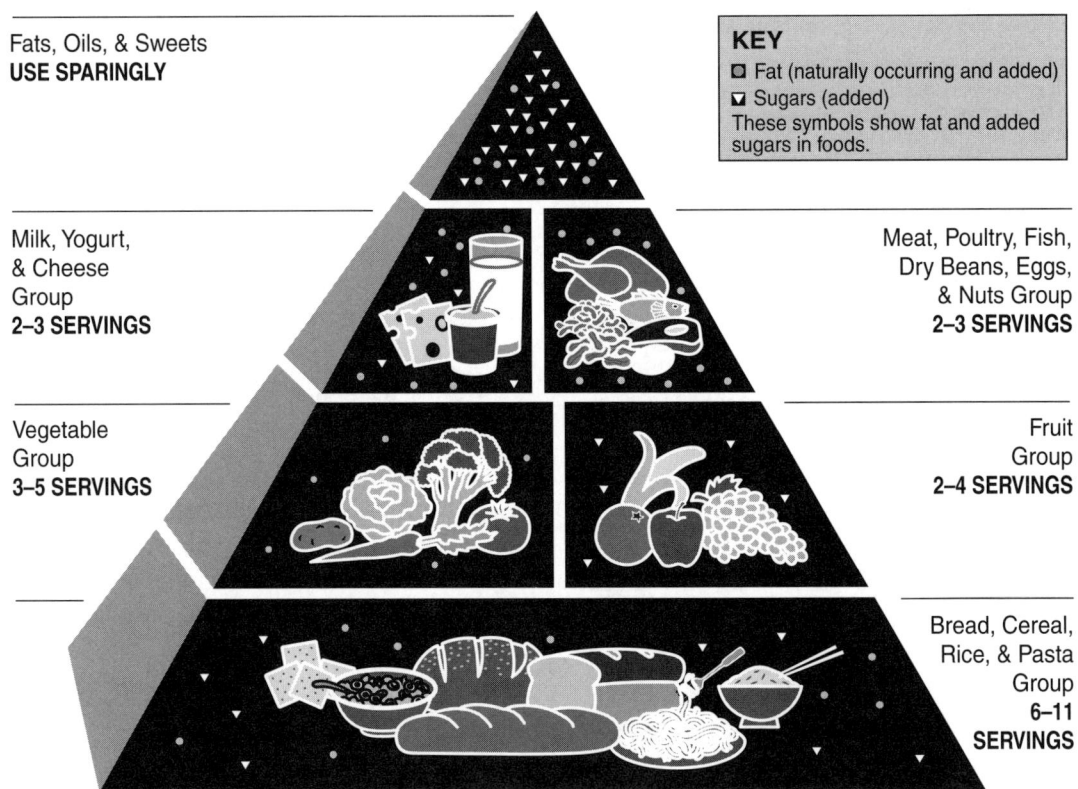

Fats, Oils, & Sweets
USE SPARINGLY

KEY
▫ Fat (naturally occurring and added)
◩ Sugars (added)
These symbols show fat and added sugars in foods.

Milk, Yogurt,
& Cheese
Group
2–3 SERVINGS

Meat, Poultry, Fish,
Dry Beans, Eggs,
& Nuts Group
2–3 SERVINGS

Vegetable
Group
3–5 SERVINGS

Fruit
Group
2–4 SERVINGS

Bread, Cereal,
Rice, & Pasta
Group
**6–11
SERVINGS**

Source: U.S. Department of Agriculture/U.S. Department of Health and Human Services

Getting Better: The Food Pyramid Way

For the next week fill out this Food Pyramid Diary. While it's recommended that you try to eat foods from each food group during each meal, to record the information here you merely need to check off the number of servings you eat throughout the day.

Food Pyramid Diary

Date _____

Food Groups Eaten Today

Dairy (milk, yogurt and cheese)
2–3 servings/day   —   —   —

Protein (meat, poultry, fish, nuts,
eggs, soy) 2–3 servings/day   —   —   —

Fruits (2–4 servings/day)   —   —   —   —

Vegetables (3–5 servings/day)   —   —   —   —

Carbohydrates (breads, cereals, rice,
pasta and grains) 6–11 servings/day   —   —   —   —   —   —   —   —   —   —   —

Fats, oils, sweets (use sparingly)   —   —   —

Water (8 oz, 8 glasses/day)   —   —   —   —   —   —   —   —

Feelings I had throughout the day:

_____

_____

_____

Positive food choices I made:

_____

_____

_____

Nutrition Exercise II

Eating a healthy diet is important. The list below is based on the USDA Food Pyramid. You should eat something from each group, every day, in order to stay healthy. Pick out the foods you like best:

Protein

____ Beans	____ Beef
____ Soy products	____ Chicken
____ Fish	____ Lamb
____ Pork	____ Nuts
____ Turkey	____ Eggs

You should have at least 2–3 servings of protein a day.

Dairy

___ Milk	___ Yogurt
___ Cheese	

You should have 2–3 servings of dairy a day.

Vegetables

____ Lettuce	____ Tomatoes
____ Onions	____ Cucumber
____ Spinach	____ Broccoli
____ Celery	____ Carrots
____ Mushrooms	____ Brussels sprouts
____ Cauliflower	____ Radishes
____ Beans	____ Cabbage
____ Peas	____ Artichokes
____ Asparagus	____ Beets
____ Corn	____ Eggplant
____ Green beans	____ Lima beans
____ Okra	____ Squash

You should have 3–5 servings of vegetables every day.

Fruit

____ Apple	____ Banana
____ Orange	____ Grapes
____ Grapefruit	____ Strawberries
____ Avocado	____ Kiwi
____ Mango	____ Apricots
____ Berries	____ Melons
____ Dates	____ Figs
____ Nectarine	____ Papaya
____ Peach	____ Pear
____ Pineapple	____ Watermelon
____ Other _____	

You should have 2–4 servings of fruits a day.

Carbohydrates

____ Bread	____ Pasta
____ Cereal	____ Grains
____ Potato	____ Rice
____ Bagel	____ Pancakes

You should have 6–11 servings of starch a day.

Fats

____ Butter	____ Vegetable oil
____ Corn oil	____ Margarine

You should limit your daily intake of fats.

Sweets

____ Candy	____ Cake
____ Pie	____ Ice cream
____ Doughnuts	____ Coffee rolls

You shouldn't eat too many sweets. Try having just a couple of desserts each week or reduce your portion size. You can substitute fruit for a dessert. It'll still taste sweet, but it's much better for you.

Willet's Healthy Eating Pyramid

Walter Willet, in his book, *Eat, Drink and Be Healthy: The Harvard Medical School Guide to Healthy Eating* suggests an alternative food pyramid based on eating whole plant foods and good fats. This eating plan is particularly good for people who are vegetarians or have lactose intolerance.

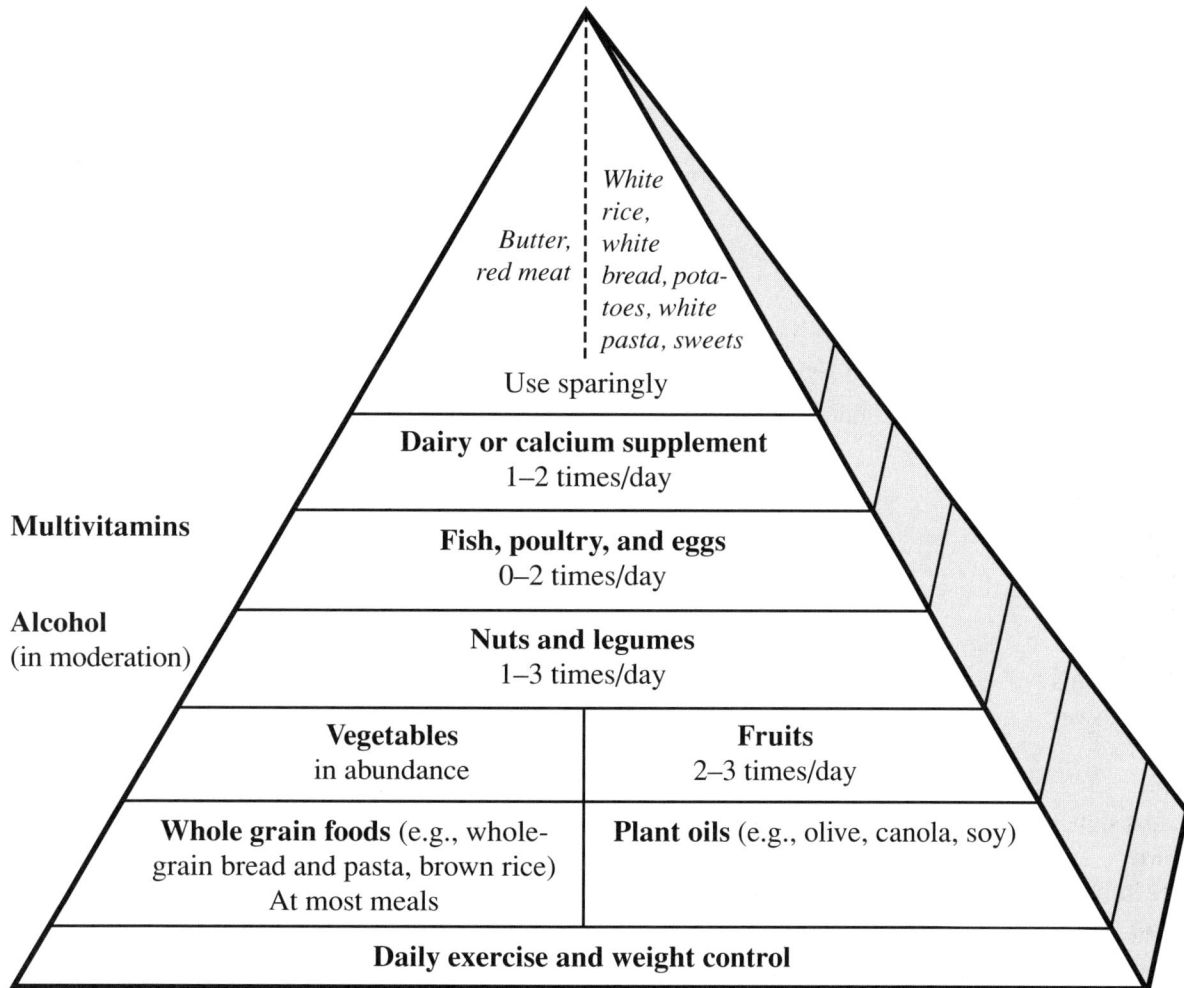

Butter, red meat   *White rice, white bread, potatoes, white pasta, sweets*

Use sparingly

Dairy or calcium supplement
1–2 times/day

Multivitamins

Fish, poultry, and eggs
0–2 times/day

Alcohol
(in moderation)

Nuts and legumes
1–3 times/day

Vegetables
in abundance   **Fruits**
2–3 times/day

Whole grain foods (e.g., whole-grain bread and pasta, brown rice)
At most meals   **Plant oils** (e.g., olive, canola, soy)

Daily exercise and weight control

Source: Willet, 2002

The list below is based on Willet's Healthy Eating Pyramid. You should eat something from each group, every day, in order to stay healthy. Pick out the foods you like best:

Protein

___ Fish	___ Poultry
___ Eggs	

You should have at least 0–2 servings of protein a day.

___ Nuts	___ Legumes

You should eat at least 1–3 servings of nuts and legumes a day.

Dairy

___ Milk	___ Yogurt
___ Cheese	___ Calcium supplement

You should have 1–2 servings of dairy a day.

Vegetables

___ Lettuce	___ Tomatoes
___ Onions	___ Cucumber
___ Spinach	___ Broccoli
___ Celery	___ Carrots
___ Mushrooms	___ Brussels sprouts
___ Cauliflower	___ Radishes
___ Beans	___ Cabbage
___ Peas	___ Artichokes
___ Asparagus	___ Beets
___ Corn	___ Eggplant
___ Green beans	___ Lima beans
___ Okra	___ Squash
___ Other: _____	

You can have an abundance of vegetables every day.

Fruit

___ Apple	___ Banana
___ Orange	___ Grapes
___ Grapefruit	___ Strawberries
___ Avocado	___ Kiwi
___ Melon	___ Mango
___ Apricots	___ Berries
___ Dates	___ Figs
___ Nectarine	___ Papaya
___ Peach	___ Pear
___ Pineapple	___ Watermelon
___ Other: _____	

You should have 2–3 servings of fruits a day.

Whole Grain Foods

___ Whole-grain bread	___ Whole-grain pasta
___ Brown rice	

You should have a serving of a whole grain food at most meals.

Plant Oils

___ Olive	___ Canola oil
___ Soy	___ Flaxseed

Plant oils can make up to 30–45% of your daily caloric intake.

You shouldn't eat too many sweets. Try having just a couple of desserts each week or reduce the portion size. You can substitute fruit for a dessert. It'll still taste sweet, but it's much better for you.

Food Diary

Write down what you eat for each meal for the next couple of days. Include portion sizes.

Breakfast

Lunch

Dinner

Snacks

Take a look at what you ate. Are you eating healthy foods? If you think you might want to make changes in your diet, write them down below:

Food Collage

Breakfast

It is important to choose the right types of foods for each meal. Today we're going to select healthy foods you can eat for breakfast. Try to include a protein, vegetable, fruit, and carbohydrate in your meal selection. Be sure to limit the fat, sugar, and salt content in your choices.

Lunch

It is important to choose the right types of foods for each meal. Today we're going to select healthy foods you can eat for lunch. Try to include a protein, vegetable, fruit, and carbohydrate in your meal selection. Be sure to limit the fat, sugar, and salt content in your choices.

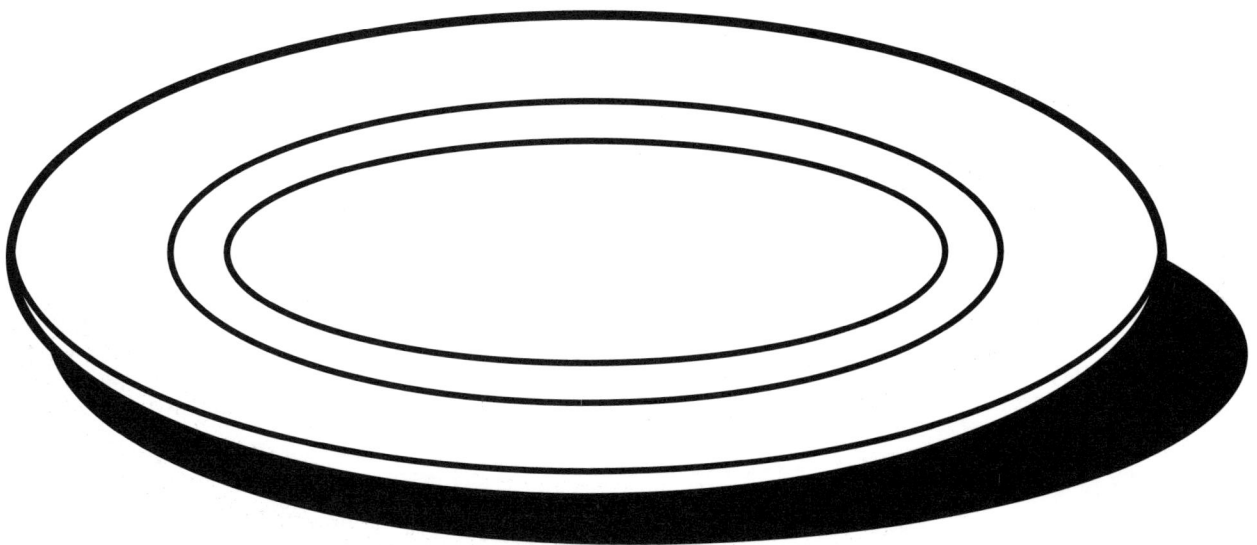

Dinner

It is important to choose the right types of foods for each meal. Today we're going to select healthy foods you can eat for dinner. Try to include a protein, vegetable, fruit, and carbohydrate in your meal selection. Be sure to limit the fat, sugar, and salt content in your choices.

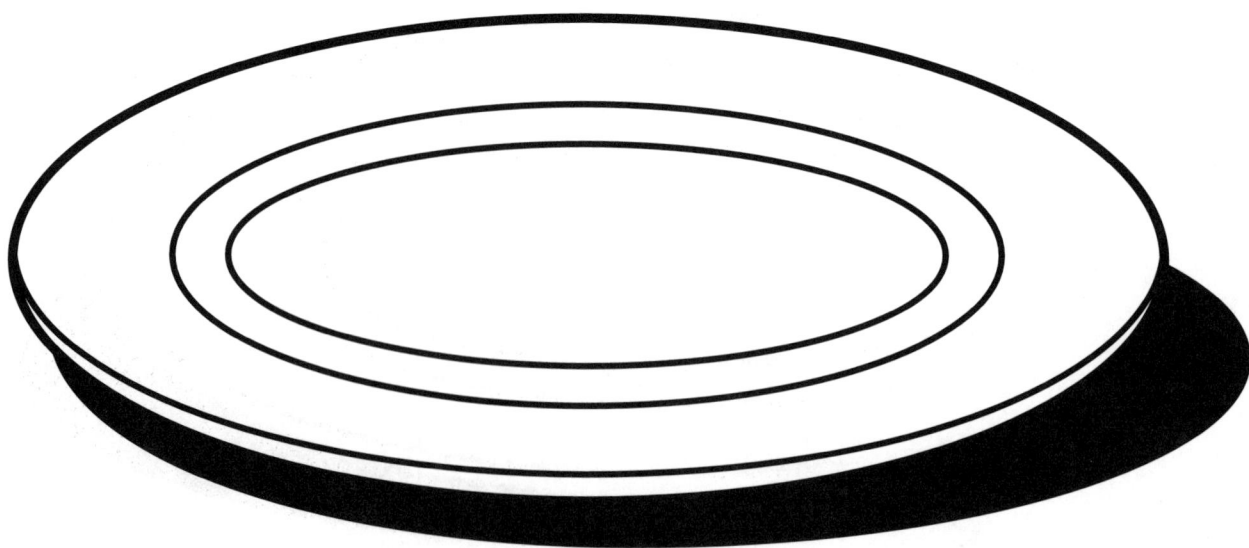

Snack

It is important to choose the right types of foods—even for snacks. Today we're going to select healthy foods you can eat as a snack. Try to include a protein, vegetable, fruit, and carbohydrate in your snack selection. Be sure to limit the fat, sugar, and salt content in your choices.

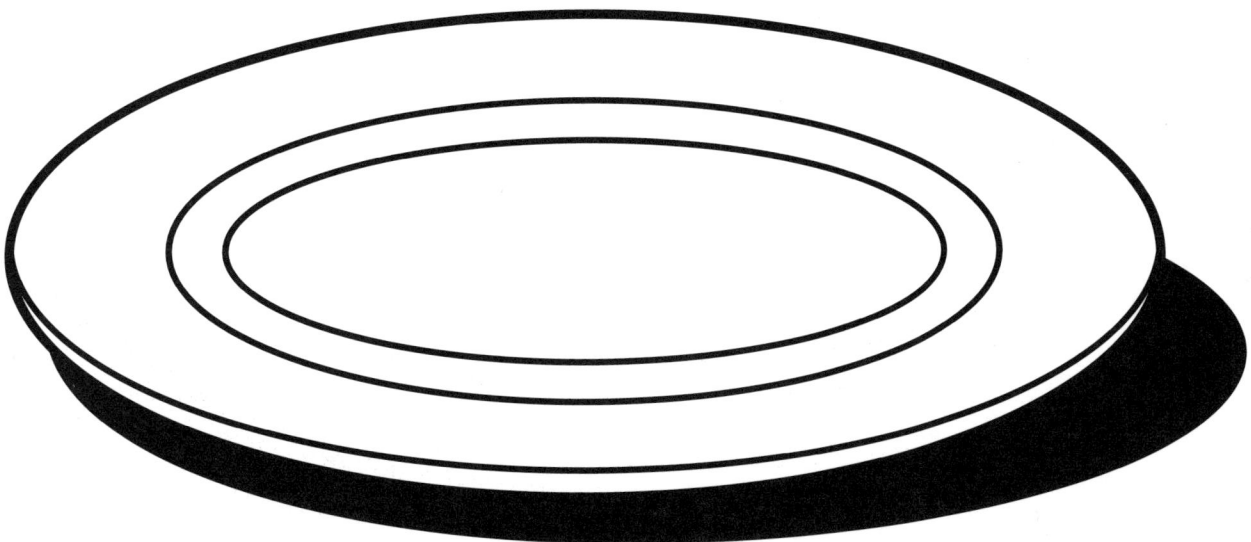

Chapter Twenty-One
Sleep Hygiene

Insomnia is quite common. In the United States, more than 100 million people suffer from poor sleep. First and foremost, it is important to educate clients that insomnia is a symptom and not a disease. There are many contributing factors for insomnia. When working with clients who have sleeping problems, assess the following:

- the client's reported history of onset and length of insomnia
- the types and dosage of medications the client is taking and the time of day he or she regularly takes the medications.
- the client's anxiety level and/or possible history of a psychiatric disorder.
- the client's history of alcohol and/or drug abuse
- if the client is currently being treated for pain management

When treating a client with insomnia, much of the protocol includes evaluating the client's current sleeping habits and recommending appropriate behavior changes. Poor sleep is often caused by faulty beliefs and attitudes about sleep. A sleep diary has been included to assist the client in observing his or her current sleep behaviors.

A 2003 study conducted at the Psychology Services, VA Medical Center in Durham, North Carolina, found that an abbreviated cognitive behavioral insomnia therapy (ABCT) program was effective in treating veterans with chronic primary insomnia (Edinger, Wohlgemuth, Radtke, Marsh & Quillian, 2001).

Patients with insomnia were effectively treated at the University of Luebeck, Germany, for Psychiatry and Psychotherapy in 2001. They took part in a six-week program which included sessions of progressive muscle relaxation, cognitive relaxation, modified stimulus control with bedtime restriction, thought stopping, and cognitive restructuring (Backhaus, Hohagen, Voderholzer & Riemann, 2001).

Special Considerations

Sleep hygiene is an important component of a stress reduction program. Clients may need some assistance in learning about sleep hygiene. Two separate programs are offered in this workbook. The first program (Sleep Hygiene Exercise I) should be utilized for clients with full cognition and who are able to function independently. The second program (Sleep Hygiene Exercise II) is for clients who may have some cognitive limitations. Sleep diaries are provided for the clients to record their sleeping patterns before and after you conduct a group or individual session about sleep hygiene.

Photocopy the sleep diaries before you begin the sleep hygiene portion of your program with clients. For best results, ask the client to complete the diaries for three days prior to the sleep hygiene program and to continue them for three days to two weeks after the session.

Recommended Resources

Hauri, P. and Linde, S. (1996). *No more sleepless nights* (2nd ed.). New York, NY: John Wiley and Sons.

Jacobs, G. (1998). *Say goodnight to insomnia—The six-week solution*. New York, NY: Henry Holt.

References

Backhaus, J., Hohagen, F., Voderholzer, U., and Riemann, D. (2001). Long-term effectiveness of a short-term cognitive-behavioral group treatment for primary insomnia. *European Archives of Psychiatry and Clinical Neuroscience, 251*(1), 35–41.

Edinger, J.D., Wohlgemuth, W.K., Radtke, R.A., Marsh, G.R., and Quillian, R.E. (2001). Does cognitive-behavioral insomnia therapy alter dysfunctional beliefs about sleep? *Sleep, 24*(5), 591–599.

Sleep Hygiene Exercise I

Sleep Diary

Keeping track of your sleep patterns will help you and your therapist determine the causes of your insomnia. For best results, complete the sleep diary for three days prior to beginning a sleep hygiene program. This will give you a baseline record of your sleep patterns.

Day of the Week _____   Date _____

What time to you get into bed? _____

How long did it take you to fall asleep? _____

Did you take a sleeping medication to fall asleep?   ❐ Yes   ❐ No

If yes, what was the name of the medication and what was the dosage? _____

Did you drink any alcohol last night?   ❐ Yes   ❐ No

If yes, what type of alcohol were you drinking and how many glasses? _____

What time did you wake up in the morning? _____

How many hours did you sleep last night? _____

How many times did you awaken during the night? _____

Rate how difficult it was for you to fall asleep last night: Easy   1   2   3   4   5   Difficult

Rate the quality of your sleep: Excellent   1   2   3   4   5   Poor

Rate how rested do you feel this morning?   Very rested   1   2   3   4   5   Not rested at all

Rate the level of your physical tension/discomfort when you went to bed last night?

        No physical tension   1   2   3   4   5   High physical tension

If you were experiencing a high level of physical tension, what was its source? _____

_____

Rate the level of your mental activity prior to going to bed last night?

        Not mentally stimulated   1   2   3   4   5   Very mentally stimulated

If you were very mentally stimulated, what activity were you involved in? _____

_____

Notes:

_____

_____

_____

Tips For Improving Sleep Hygiene

Do you have trouble falling asleep? Or, do you have problems staying asleep? Perhaps you wake up too early every day. If you don't get enough sleep at night, you might end up feeling groggy and grouchy and generally miserable the next day.

The important thing to remember is that insomnia is not a disease, it is a symptom. For many people, sleeping problems have to do with poor sleep hygiene. Below is a checklist of bad habits you might have developed which are causing you to have insomnia, along with some suggestions about how to improve your sleep.

1. Consider turning off your television by mid-evening.

Watching television is a national pastime, but it has its drawbacks. Try not to watch the eleven o'clock news. What you really don't need before going to bed is worry about the affairs of the world. Watch an earlier broadcast if you like to know what's going on in the news. Furthermore, limit the amount of time spent watching violent shows before going to bed.

2. Consider turning off your telephone by mid-evening.

Try to have a reasonable cut off time regarding the telephone. Tell your friends and family members to not call you after 10 o'clock. The fact is, you become too stimulated when you are on the phone.

3. Try not to work into the late evening.

Are you the kind of person who brings projects home from work? Do you think you can get more work done at home without interruptions? If at all possible, be sure to give yourself a work deadline. Tell yourself you will stop working at 10 o'clock and stick to it. If your work has been too stimulating, read a book or listen to music to calm your mind.

4. Monitor your anxiety level.

It's difficult to turn off anxiety, but it's the best thing you can do before going to sleep. If you suffer from an anxiety disorder, be sure to speak with your therapist and/or physician if you are having sleeping problems. Give yourself an hour each night, early in the evening to allow yourself to worry about whatever is making you anxious. But then, when the hour is up, tell yourself you'll focus on something else. Practice meditation or progressive relaxation techniques when you are feeling particularly anxious.

5. Turn off your computer by mid-evening.

Computers are addictive—and they're very stimulating. Stay away from your computer after 10 o'clock every night.

6. Seek help from a healthcare professional if you are experiencing insomnia and you are currently being treated for a medical condition.

If you are being treated for a medical problem and are experiencing insomnia, you need to speak to your physician about it. Don't hesitate to discuss it with your doctor. He or she will be able to determine whether your medical problem is interfering with your quality of sleep.

7. If you are on medication, discuss with a pharmacist the problems you are having with insomnia.

Many medications can cause sleeping problems. Some medications are stimulating while others can make you drowsy. If you are on several medications, they could be interacting with one another and causing sleep disruptions. It is very important to speak to your doctor or pharmacist about any medications you take, particularly if you are having trouble sleeping.

8. Consider creative visualization to deal with insomnia associated with pain problems.

It's very difficult to fall asleep when you are in pain. Consider doing creative visualization exercises before going to sleep. If you can imagine yourself away from your pain, you can fall asleep with less discomfort.

9. Stop worrying about whether you are getting enough sleep.

Most people tend to worry about the way they think they will feel the following day if they have a bad night with insomnia—that causes a vicious circle. Don't judge how much sleep you are getting. Turn your clock away from view. If you can't fall asleep, get up out of bed and read or do something else that's relaxing in nature. Even if you go back to bed and can't fall asleep, get up again and again until you are finally tired.

10. Turn your clocks away from you or cover them.

Most people with insomnia tend to look repeatedly at their clocks throughout the night and become more and more anxious as it gets later and later. If you are one of those people, turn your clock away from view and stop judging your ability to sleep.

11. Do not exercise before you go to bed.

Research shows that they optimum time to exercise is three to six hours before going to bed. Do not exercise just before going to bed. It will alter your temperature and make it much more difficult to fall asleep.

12. Do not consume caffeine after 4:00 p.m.

Caffeine is the worst offender in one's failure to fall asleep. Coffee is not the only offender that contains caffeine. Read the labels of the soft drinks you enjoy. Both black and green tea contain caffeine. Try not to consume caffeinated drinks after 4 o'clock in the afternoon. If you still have problems falling asleep at night, cut off your caffeine intake earlier in the day.

13. If you smoke, consider quitting, or curtail the number of cigarettes you smoke after dinner.

Nicotine is a stimulant. Try to quit smoking or at least taper off the number of cigarettes you smoke during the evening hours.

14. Curtail eating chocolate after dinner.

Chocolate has a lot of caffeine in it. It might taste just dandy, but it may be keeping you up at night. The best bet is to curtail your chocolate intake after 4 o'clock in the afternoon.

15. Try not to eat anything just before going to bed.

If your stomach is busy digesting food, it can keep you awake. Try to eat earlier in the evening.

16. If you drink alcohol, decrease the amount you drink before going to bed.

Alcohol is a sedative and will help you initially fall asleep. Once it wears off, however, you may wake up in the middle of the night and have a difficult time falling back to sleep. Alcohol contributes to a reduction of REM sleep—the deepest stage of sleep.

17. Wake up at the same time every morning, even if you have had a bad night's sleep.

Many people with insomnia will sleep late to make up for not being able to sleep well at night. However, this is not a good idea. Get up at a designated time every morning. What you will find is that eventually you will be able to fall asleep better and earlier.

18. Don't take naps or limit the time of your naps.

Sometime a nap feels so good, especially if you haven't slept well the night before. Research shows that you should not take a nap after 4:00 p.m. if you want to get a good night's sleep. Best bet is to "time" your naps. Don't nap for more than 45 minutes. To ensure you take a short nap, set your alarm for just 45 minutes or ask someone to wake you up at a designated time.

19. Get out of bed if you can't sleep.

Lying in bed and tossing and turning is only going to make it more difficult to fall asleep. Get up and try to do something relaxing. Consider reading, knitting, drawing, or meditating. Don't go back to bed until you're very tired. If you return to your bed and still can't sleep, get back up and continue with a calming activity.

20. Consider taking a sleeping medication only when absolutely necessary.

There are newer medications on the market which are not addictive and can be used effectively for sleep management. Discuss this option with your doctor.

Sleep Diary

Now that you have started making the necessary changes outlined in the Tips for Improving Sleep Hygiene, you will more than likely find improvement in your sleep. Record your sleeping patterns for the next two weeks:

Day of the Week _____   Date _____

What time do you get into bed? _____

How long did it take you to fall asleep? _____

Did you take a sleeping medication to fall asleep?   ❏ Yes   ❏ No

If yes, what was the name of the medication and what was the dosage? _____

Did you drink any alcohol last night?   ❏ Yes   ❏ No

If yes, what type of alcohol were you drinking and how many glasses? _____

What time did you wake up in the morning? _____

How many hours did you sleep last night? _____

How many times did you awaken during the night? _____

Rate how difficult it was for you to fall asleep last night: Easy   1   2   3   4   5   Difficult

Rate the quality of your sleep: Excellent   1   2   3   4   5   Poor

Rate how rested do you feel this morning?   Very rested   1   2   3   4   5   Not rested at all

Rate the level of your physical tension or discomfort when you went to bed last night?

                              No physical tension   1   2   3   4   5   High physical tension

If you were experiencing a high level of physical tension, what was its source? _____

_____

Rate the level of your mental activity prior to going to bed last night?

                              Not mentally stimulated   1   2   3   4   5   Very mentally stimulated

If you were very mentally stimulated, what activity were you involved in? _____

_____

What changes would you like to make to improve your sleep tonight? _____

_____

Notes:

_____

_____

_____

_____

Sleep Hygiene Exercise II

Sleep Diary

For the next three days, write down the time you went to sleep and the time you woke up. How many hours did you sleep?

Day 1

Date: _____

Time I went to sleep: _____

Time I woke up: _____

Number of hours I was asleep:

_____

Day 2

Date: _____

Time I went to sleep: _____

Time I woke up: _____

Number of hours I was asleep:

_____

Day 3

Date: _____

Time I went to sleep: _____

Time I woke up: _____

Number of hours I was asleep:

_____

How did it go for the last three days? Did you have problems sleeping? Check below if you:

❏ Watch television late at night

❏ Talk on the phone late at night

❏ Drink coffee during the evening hours

❏ Eat chocolate during the evening hours

❏ Smoke cigarettes during the evening hours

❏ Eat a big snack at night

❏ Don't exercise

❏ Exercise just before going to bed

❏ Watch the clock all the time

❏ Sleep late to make up for not sleeping during the night

❏ Worry all the time

❏ Take medication

❏ Drink alcohol or take drugs

Guess what? Even though you have had problems sleeping, help is on the way. By changing certain habits, you will be able to sleep better. Check off changes you can make to develop better sleeping habits:

❏ I will exercise 3 to 6 hours before going to sleep

❏ I will stop watching television after 10:00 p.m.

❏ I will stop drinking coffee, tea, and soda after 4:00 p.m.

❏ I will not eat chocolate after 4:00 p.m.

❏ I will not eat a big snack just before going to bed.

❏ I will stop smoking cigarettes.

❏ I will wake up every morning at the same time even if I'm still tired.

❏ I will turn my clocks away from view before going to sleep.

❏ I will talk to my doctor about my medication(s) to see if it's interfering with my sleeping patterns.

❏ I'll curtail worrying to a specific time each day. If I start worrying before going to sleep, I'll tell myself to worry earlier in the day.

❏ I will take a hot bath before going to bed.

❏ I will listen to soft music before going to sleep.

❏ I will do a relaxation exercise before going to sleep.

❏ I will turn my telephone off after 10:00 p.m.

❏ I will stop drinking alcohol or taking drugs.

Now that you have completed this exercise, you are more prepared to make smart decisions about your sleep habits. Record your sleep patterns for another three days.

Day 1

Date: _____

Time I went to sleep: _____

Time I woke up: _____

Number of hours I was asleep:

_____

Day 2

Date: _____

Time I went to sleep: _____

Time I woke up: _____

Number of hours I was asleep:

_____

Day 3

Date: _____

Time I went to sleep: _____

Time I woke up: _____

Number of hours I was asleep:

_____

Appendix A
Support Groups

The following resources were retrieved from Sourcebook Home—Mental Help Net

1-800-SUICIDE   1-800-SUICIDE; 1-800-784-2433

1-888-MARIJUANA   1-888-MARIJUANA
                         1-888-627-4582

A Special Wish Foundation   1-800-486-9474

Abledata   1-800-227-0216

Access Board   1-800-872-2253

Access Project   1-800-734-7104

Action, Parent and Teen Support   1-800-282-5660

Aerobics and Fitness Association of America
                                 1-800-445-5950

Agency for Health Care Research and Policy
                                 1-800-358-9295
                                 301-495-3453

AIDS Clinical Trials Information Service
                                 1-800-874-2572

AIDS Hotline (USA)   1-800-FOR-AIDS

Al-Anon for Families of Alcoholics 1-800-344-2666

Alcohol & Drug Abuse Hotline   1-800-729-6686

Alcohol and Drug Helpline   1-800-821-4357

Alcohol Hotline   1-800-331-2900

Alliance for Aging Research   1-800-639-2421

Alliance for Lung Cancer Advocacy,
Support and Education   1-800-298-2436

Alzheimer's Disease Education and
Referral Center   1-800-438-4380

America's Crisis Pregnancy Helpline
                                 1-800-67-BABY-6

American Association on Mental Retardation
                                 1-800-424-3688

American Cancer Society   1-800-227-2345

American Council for Drug Education
                1-800-DRUG-HELP (English/Spanish)
                1-800-HEROIN; 1-800-RELAPSE
                1-800-COCAINE; 1-888-MARIJUANA
                1-800-488-DRUG; 1-212-595-2553 (fax)
                1-212-595-5810 ext. 7582 (Admin.)

American Council on Alcoholism   1-800-527-5344
                                 1-410-889-0100 (in MD)

American Dietetic Association
                1-800-366-1655 (English/Spanish)

American Foundation for the Blind   1-800-232-5463
                                 212-502-7662 (TDD)

American Foundation for Urologic Disease
                                 1-800-828-7866
                                 1-800-242-2383 (booklets)

American Foundation of Thyroid Patients
                                 1-888-996-4460

American Health Assistance Foundation
                                 1-800-437-2423

American Heart Association   1-800-242-8721

American Humane Association   1-800-227-4645

American Kidney Fund   1-800-638-8299

American Lyme Disease Foundation 1-800-876-5963

American Running and Fitness Association
                                 1-800-776-2732

American SIDS Institute   1-800-232-SIDS

American Suicide Foundation   1-800-531-4477

American Trauma Society   1-800-556-7890

Anorexia and Bulimia Crisis   1-800-227-4785

ASHA Hearing and Speech Helpline
                    1-800-638-8255 (voice/TDD)

Asthma and Allergy Network   1-800-878-4403
                    1-703-573-7794 (fax)

Asthma and Allergy Referral Line   1-800-822-2762
                    414-272-6071

Attorney Referral Network   1-800-624-8846

Be Sober Hotline   1-800-237-6237

Boy's Town National Hotline
                    1-800-448-3000 (English/Spanish)

Braille Institute   1-800-272-4553

California Smoker's Helpline   1-800-NOBUTTS
            (Toll-free for California residents only)

Cancer Care, Inc.   1-800-813-HOPE
                    973-379-7500

Cancer Hope Network   1-877-HOPE-NET

Cancer Information Service   1-800-4-CANCER

Cancer Research Institute   1-800-99-CANCER

Canine Companions   1-800-572-BARK

Captioned Media Program   1-800-237-6213
                    1-800-237-6819 (TTY)

CDC National AIDS/HIV+ Hotline 1-800-342-AIDS

CDC National Prevention Information Network
                    1-800-458-5231

CDC National STD Hotline   1-800-227-8922

CDC National STD Hotline   1-877-HPV-5868

Center for Disease Control (CDC) AIDS Information
                    1-800-342-2437

Center for Food Safety and Applied Nutrition
                    1-800-332-4010

Center for Patient Advocacy   1-800-846-7444

Center for the Study of Inherited and
Neurological Disorders   1-800-283-4316
                    919-684-6515

Centers for Disease Control and Prevention
                    1-800-311-3435

Child Abuse Hotline   1-800-540-4000

Child Find of America Hotline   1-800-I-AM-LOST

Child Help USA Hotline   1-800-422-4453

Children's Defense Fund   1-800-233-1200

Children's Hospice International   1-800-242-4453

Children's Organ Transplant Association
                    1-800-366-2682

Christopher Reeves Paralysis Foundation
                    1-800-225-0292

Clearinghouse for Immigrant Education
                    1-800-441-7192

Cocaine Anonymous   1-800-347-8998

Consumer Credit Counseling Services
                    1-800-388-2227

Crisis Helpline   1-800-233-4357

Crisis Line for the Handicapped   1-800-426-4263

Crisis Pregnancy Center   1-800-560-0717

Cure for Lymphoma Foundation   1-800-CFL-6848

Cystic Fibrosis Foundation   1-800-344-4823

Dana Farber Cancer Institute Family Studies
Cancer Risk Line   1-800-828-6622

DB-Link (National Information Clearinghouse
for Children Who Are Deaf/Blind)
                    1-800-438-9376 (voice)
                    1-800-854-7013 (TTY)

Depression Awareness, Recognition and
Treatment Helpline   1-800-421-4211

Depression/Alcohol and Drug Addiction
Trauma Hotline   1-800-544-1177

Disability Rights Education and Defense Fund
                    1-800-466-4232

Donated Dental Services   1-888-471-6334

Down Syndrome Hotline   1-800-221-4602

Drug Abuse Information and Referral Line
                    1-800-662-HELP

Drug Policy Information Clearinghouse
                    1-800-666-3332

Easter Seals National Headquarters
Disability Helpline   1-800-221-6827

Eat Right Hotline	1-800-231-DIET
Eldercare Locator	1-800-424-9046
	202-479-0735 (fax)
Epilepsy Information Service	1-800-642-0500
ERIC Clearinghouse on Disabilities and Gifted Education	1-800-328-0272
Families and Advocates Partnership for Education	1-888-248-0822
Families Anonymous	1-800- 736-9805
Family Support Network	1-800-TLC-0042
FDA Consumer Affairs	1-888-463-6332
Federal Student Aid Information Center	1-800-433-3243
Foot Care Information Center	1-800-366-8227
Gay and Lesbian National Hotline	1-888-843-4564
	1-212-633-7492
Gilda Radner Familial Ovarian Cancer Registry	1-800-682-7426
Glaucoma Research Foundation	1-800-826-6693
Grant-A-Wish Foundation	1-800-933-5470
Grief Recovery Helpline	1-800-445-4808
Guide Dog Foundation	1-800-548-4337
	516-361-5192 (fax)
Gynecologic Cancer Foundation	1-800-444-4441
Hereditary Cancer Institute	1-800-648-8133
HIV/AIDS Treatment Information Service	1-800-448-0440
Hospice Foundation of America	1-800-854-3402
Hospice Link Institute	1-800-331-1620
HUD (Housing and Urban Development)	1-800-998-9999
Impotence Information Center	1-800-843-4315
Impotence World Association	1-800-669-1603
Incontinence Information Center	1-800-543-9632
Indoor Air Quality Information Clearinghouse	1-800-438-4318
Insurance Information Clearinghouse	1-800-331-9146

International Association for Marriage and Family Counselors	1-800-545-AACD
International Cancer Alliance	1-800-I-CARE-61
International Dyslexia Association	1-800-ABCD-123
International Myeloma Foundation	1-800-452-2873
IRS Federal Tax Information	1-800-829-1040
Juvenile Justice Clearinghouse	1-800-638-8736
KID SAVE	1-800-543-7283
	1-800-334-4KID
Make-A-Wish Foundation	1-800-722-9474
Medic Alert Foundation International	1-800-432-5378
Medicare Hotline	1-800-MEDICARE
Medicare+ Choice Helpline Assistant	1-800-MEDICARE
Meningitis Foundation	1-800-668-1129
Minority Health Resource Center	1-800-444-6472
Minority Organ Tissue Transplant Education Program	1-800-393-2839
Missing Children Help Center	1-800-872-5437
Multiple Sclerosis Foundation	1-800-441-7055
Muscular Dystrophy Family Foundation, Inc.	1-800-544-1213 (days)
	317-443-2054
NAPARE Alcohol, Drug and Pregnancy	1-800-368-BABY
National Accessible Apartment Clearinghouse	1-800-421-1221
National Adoption Center	1-800-TO-ADOPT
National Alliance for Hispanic Health	1-800-504-7081 (Spanish/English)
National Alliance for Research on Schizophrenia & Depression	1-800-829-8289
National Alliance of Breast Cancer Organizations	1-888-80-NABCO
	212-889-0606
National Association for Children of Alcoholics	1-888-554-2627

National Association for Continence   1-800-252-3337
864-579-7900

National Association for Family Child Care
1-800-359-3817 (child care)
1-800-628-9163 (day care)

National Association for the Education of
Young Children   1-800-424-2460

National Association of Hospital Hospitality Houses
1-800-542-9730

National Association of Radiation Survivors
1-800-798-5102

National Braille Press   1-800-548-7323

National Cancer Hotline   1-800-433-0464

National Center for Learning Disabilities
1-888-575-7373

National Center for Missing and Exploited Children
1-800-843-5678

National Center on Complementary and
Alternative Medicine   1-888-644-6226

National Child At-Risk Hotline   1-800-792-5200

National Child Abuse Hotline   1-800-422-4453

National Child Abuse Hotline   1-800-4-A-CHILD

National Childhood Cancer Foundation
1-800-458-6223
626-447-6359 (fax)

National Clearinghouse Family Support/Children's
Mental Health   1-800-628-1696

National Clearinghouse for Alcohol and Drug
Information   1-800-729-6686

National Clearinghouse on Child Abuse and
Neglect Information   1-800-394-3366

National Council on Alcoholism and Drug Dependence
1-800-622-2255
1-800-654-HOPE

National Council on Alcoholism and Drug
Dependence Hopeline   1-800-622-2255

National Council on Problem Gambling
1-800-522-4700

National Domestic Violence Hotline
1-800-799-7233
1-800-787-3224 (TDD)

National Family Association for Deaf-Blind
1-800-255-0411 ext. 275

National Foundation for Depressive Illness
1-800-248-4344

National Foundation for Transplants   1-800-489-3863

National Help Line for Substance Abuse
1-800-262-2463

National Helpline   1-800-COCAINE

National Hospice Helpline   1-800-658-8898

National Hotline for Missing and Exploited Children
1-800-843-5678

National Immunizations Information Hotline
1-800-232-2522 (English/Spanish)
1-800-232-0233 (Spanish)

National Information Center for Children and Youth
with Disabilities   1-800-695-0285 (voice/TTY)
202-884-8200

National Inhalant Prevention Center   1-800-269-4237

National Institute for Occupational Safety and Health
1-800-356-4674
513-533-8326

National Institute of Allergy and Infectious Disease
1-800-243-7644

National Institute of Diabetes and Digestive and
Kidney Diseases   1-800-891-5390

National Institute of Mental Health Information Line
1-800-647-2642

National Institute of Neurological Disorders
1-800-352-9424

National Institute on Aging   1-800-222-2225

National Institute on Deafness and Other
Communication Disorders   1-800-241-1044
1-800-241-1055 (TTY)

National Institute on Drug Abuse   1-888-644-6432

National Institute on Drug Abuse Hotline
1-800-662-4357

National Insurance Consumer Helpline
1-800-942-4242

National Job Corps Information Line 1-800-733-5627

National Job Corps Information Line 1-800-733-5627

National Kidney Foundation 1-800-622-9010

National Lead Information Center and Clearinghouse 1-800-424-LEAD

National Library of Medicine 1-888-346-3656

National Literacy Hotline 1-800-228-8813

National Lyme Disease Foundation 1-800-886-LYME

National Marrow Donor Program 1-800-627-7692

National Mental Health Association 1-800-969-6642

National Organization for Rare Disorders 1-800-999-6673

National Parent-to-Parent Support and Information System 1-800-651-1151

National Parkinson's Foundation 1-800-327-4545

National Pediatric and Family HIV Resource Center 1-800-362-0071

National Rehabilitation Information Center 1-800-346-2742

National Reye's Syndrome 1-800-233-7393

National Rosacea Society 1-888-662-5874

National Runaway for the Hearing Impaired 1-800-621-0394

National Runaway Switchboard 1-800-621-4000

National Runaway Switchboard 1-800-621-4000

National Sexually Transmitted Diseases Hotline 1-800-227-8922

National Spinal Cord Injury Hotline 1-800-526-3456

National US Child Abuse Hotline 1-800-422-4453

National Veterans Service Fund, Inc. 1-800-521-0198

National Youth Crisis Hotline 1-800-HIT-HOME

NIH Clinical Center—Patient Recruitment for Clinical Trial 1-800-411-1222

NIH National Diabetes Outreach Program Helpline 1-800-438-5383 (English/Spanish)

NIH National Heart, Lung and Blood Institute Helpline 1-800-575-WELL

NIH Osteoporosis and Related Bone Diseases Resource Center 1-800-624-BONE

Occupational Therapy Consumer Line 1-800-668-8255 (English/Spanish)

OCD Literature Request Line 1-800-639-7462

Office for Civil Rights 1-800-368-1019

Office for Victims of Crime Resource Center 1-800-627-6873

Office on Smoking and Health 1-800-232-1311 770-488-5705

Osteoporosis Helpline 1-888-934-2663

Ovarian Cancer Research Fund 1-800-873-9569

Paralyzed Vets of America 1-800-424-8200

Patient Advocate Foundation 1-800-532-5274

Pharmaceutical Patient Assistance Directory Line 1-800-762-4636

Planned Parenthood 1-800-829-7732

Pregnancy Hotline 1-800-848-5683

Prevent Blindness America 1-800-331-2020 1-800-221-3004

Prevent Child Abuse America 1-800-CHILDREN (244-5373)

Recording For The Blind and Dyslexic 1-800-221-4792

Runaway Hotline 1-800-231-6946

Rural Information Center 1-800-633-7701

SAFE (Self-Abuse Finally Ends) Alternative Information Line 1-800-DONT-CUT (366-8288)

Sanctuary Crisis Line 1-800-548-5222

Sexually Transmitted Diseases Hotline 1-800-227-8922

Shoplifters Anonymous 1-800-848-9595

Shriner's Hospital 1-800-237-5055

SIDS Alliance 1-800-221-7437

Skin Cancer Foundation 1-800-SKIN-490

SNAP (Special Needs Advocate for Parents) 1-888-310-9889 310-201-9614

Social Security 1-800-772-1213

Stuttering Foundation of America 1-800-992-9392

Teen AIDS Line	1-800-234-TEEN
	1-800-440-TEEN
Teen Pregnancy Hotline	1-800-522-5006

TEENS TAP (Teens Teaching AIDS Prevention)

1-800-234-TEEN

The Teen AIDS Hotline	1-800-440-TEEN
Through the Looking Glass	1-800-644-2666
	510-848-1112
Thyroid Foundation of America	1-800-832-8321

Thyroid Society for Education and Research

1-800-849-7643

713-799-9909

United Student Aid Funds	1-800-428-9250
United Way	1-800-204-2803
VA Persian Gulf Helpline	1-800-749-8387

Vanished Children Alliance

1-800-VANISHED (24 hrs)

408-296-1113

Vision World Wide	1-800-431-1739
	317-254-1332

Visiting Nurse Association of America

1-888-866-8773

617-227-4843 (fax)

Women's Sport Foundation	1-800-227-3988
	516-542-4700

Review of Cited Literature

Selections listed alphabetically by subject.

Acupressure

Chen, M.L., Lin, L.C., Wu, S.C., and Lin, J.G. (1999). The effectiveness of acupressure in improving the quality of sleep of institutionalized residents. *Journals of Gerontology: Series A, Biological Sciences and Medical Sciences, 54*(8), M389–394.

Background: Elderly people often suffer from disturbed sleep. Because traditional Chinese medicine indicates that acupressure therapy may induce sedation, testing the effectiveness of acupressure in enhancing the quality of sleep of institutionalized residents with a well-designed scientific study is needed. *Methods:* A randomized block of experimental designed was used. The Pittsburgh Sleep Quality index (PSQI) questionnaire was used as a screening tool to select subjects with sleep disturbance. By matching the effects of hypertension, hypnosis, naps, and exercise, subjects were randomly assigned to an acupressure group, a sham acupressure group, and a control group. Each group has 28 subjects for a total of 84 subjects. The same massage routine was used in the acupressure group and the sham acupressure group, whereas only conversation was employed in the control group. *Results:* There were significant differences in PSQI subscale scores of the quality, latency, duration, efficiency, disturbances of sleep, and global PSQI scores among subjects in the three groups before and after interventions. Furthermore, there was a significant reduction in the frequencies of nocturnal awakening and night wakeful time in the acupressure group compared to the other two groups. *Conclusions:* This study confirmed the effectiveness of acupressure in improving the quality of sleep of elderly people and offered a nonpharmacological therapy method for sleep-disturbed elderly people.

Types: Clinical trial. Randomized controlled trial.
PMID: 10496543

Felhendler, D. and Lisander, B. (1999). Effects of non-invasive stimulation of acupoints on the cardiovascular system. *Complementary Therapies in Medicine, 7*(4), 231–234.

Objective: To study the effect of two noninvasive methods to stimulate acupoints on the cardiovascular system. *Design:* Blind randomized-controlled trial. *Setting:* An experimental setting in a university-affiliated hospital. *Interventions:* The subjects (24 healthy male volunteers) were randomized to receive either an active stimulation consisting of pressure on acupoints (P), an active stimulation consisting of stroking along meridians (S), or a control stimulation (C). *Main Outcome Measures:* Data on skin blood flow, arterial pressure, heart rate, and EKG were recorded continuously from 20 minutes before stimulation to 30 minutes after. *Results:* In P group there was a decrease in systolic arterial pressure, diastolic arterial pressure, mean arterial pressure, heart rate and skin blood flow. These changes were significantly different from those in C group and, as regards diastolic pressure mean pressure, also from those in S group. There were no significant differences between S and C groups. *Conclusions:* Pressure on acupoints can significantly influence the cardiovascular system.

Types: Clinical trial. Randomized control trial.
PMID: 10709307

Maa, S.H., Gauthier, D., and Turner, M. (1997). Acupressure as an adjunct to a pulmonary rehabilitation program. *Journal of Cardiopulmonary Rehabilitation, 17*(4), 268–276.

Background: Acupressure is a therapy in which gentle pressure is applied with fingers at specific acupoints on the body. It is reported to relieve pain and have other beneficial effects. This study was designed to ascertain the value of self-administered acupressure as an adjunct to a pulmonary rehabilitation program (PRP) for relief of dyspnea and other symptoms in patients with chronic obstructive pulmonary disease (COPD). *Methods:* A single-blind pretest-posttest, crossover design was used. Thirty-one new patients beginning a twelve-week PRP at two private hospitals were randomly assigned to one of two groups. Patients in group 1 were taught acupressure and practiced it daily at home for six weeks, then sham acupressure for the following six weeks. In group 2, the order of acupressure and sham acupressure was reversed. During weeks 1, 6, and 12, patient dyspnea, other symptoms associated with COPD, activity tolerance, lung function, and functional exercise capacity were assessed. *Results:* Real acupressure was more effective than sham acupressure for reducing dyspnea as measured by a visual analog scale (P=.009, one-tailed), and was minimally effective for relieving decathexis (P=.044, one-tailed). Sham acupressure seemed to be more effective than real acupressure for reducing peripheral sensory symptoms (P=.002, two-tailed), but the presence of these symptoms may also be an indication that the acupressure is affecting the body. *Conclusions:* Acupressure seems to be useful to patients with COPD as an adjunct to a PRP in reducing dyspnea. Some persons who are not initially familiar with traditional Chinese medicine can learn and will accept self-administered acupressure as part of their self-care.

Types: Clinical trial. Randomized controlled trial.
PMID: 9271771

Aromatherapy

Balinski, A.A. (1998). Use of Western Australian flower essences in the management of pain and stress in the hospital setting. *Complementary Therapies in Nursing & Midwifery, 4*(4), 111–117.

This article explores the use of the unique flora from Western Australia. These wildflower essences are collected from across the state and are made into flower essences. These essences are made in a form similar to homeopathy. The essences can be given internally, or applied to the external body and acupressure points. Angela and Craig Balinski have used the Western Australian flower essences in their complementary therapy practice where patients are treated for stress and pain management. This programme is currently being utilized at nine of Perth's hospitals. The Western Australian flower essences and their specific application techniques are compatible within the hospital environment because they are safe, produce consistent results, and take little time to apply to the patient. One of the

other outstanding features of these essences is that they can be used without any interference to medical procedures. The Western Australian flower essenses and the techniques for their use are unique and have, over the last two years, been presented at all of the major nursing conferences in Australia. At present, across Australia there are over 16 hospitals which are currently offering these treatments to their patients.

Types: Case reports. Review. Review, tutorial.
PMID: 9830938

Ballard, C.G., O'Brien, J.T., Reichelt, K., and Perry, E.K. (2002). Aromatherapy as a safe and effective treatment for the management of agitation in severe dementia: The results of a double-blind, placebo-controlled trial with *Melissa. Journal of Clinical Psychiatry, 63*(7), 553–558.

Background: Behavioral and psychological symptoms in dementia are frequent and are a major management problem, especially for patients with severe cognitive impairment. Preliminary reports have indicated positive effects of aromatherapy using select essential oils, but there are no adequately powered placebo-controlled trials. We conducted a placebo-controlled trial to determine the value of aromatherapy with essential oil of *Melissa officinalis* (lemon balm) for agitation in people with severe dementia. *Method:* Seventy-two people residing in National Health Service (UK) care facilities who had clinically significant agitation in the context of severe dementia were randomly assigned to aromatherapy with *Melissa* essential oil (N=36) or placebo (sunflower oil; N=36). The active treatment or placebo oil was combined with a base lotion and applied to patients' faces and arms twice a day by caregiving staff. Changes in clinically significant agitation (Cohen-Mansfield Agitation Inventory [CMAI]) and quality of life indices (percentages of time spent socially withdrawn and percentage of time engaged in constructive activities, measured with Dementia Care Mapping) were compared between the two groups over a four-week period of treatment. *Results:* Seventy-one patients completed the trial. No significant side effects were observed. Sixty percent (21/35) of the active treatment group and 14% (5/36) of the placebo-treated group experienced a 30% reduction of CMAI score, with an overall improvement in agitation (mean reduction in CMAI score) of 35% in patients receiving *Melissa* balm essential oil and 11% in those treated with placebo (Mann-Whitney U test; Z=4.1, p<.0001). Quality of life indices also improved significantly more in people receiving essential balm oil (Mann-Whitney U test;

percentage of time spent socially withdrawn: Z=2.6, p=.005; percentage of time engaged in constructive activities: Z=3.5, p=.001). *Conclusion:* The finding that aromatherapy with essential balm oil is a safe and effective treatment for clinically significant agitation in people with severe dementia, with additional benefits for key quality of life parameters, indicates the need for further controlled trials.

Types: Clinical trial. Randomized control trial.
PMID: 12143909

Louis, M. and Kowalski, S.D. (2002). Use of aromatherapy with hospice patients to decrease pain, anxiety, and depression and to promote an increased sense of well-being. *Journal of Hospice and Palliative Care, 19*(6), 381–386.

This study measured the response of 17 cancer hospice patients to humidified essential lavender oil aromatherapy. Vital signs as well as levels of pain, anxiety, depression, and sense of well-being were measured (using 11-point verbal analogs). Each subject was measured on three different days before and after a 60-minute session consisting of (1) no treatment (control); (2) water humidification (control); (3) three-percent lavender aromatherapy. Results reflected a positive, yet small, change in blood pressure and pulse, pain, anxiety, depression, and sense of well-being after both the humidified water treatment and the lavender treatment. Following the control session (no treatment), there was also slight improvement in vital signs, depression, and sense of well-being, but not in pain or anxiety levels.

PMID: 12442972

Autogenics

Lysaght, R. and Bodenhamer, E. (1990). The use of relaxation training to enhance functional outcomes in adults with traumatic head injuries. *American Journal of Occupational Therapy, 44*(9), 797–802.

Impaired anxiety management and poor emotional control have a negative effect on the adaptive functioning of persons with head injuries who are in the postacute stages of recovery. This paper outlines a relaxation training program administered individually with four adults with severe head injuries. Each subject was in the postacute phase of recovery and had reported stress to be a persistent problem in daily living. The relaxation training protocol combined biofeedback, imagery, autogenic training, and deep breathing. Significant

improvement in function, measured by scores on a scale of illness-related dysfunction, support the potential benefits of stress management training as part of functional training programs for persons with traumatic head injuries.

PMID: 2220998

Wright, S., Courtney, U. and Crowther, D. (2002). A quantitative and qualitative pilot study of the perceived benefits of autogenic training for a group of people with cancer. *European Journal of Cancer Care, 11*(2), 122–130.

This paper describes the application of autogenic training (AT), a technique of deep relaxation and self-hypnosis, in patients diagnosed with cancer, with the aim of increasing their coping ability, and reports the results of a questionnaire survey performed before and after an AT course. A reduction in arousal and anxiety can help individuals to perceive their environment as less hostile and threatening, with implications for improved perceived coping ability. Complementary therapies are considered useful in enhancing symptom relief, overall well-being and self-help when used as adjuvant therapies to allopathic medical interventions. The present study aimed to validate, in an Irish context, the effectiveness of AT as a complementary therapy for patients with cancer. Each participant completed a Hospital Anxiety and Depression Scale and Profile of Mood States questionnaire before and after a 10-week AT course. The results indicated a significant reduction in anxiety and increase in 'fighting spirit' after compared with before training, with an improved sense of coping and improved sleep being apparent benefits of AT practice.

PMID: 12099948

Breathing

Forbes, E.J. and Pekala, R.J. (1993). Psychophysiological effects of several stress management techniques. *Psychological Reports, 72*(1), 19–27.

The purpose of this study was to assess the psychophysiological stress-reducing properties of progressive relaxation compared with hypnosis, and deep abdominal breathing compared with a baseline condition, while controlling for hypnotizability. Two hundred thirty-one nursing students experienced the baseline procedure and progressive relaxation in Session 1 and deep abdominal breathing and hypnosis in Session 2 about a week later. Before and after each technique peripheral skin temperature and pulse rate were assessed. Separate analyses of variance, computed for the first and second sets of techniques, indicated that progressive relaxation and hypnosis both increased skin temperature and reduced pulse rate, suggesting reduced psychophysiological responsivity. Deep abdominal breathing was associated with a significant reduction in physiological responsivity (skin temperature) relative to baseline. Hypnotic susceptibility had no effect on the psychophysiological measures.

PMID: 8451354

Coping Skills

Brown, D.R., Wang, Y., Ward, A., Ebbeling, C.B. Fortlage, L., Puleo, E., Benson, H., and Rippe, J.M. (1995). Chronic psychological effects of exercise and exercise plus cognitive strategies. *Medicine and Science in Sports and Exercise, 27*(5), 765–775.

Psychological changes associated with 16-week moderate and low intensity exercise training programs, two of which possessed a cognitive component, were evaluated. Subjects were healthy, sedentary adults, 69 women (mean age = 54.8 ± 8.3 yrs) and 66 men (mean age = 50.6 ± 8.0 yrs). Participants were randomly assigned to a control group (C), moderate intensity walking group (MW), low intensity walking group (LW), low intensity plus relaxation response group (LWR), or mindful exercise (ME) group, a tai chi program. Women in the ME group experienced reductions in mood disturbance (tension, P<0.01; depression, P<0.05; anger, P<0.008; confusion, P<0.02, and total mood disturbance, P< 0.006) and an improvement in general mood (P<0.04). Women in the MW group noted greater satisfaction with physical attributes (body cathexis, P<0.03), and men in MW reported increased positive affect (P< 0.006). No other differences were observed between groups on measures of mood, self-esteem, personality, or life satisfaction. Equivocal support provides for the hypothesis that exercise plus cognitive strategy training programs are more effective than exercise programs lacking a structured cognitive component in promoting psychological benefits.

Types: Clinical trial. Randomized control trial.
PMID: 7674883

Grover, N., Kumaraiah, V., Prasadrao, P.S., and D'souza, G. (2002). Cognitive behavioural intervention in bronchial asthma. *Journal of the Association of Physicians of India, 50,* 896–900.

Objective: The aim of the present study was to find out the efficacy of cognitive behaviour therapy, as an adjunct to standard pharmacotherapy in bronchial asthma. *Design:* An experimental design with pre- and post-therapy assessments was adopted. *Setting:* The Medicine Outpatient Department of St. John's Medical College and Hospital, and Department of Clinical Psychology, NIMHANS, Bangalore. *Patients:* Ten asthma patients who fulfilled the inclusion and exclusion criteria, matched for use of drugs, were sequentially allotted to two groups: (a) experimental group, who were exposed to cognitive behaviour therapy along with standard pharmacotherapy, (b) control group, who were exposed to standard pharmacotherapy alone. *Intervention:* Cognitive behaviour therapy included 15 individual sessions consisting of asthma education, Jacobson progressive muscle relaxation (JPMR), behavioural techniques, cognitive restructuring, cognitive coping skills and behavioural counseling to significant others. *Measurements:* The measures used for pre- and post-therapy assessments were—Asthma symptom checklist, asthma diary, state trait anxiety inventory—Y1 and Y2, Beck depression inventory, asthma quality of life questionnaire and peak expiratory flow rate. *Results:* There was significant decrease on asthma symptoms, anxiety and depression; and significant increase in quality of life in the experimental group (p<0.05) at the post-assessment. The control group did not show any significant change at the post-assessment. *Conclusion:* Cognitive behaviour therapy helps in improving the management of asthma.

Types: Clinical trial. Controlled clinical trial.
PMID: 12126343

Williams, A.C., Nicholas, M.K., Richardson, P.H., Pither, C.E., Justins, D.M., Chamberlain, J.H., Harding, V.R., Ralphs, J.A., Jones, S.C., Dieudonne, I. et al. (1993). Evaluation of a cognitive behavioural programme for rehabilitating patients with chronic pain. *British Journal of General Practice, 43*(377), 513–518.

The aim of this prospective longitudinal study was to evaluate an inpatient cognitive behavioural pain management programme for patients with chronic pain. A physical and psychological assessment of patients was carried out before and after treatment, and at one and six months follow up. A total of 212 patients with disabling chronic pain of mean duration 10.5 years, for whom no further medical and psychiatric treatment was appropriate or available, were admitted; their mean age was 50 years and 65% were women. The four-week programme was delivered by a multidisciplinary team of two psychologists, a physiotherapist, nurse, occupational therapist, and anaesthetist. The main components of therapy included: education, teaching behavioural and cognitive skills, a stretch and exercise programme, medication reduction, goal setting and pacing, and relaxation training. Outcome measures assessed quality of life, physical performance (for example, speed walking), pain intensity and distress, depression severity and confidence. Assessment immediately after treatment revealed significant improvement on all measures. Improvements were well-maintained at six-month follow up. Cognitive behavioural treatment can be of value in improving the day-to-day functioning and quality of life of patients with chronic pain for whom conventional medical treatments have apparently failed.

PMID: 8312023

Creative Visualization

Bakke, A.C., Purtzer, M.Z., and Newton, P. (2002). The effect of hypnotic-guided imagery on psychological well-being and immune function in patients with prior breast cancer. *Journal of Psychosomatic Research, 53*(6), 1131–1137.

Objective: To determine the effect of hypnotic-guided imagery on immune function and psychological parameters in patients being treated for Stage I and II breast cancer. *Methods:* To determine the effects of hypnotic-guided imagery on immune function and, the following study was undertaken. Psychological profiles, natural killer (NK) cell number and activity were measured at baseline, after the eight-week imagery training program, and at the three-month follow-up. *Results:* There were significant increases in improvement in depression (P < .04) and increase in absolute number of NK cells, but these were not maintained at the three-month follow-up. Hypnotic-guided imagery did cause some transient changes in psychological well-being and immune parameters. However, these changes were not retained after the treatment ended. *Conclusions:* Many studies during the last 15 years have demonstrated interactions between the central nervous and immune systems. While a negative effect of stress on immune

responses has been demonstrated, there have also been published reports that psychological treatments can positively alter the immune system. However, given the complexities of immune system kinetics, the transient nature of any psychological effect and the insensitivity of immune assays, our study indicates that there is a role for hypnotic-guided imagery as an adjunctive therapy.

PMID: 12479996

Esplen, M.J. and Garfinkel, P.E. (1998). Guided imagery treatment to promote self-soothing in bulimia nervosa: A theoretical rationale. *Journal of Psychotherapy Practice and Research, 7*(2), 102–118.

Bulimia nervosa (BN) has been described as involving impairment in affect regulation and in self-soothing. Such a conceptualization suggests the need to design treatments that specifically target these problems in order to assist individuals with BN in comforting themselves. A model of guided imagery therapy suggests that imagery therapy has multiple levels of action and can assist these individuals in the regulation of affect by providing an external source of soothing and also by enhancing self-soothing. The authors illustrate the model with a case example and report the results of a study in a clinical sample of BN.

Types: Case reports. Review. Review, tutorial.
PMID: 9527955

Wichowski, H.C. and Kubsch, S.M. (1999). Increasing diabetic self-care through guided imagery. *Complementary Therapies in Nursing and Midwifery, 5*(6), 159–163.

Background: Findings from the literature and clinical practice describe the various strategies necessary on a regular basis to control blood sugar levels in people with diabetes and suggests guided imagery techniques aid clients in adhering to the rigorous diabetic routine. *Methods and Results:* An imagery script was developed and used to aid diabetic clients in maintaining their diabetic regimen. Participants in this cognitive experience indicated that the motivation script used with them by healthcare practitioners was effective. The major treatment areas were blood testing, regular exercise, weight management, and consumption of a restricted lifetime diet. Several of these areas showed modification after use of guided imagery.

Type: Case reports.
PMID: 10887879

Meditation

Barnes, V.A., Treiber, F.A., and Davis, H. (2001). Impact of transcendental meditation on cardiovascular function at rest and during acute stress in adolescents with high normal blood pressure. *Journal of Psychosomatic Research, 51*(4), 597–605.

Objective: This study examined the impact of the transcendental meditation (TM) program on cardiovascular (CV) reactivity in adolescents with high normal blood pressure (BP). *Method:* Thirty-five adolescents [34 African-Americans (AAs), 1 Caucasian American (CA); ages 15–18 years] with resting blood pressure (SBP) between 85th and 95th percentile for their age and gender on three consecutive occasions, were randomly assigned to either TM (n=17) or health education control (CTL, n=18) groups. The TM group engaged in 15-minute meditation twice each day for 2 months including sessions during school lunch break. Primary CV outcome measures were changes in blood pressure (BP), heart rate (HR), and cardiac output (CO) at rest and in response to two laboratory stressors, a simulated car driving stressor and interpersonal social stressor interview. *Results:* The TM group exhibited greater decreases in resting SBP (P<.03) from pre- to post-intervention, compared to the CTL group. The TM group exhibited greater decreases from pre- to postintervention in SBP, HR, and CO reactivity (P's<.03) to the simulated car driving stressor, and in SBP reactivity (P<.03) to the social stressor interview. *Conclusion:* The TM program appears to have a beneficial impact upon CV functioning at rest and during acute laboratory stress in adolescent at-risk for hypertension.

Types: Clinical trial. Randomized control trial.
PMID: 11595248

Keefer, L. and Blanchard, E.B. (2002). A one-year follow-up of relaxation response meditation as a treatment for irritable bowel syndrome. *Behavior Research and Therapy, 40*(5), 541–546.

Ten of thirteen original participants with irritable bowel syndrome (IBS) participated in a one-year follow-up study to determine whether the effects of relaxation response meditation (RRM) on IBS symptom reduction were maintained over the long term. From a pretreatment to one-year follow-up, significant reductions were noted for the symptoms of abdominal pain (p=0.017), diarrhea (p=0.045), flatulence (p=0.030), and bloating (p=0.018). When we examined changes from the original three-month follow-up point to the one-year follow-up, we noted significant reductions in pain (p=0.03), and bloating (p=0.04), which tended to be the most distressing symptoms of IBS. It appears that: (1) continued use of meditation is particularly effective in reducing the symptoms of pain and bloating; and (2) RPM is a beneficial treatment for IBS in both the short term and the long term.

PMID: 12038646

King, M.S., Carr, T. and D'Cruz, C. (2002). Transcendental meditation, hypertension and heart disease. *Australian Family Physician, 31*(2), 164–168.

Background: Accumulating evidence that stress contributes to the pathogenesis and expression of coronary heart disease has led to the increasing use of stress reduction techniques in its prevention and treatment. The most widely used and tested technique is transcendental meditation. *Objective:* To describe transcendental meditation and review research on its use in the treatment and prevention of coronary heart disease. *Discussion:* Transcendental meditation shows promise as a preventative and treatment method for coronary heart disease. Transcendental meditation is associated with decreased hypertension and atherosclerosis, improvements in patients with heart disease, decreased hospitalisation rates and improvements in other risk factors including decreased smoking and cholesterol. These findings cannot be generalised to all meditation and stress reduction techniques as each technique differs in its effects. Further research is needed to delineate the mechanisms involved and to verify preliminary findings concerning atherosclerosis and heart disease and the findings of short-term hypertension studies.

Type: Review. Review, tutorial.
PMID: 11917830

Witoonchart, C. and Bartlet, L. (2002). The use of a meditation programme for institutionalized juvenile delinquents. *Journal of the Medical Association of Thailand, 85*(2), S790–793.

The study applied intensive, seven-consecutive-days meditation programme in 101 late adolescent male delinquents in Upekkha Detention Centre. All of the boys completed the programme and answered the questionnaires. All of them felt that the meditation practice had been beneficial. Seventy percent of the subjects described feelings of contentment and calm,

53% requested the programme to be repeated, 52% of the subjects declared a clearer understanding of the doctrine of Karma, 44% referred to improved concentration and awareness, 36% felt less compulsive, 22% had flashbacks of their criminal behavior and their victims. In conclusion, the boys in Upekkha Detention Centre had the willingness to join and complete the intensive meditation programme. Their self-assessment reports showed a positive attitude to the programme. It is possible to develop a meditation programme as an adjunctive therapy for institutionalized juvenile delinquents.

PMID: 12403262

Music Relaxation

Gregory, D. (2002). Music listening for maintaining attention of older adults with cognitive impairments. *Journal of Music Therapy, 39*(4), 244–264.

Twelve older adults with cognitive impairments who were participants in weekly community-based group music therapy sessions, 6 older adult in an Alzheimer's caregivers' group, and 6 college student volunteers listened to a 3.5 minute prepared audiotape of instrumental excerpts of patriotic selections. The tape consisted of 7 excerpts ranging from 18 s to 34 s in duration. Each music excerpt was followed by a 7–9 s period of silence, a "wait" excerpt. Listeners were instructed to move a continuous response digital interface (CRDI) to the name of the music excerpt depicted on the CRDI overlay when they heard the music excerpt. Likewise, they were instructed to move the dial to the word "WAIT" when there was no music. They were also instructed to maintain the dial position for the duration of each music or silence excerpt. Statistical analysis indicated no significant differences between the caregivers' and the college students' group means for total dial changes, correct and incorrect recognitions, correct and incorrect responses to silence excerpts, and reaction times. The mean scores of these 2 groups were combined and compared with the mean scores of the group of elderly adults with cognitive impairments. The mean total dial changes were significantly lower for the listeners with cognitive impairments, resulting in significant differences in all of the other response categories except incorrect recognitions. In addition, their mean absence of response to silent excerpts was significantly higher than their mean absence of responding to music excerpts. Their mean reaction time was significantly slower than the comparison group's reaction time. To evaluate training effects, 10 of the original 12 music therapy participants repeated the listening task with assistance from the therapist (treatment) immediately following the first listening (baseline). A week later the order was reversed for the 2 listening trials. Statistical and graphic analysis of responses between first and second baseline responses indicate significant improvement in responses to silence and music excerpts over the 2 sessions. Applications of the findings to music listening interventions for maintaining attention, eliciting social interaction between clients or caregivers and their patients, and evaluation this population's affective responses to music are discussed.

PMID: 12597728

Remington, R. (2002). Calming music and hand massage with agitated elderly. *Nursing Research, 51*(5), 317–323.

Background: Agitated behavior is a widespread problem that adversely affects the health of nursing home residents and increases the cost of their care. *Objective:* To examine whether modifying environmental stimuli by the use of calming music and hand massage affects agitated behavior in persons with dementia. *Method:* A four-group, repeated measures experimental design was used to test the effect of a 10-minute exposure to either calming music, hand massage, or calming music and hand massage simultaneously, or no intervention (control) on the frequency and type of agitated behaviors in nursing home residents with dementia (N=68). A modified version of the Cohen-Mansfield Agitation inventory was used to record agitated behaviors. *Results:* Each of the experimental interventions reduced agitation more than no intervention. The benefit was sustained and increased up to on hour following the intervention (F=6.47, p<.01). The increase in benefit over time was similar for each intervention group. When types of agitated behaviors were examined separately, none of the interventions significantly reduced physically aggressive behaviors (F=1.93, p=.09), while physically non-aggressive behaviors decreased during each of the interventions (F=3.78, p=01). No additive benefit resulted from simultaneous exposure to calming music and hand massage. At one hour following any intervention, verbally agitated behavior decreased more than no intervention. *Conclusions:* Calming music and hand massage alter the immediate environment of agitated nursing home residents to a calm structured surrounding, offsetting disturbing stimuli, but no additive benefit was found by combining interventions simultaneously.

Types: Clinical trial. Randomized controlled trial.
PMID: 12352780

Progressive Relaxation

Cheung, Y.L., Molassiotis, A., and Chang, A.M. (2003). The effect of progressive muscle relaxation training on anxiety and quality of life after stoma surgery in colorectal cancer patients. *Psycho-oncology, 12*(3), 254–266.

The aim of the study was to evaluate the effects of the use of progressive muscle relaxation training (PMRT) on anxiety and quality of life in colorectal cancer patients after stoma surgery. A randomised controlled trial was used with repeated measures assessment over 10 weeks post-stoma surgery. Fifty-nine patients participated in the study and were randomised to a control group receiving routine care (n=30) and an experimental group receiving routine care and PMRT through two teaching sessions and practice at home for the first 10 weeks. The State-Trait Anxiety Inventory and two Quality of Life Scales were used to collect the data of interest in three occasions, namely during hospitalisation, at week 5, and at week 10 post-surgery. The use of PMRT significantly decreased state anxiety and improved generic quality of life in the experimental group (P<0.05), especially in the domains of physical health, psychological health, social concerns and environment. Social relationships decreased in both groups. In relation to the disease-specific quality of life measure, differences were observed only in the 10-week assessment, with the experimental group reporting better quality of life at 10 weeks, but not over time as compared to the control group. The use of PMRT should be incorporated in the long-term care of colorectal cancer patients, as it can improve their psychological health and quality of life. This may be a cost-effective intervention that needs minimal training and could easily be offered to those patients that they would like to use it as part of the specialist care provided to stoma patients.

Types: Clinical trial. Multicenter study. Randomized control trial.
PMID: 12673809

de Paula, A.A., de Carvalho, E.C., and dos Santos, C.B. (2002). The use of the "progressive muscle relaxation" technique for pain relief in gynecology and obstetrics. *Revista Latino-Americana de Enfermagem, 10*(5), 654–659.

Pain is one of the most frequent symptoms observed in patients and various treatments are proposed for its relief, including relaxation techniques. With the purpose of testing the effect of a specific intervention (progressive muscle relaxation) in a determined situation (pain), this study aimed at verifying the level of pain in post-surgery patients prior to and after the application of the progressive muscle relaxation techniques. The subjects, 61 patients, have been submitted to abdominal surgical interventions, of which 52.5% had a gynecological nature and 47.5% obstetrical. Our data showed statistically significant alterations in life parameters as well as muscular alterations after the application of the progressive muscle relaxation technique. It was concluded that the use of the progressive muscle relaxation technique enabled the subjects to determine that their pain levels decreased.

PMID: 12641051

Pawlow, L.A. and Jones, G.E. (2002). The impact of abbreviated progressive muscle relaxation on salivary cortisol. *Biological Psychology, 60*(1), 1–16.

The purpose of this study was to examine whether acute relaxation training, conducted on two separate occasions, would be associated with reliable reductions in subjective and physiological indices of stress. Forty-six experimental subjects were led through abbreviated progressive relaxation training (APRT) exercises during two laboratory sessions spaced exactly one week apart. Fifteen control subjects experienced two laboratory sessions where they sat quietly for an equal amount of time. Results indicated that a brief relaxation exercise led to experimental subjects having significantly lower levels of postintervention heart rate, state anxiety, perceived stress, and salivary cortisol than control subjects, as well as increased levels of self-report levels of relaxation. The results of this study may have implications for the use of relaxation training in enhancing immune function.

PMID: 12100842

Sloman, R. (2002). Relaxation and imagery for anxiety and depression control in community patients with advanced cancer. *Cancer Nursing, 25*(6), 432–435.

A community-based nursing study was conducted in Sydney, Australia, to compare the effects of progressive muscle relaxation and guided imagery on anxiety, depression, and quality of life in people with advanced cancer. In this study, 56 people with advanced cancer who were experiencing anxiety and depression were randomly assigned to 1 of 4 treatment conditions: (1) progressive muscle relaxation training, (2) guided imagery training, (3) both of these treatments, and (4) control group. Subjects were tested before and after learning muscle relaxation and guided imagery techniques for anxiety, depression, and quality of life using the Hospital Anxiety and Depression scale and the Functional Living Index-Cancer scale. There was no significant improvement for anxiety; however, significant positive changes occurred for depression and quality of life.

Types: Clinical trial, randomized controlled trial.
PMID: 12464834

Wilk, C. and Turkoski, B. (2001). Progressive muscle relaxation in cardiac rehabilitation: A pilot study. *Rehabilitation Nursing, 26*(6), 238–242.

Learning to manage stress is an important lifestyle change for participants in cardiac rehabilitation programs. Progressive muscle relaxation (PMR) is one stress management approach that has produced positive benefits among different patient populations. The purpose of this study was to identify the effects of learning and practicing PMR in a population of cardiac rehabilitation patients. Blood pressure and heart rate data, and scores on the Spielberger State-Trait Anxiety Inventory (STAI) were collected from a treatment group and a control group of patients enrolled in phases II and III of cardiac rehabilitation. Analysis of the data revealed positive effects of PMR on the variables heart rate and state of anxiety. In addition, written evaluations of PMR from patients in the treatment group indicated a high degree of subjective satisfaction with PMR as a means to reduce stress in their lives.

PMID: 12035725

Self-Hypnosis

Anbar, R.D. (2001). Self-hypnosis for the treatment of functional abdominal pain in childhood. *Clinical Pediatrics, 40*(8), 447–451.

Functional abdominal pain, defined as recurrent abdominal pain in the absence of an identifiable physiologic cause, can respond to psychological intervention in appropriate patients. In this patient series, functional abdominal pain of 4 of 5 patients resolved within 3 weeks after a single session of instruction in self-hypnosis. The potential impact of widespread application of such hypnotherapy may be large, because abdominal pain is thought to be the most common recurrent physical symptom attributable to psychological factors among children and adolescents.

PMID: 11516052

Langenfeld, M.C., Cipani, E., and Borckardt, J.J. (2002). Hypnosis for the control of HIV/AIDS-related pain. *International Journal of Clinical and Experimental Hypnosis, 50*(2), 170–188.

This intensive case study used and A-B time-series analysis design to examine whether 5 adult patients with various AIDS-related pain symptoms benefited from a hypnosis-based pain management approach. The 3 dependent variables in this study were: (a) self-ratings of the severity of pain, (b) self-ratings of the percentage of time spent in pain, and (c) amount of p.r.n. pain medication taken. Data were collected over a period of 12 weeks, including a 1-week baseline period and an 11-week treatment period. Autoregressive integrated moving-average (ARIMA) models were used to determine the effects of the hypnotic intervention over and above autoregressive components of the data. All 5 patients showed significant improvement on at least 1 of the 3 dependent variables as a result of the hypnotic intervention. Four of the 5 patients reported using significantly less pain medication during the treatment phase.

PMID: 11939277

Montgomery, G.H., David, D., Winkel, G., Silverstein, J.H., and Bovbjerg, D.H. (2002). The effectiveness of adjunctive hypnosis with surgical patients: A meta-analysis. *Anesthesia and Analgesia, 94*(6), 1639–1645.

Hypnosis is a nonpharmacologic means for managing adverse surgical side effects. Typically, reviews of the hypnosis literature have been narrative in nature, focused on specific outcome domains (e.g., patients' self-reported pain), and rarely address the impact of different modes of the hypnosis administration. Therefore, it is important to take a quantitative approach to assessing the beneficial impact of adjunctive hypnosis for surgical patients, as well as to examine whether the beneficial impact of hypnosis goes beyond patients' pain and method of the administration. We conducted meta-analyses of published controlled studies (n=20) that used hypnosis with surgical patients to determine: (1) overall, whether hypnosis has a significant beneficial impact, (2) whether there are outcomes for which hypnosis is relatively more effective, and (3) whether the method of hypnotic induction (live versus audiotape) affects hypnosis efficacy. Our results revealed a significant effect size (D=1.20), indicating that surgical patients in hypnosis treatment groups had better outcomes than 89% of patients in control groups. No significant differences were found between clinical outcome categories or between methods of the induction of hypnosis. These results support the position that hypnosis is an effective adjunctive procedure for a wide variety of surgical patients. *Implications:* A meta-analysis review of studies using hypnosis with surgical patients was performed to determine the effectiveness of the procedure. The results indicated that patients in hypnosis treatment groups had better clinical outcomes than 89% of patients in control groups. These data strongly support the use of hypnosis with surgical patients.

Type: Meta-analysis
PMID: 12032044

Taylor, D.N. (1995). Effects of a behavioral stress management program on anxiety, mood, self-esteem, and T-cell count in HIV-positive men. *Psychological Reports, 76*(2), 451–457.

This study evaluated the effects of a behavioral stress management program on anxiety, mood, self-esteem, and T-cell count in a group of HIV-positive men who were asymptomatic except for T-cell counts below 400. The program consisted of 20 biweekly sessions of progressive muscle relaxation and electromyograph biofeedback-assisted relaxation training, meditation, and hypnosis. Ten subjects were randomly assigned to either a treatment group or a no-treatment control group, and the two groups were compared on pre- to posttreatment changes in the dependent measures. Analysis showed that, compared to the no-treatment group, the treatment group showed significant improvement on all the de-

pendent measures, which was maintained at a one-month follow-up. Since stress is known to compromise the immune system, these results suggest that stress management to reduce arousal of the nervous system and anxiety would be an appropriate component of a treatment regimen for HIV infection.

Type: Clinical trial. Randomized control trial.
PMID: 7667456

Sleep Hygiene

Backhaus, J., Hohagen, F., Voderholzer, U., and Riemann, D. (2001). Long-term effectiveness of a short-term cognitive-behavioral group treatment for primary insomnia. *European Archives of Psychiatry and Clinical Neuroscience, 251*(1), 35–41.

The long-term effectiveness of a short-term cognitive-behavioral therapy was evaluated. The structured group treatment consisted of six weekly sessions and included progressive muscle relaxation, cognitive relaxation, modified stimulus control with bedtime restriction, thought stopping and cognitive restructuring. Twenty patients with chronic primary insomnia took part in the study. All patients were referred by physicians for diagnosis and therapy of insomnia. During a waiting period of six weeks prior to treatment, patients did not experience any change of their sleep parameters. After therapy, patients improved their total sleep time and sleep efficiency and reduced their sleep latency and negative sleep-related cognitions. Furthermore, depression scores decreased. Most of the treatment effects were significant at the end of the treatment and remained stable over the long-term follow-up, which was evaluated after a mean of almost three years (35±6.7 months). The subjective estimated total sleep time improved from 298±109 min prior to therapy to 351±54 min at the end of treatment, to 376±75 min at the 3-month follow-up, to 379±58 min at the 12-month follow-up, and to 381±92 min at the long-term follow-up.

Type: Clinical trial.
PMID: 11315517

Edinger, J.D., Wohlgemuth, W.K., Radtke, R.A., Marsh, G.R., and Quillian, R.E. (2001). Does cognitive-behavioral insomnia therapy alter dysfunctional beliefs about sleep? *Sleep, 24*(5), 591–599.

Study Objectives: This study was conducted to examine the degree to which cognitive-behavioral insomnia therapy (CBT) reduces dysfunctional beliefs about sleep and to determine if such cognitive changes correlate with sleep improvements. *Design:* The study used a double-blind, placebo-controlled design in which participants were randomized to CBT, progressive muscle relaxation training, or a sham behavioral intervention. Each treatment was provided in 6 weekly, 30–60-minute individual therapy sessions. *Setting:* The sleep disorders center of a large university medical center. *Participants:* Seventy-five individuals (ages 40–80 years) who met strict criteria for persistent primary sleep-maintenance insomnia were enrolled in this trial. *Interventions:* n/a. *Measurements and Results:* Participants completed the Dysfunctional Belief and Attitudes About Sleep (DBAS) Scale, as well as other assessment procedures before treatment, shortly after treatment, and at six-month follow-up. Items composing a factor-analytically derived DBAS short form (DBAS-SF) were then used to compare treatment groups across time points. Results showed CBT produced larger changes on the DBAS-SF than did the other treatments, and these changes endured through the follow-up period. Moreover, these cognitive changes were correlated with improvements noted on both objective and subjective measures of insomnia symptoms, particularly within the CBT group. *Conclusions:* CBT is effective for reducing dysfunctional beliefs about sleep and such changes are associated with other positive outcomes in insomnia treatment.

Type: Clinical trial. Randomized controlled trial. PMID: 11480656

Social Support

Johnson, L., Lundstrom, O., Aberg-Wistedt, A., and Mathe, A.A. (2003). Social support in bipolar disorder: Its relevance to remission and relapse. *Bipolar Disorders, 5*(2), 129–137.

Objectives: While an association between low-level social support and depression has been found in many studies, its relevance in bipolar illness has rarely been investigated. The aim of this study was to investigate the efforts of social support in the remission and relapse of bipolar disorder. *Methods:* We obtained ratings from 94 stabilized bipolar patients using two different questionnaires that measure perceived social support: the Interview Schedule for Social Interaction and the Interpersonal Support Evaluation List. *Results:* Significantly lower social support was found in patients in partial recovery compared with those in full recovery (p=0.003). Patients who relapsed during a 1-year prospective follow-up period perceived a significantly lower level of social support than patients with no relapse (p=0.012). *Conclusions:* Bipolar patients with full interepisode remission perceive more social support than those who do not achieve full remission. Poor social support may increase the risk of relapse in bipolar disorder.

PMID: 12680903

Symister, P. and Friend, R. (2003). The influence of social support and problematic support on optimism and depression in chronic illness: A prospective study evaluating self-esteem as a mediator. *Health Psychology, 22*(2), 123–129.

The present study focuses on the mechanism through which social and problematic support affects psychological adjustment in chronic illness. The authors hypothesized that self-esteem would mediate the relations between social and problematic support and adjustment. Eighty-six end-stage renal disease patients were assessed twice for social support, problematic support, and self-esteem. Adjustment was assessed twice by depression and optimism. Mediational analysis indicated that social support operated through self-esteem to influence optimism cross-sectionally and prospectively and depression cross-sectionally. Social support was associated with high self-esteem, which in turn increased optimism and was related to decreased depression. Problematic support was unrelated to self-esteem obviating mediational analysis. Disaggregating social support into subscales showed that belonging support predicted decreases in depression, and both tangible and belonging support predicted increases in optimism.

PMID: 12683732

Stretching

Yoshimura, N. (2003). Exercise and physical activities for the prevention of osteoporotic fractures: A review of the evidence. *Nippon Eiseigaku Zasshi, 58*(3), 328–337.

According that osteoporosis is the common condition in an aging society such as in Japan, much progress has been made in understanding the treatment and prevention of osteoporosis. Among potential risk factors, exercise and physical activities have been recognized as lifestyle factors that might influence the risk of osteoporosis and osteoporotic fractures. To access the relationship between exercises including physical activities and the risk for low bone mass and osteoporosis-related fractures, a literature search over the past 13 years was conducted. Accumulating evidence indicates that exercises decrease the risk for hip fractures among middle-aged and older men and women. Exercises also help to maintain muscle strength, muscle volume, balance, and joint flexibility, which might prevent falls and fall-related fractures. One randomized controlled trial showed back-stretching exercise reduced the risk for vertebral fractures. The literature search also indicates that high-impact and/or weight-bearing exercise might increase the bone density in the elderly and the peak bone mass among young women, while there is no association between moderate or lower-impact exercise and bone mineral density. Future research should be required to evaluate the types and quantity of physical activity needed for the prevention of osteoporosis.

PMID: 14533562

Zakas, A., Vergou, A., Grammatikopoulou, M.G., Zakas, N., Sentelidis, T., and Vamvakoudis, S. (2003). The effect of stretching during warming-up on the flexibility of junior handball players. *Journal of Sports Medicine and Physical Fitness, 43*(2), 145–149.

Aim: The purpose of the investigation was to examine in field conditions the acute effects of warming-up on lower extremity joints and trunk flexibility in junior team handball players. *Methods:* Forty-seven junior team handball players participated in this study forming an experiment (n=32) and a control group (n=15). The first group performed warming-up and stretching exercises (20 min) whereas the second group only performed warming-up exercises. Passive range of joint motion was determined in hip flexion, hip extension, hip abduction, knee flexion, ankle dorsiflexion and the trunk flexion using a goniometer and a flexometer. *Results:* The warming-up session induced a significantly increased range in all lower extremity joints and trunk flexion (p<.01 to p<.001) of both groups. *Conclusion:* Flexibility improves as a result of muscle elongation during warming-up or even through an incorporated pathetic stretching program.

PMID: 12853895

Tai Chi

Lan, C., Lai, J.S., and Chen, S.Y. (2002). Tai chi chuan: An ancient wisdom on exercise and health promotion. *Sports Medicine, 32*(4), 217–224.

Tai chi chuan (TCC) is a Chinese conditioning exercise and is well-known for its slow and graceful movements. Recent investigations have found that TCC is beneficial to cardiorespiratory function, strength, balance, flexibility, microcirculation and psychological profile. The long-term practice of TCC can attenuate the age decline in physical function, and consequently it is a suitable exercise for the middle-aged and elderly individuals. TCC can be prescribed as an alternative exercise programme for selected patients with cardiovascular, orthopaedic, or neurological diseases, and can reduce the risk of falls in elderly individuals. The exercise intensity of TCC depends on training style, posture and duration. Participants can choose to perform a complete set of TCC or selected movements according to their needs. In conclusion, TCC has potential benefits in health promotion, and is appropriate for implementation in the community.

Types: Review. Review, tutorial.
PMID: 11929351

Li, J.X., Hong, Y., and Chan, K.M. (2001). Tai chi: Physiological characteristics and beneficial effects on health. *British Journal of Sports Medicine, 35*(3), 148–156.

Objectives: To access the characteristic effects of tai chi chuan (TCC) exercise on metabolism and cardiorespiratory response, and to measure its effect on cardiorespiratory function, mental control, immune capacity, and the prevention of falls in elderly people. *Design:* A review of controlled experimental studies and clinical trials designed with one of two aims: either to assess physiological responses during the performance of TCC or to access the impact of this exercise on general health and fitness. *Main Outcome Measures:* Metabolic rate, heart rate, blood pressure, ventilation, maximal oxygen uptake (VO(2)MAX), immune capacity, falls, and fall-related factors. *Subjects:* A total of 2,216 men and women. *Results:* Under review were 31 original studies, published in Chinese or English journals, that met the criteria for inclusion. Most of the papers written in Chinese had not been introduced into the Western literature. Nine of these studies showed that TCC can be classified as moderate exercise, as it does not demand more than 55% of maximal oxygen intake. When this form of exercise and others conducted at equal intensity were compared, TCC showed a significantly lower ventilatory equivalent (VE/VO(2)MAX). Evidence provided by cross-sectional and longitudinal studies suggests that TCC exercise has beneficial effects on cardiorespiratory and musculoskeletal function, posture control capacity, and the reduction of falls experienced by the elderly. *Conclusions:* TCC is a moderate intensity exercise that is beneficial to cardiorespiratory function, immune capacity, mental control, flexibility, and balance control; it improves muscle strength and reduces the risk of falls in the elderly.

Types: Review. Review literature.
PMID: 11375872

Wellness

Campbell, J. and Aday, R.H. (2001). Benefits of using a nurse-managed wellness program. A senior center model. Using community-based sites for older adult intervention and self-care activities may promote an ability to maintain an independent lifestyle. *Journal of Gerontological Nursing, 27*(3), 34–43.

Recent health initiatives have encouraged the promotion of wellness and self-care among the elderly population. This research describes the effectiveness of a nurse-managed wellness program located at a multipurpose senior center. The wellness clinic was created to provide a broad range of screening services, individual counseling services, health educational programs, and management services for chronic diseases common among older adults. Outcome measures focusing for utilization of health services, healthy behaviors, emotional well-being, and mental and physical health variables gathered from 111 older adults demonstrated significant program success. Respondents who used the wellness clinic more frequently, and in particular, those who consulted regularly with the clinical nurse, were more likely to increase their healthy behavior and subsequent health knowledge. As a result of participation in the wellness programs, respondents reported a greater psychological comfort and a more confident feeling concerning the ability to maintain an independent lifestyle.

PMID: 11915256

Sadur, C.N., Moline, N., Costa, M., Michalik, D., Mendlowitz, D., Roller, S., Watson, R., Swain, B.E., Selby, J.V., and Javorski, W.C. (1999). Diabetes management in a health maintenance organization. Efficacy of care management using cluster visits. *Diabetes Care, 22*(12), 2011–2017.

Objective: To evaluate the effectiveness of a cluster visit model led by a diabetes nurse educator for delivering outpatient care management to adult patients with poorly controlled diabetes. *Research Design and Methods:* This study involved a randomized controlled trial among patients of Kaiser Permanente's Pleasanton, California, center who were ages 16–75 years and had either poor glycemic control (HbA1c>8.5%) or no HbA1c test performed during the previous year. Intervention subjects received multidisciplinary outpatient diabetes care management delivered by a diabetes nurse educator, a psychologist, a nutritionist, and a pharmacist in cluster visit settings of 10–18 patients/month for 6 months. Outcomes included change (from baseline) in HbA1c levels; self-reported changes in self-care practices, self-efficacy, and satisfaction; and utilization of inpatient and outpatient healthcare. *Results:* After the intervention, HbA1c levels declined by 1.3% in the intervention subjects versus 0.2% in the control subjects (P<0.0001). Several self-care practices and several measures of self-efficacy improved significantly in the intervention group. Satisfaction with the program was high. Both hospital (P=0.04) and outpatient (P<0.01) utilization were significantly lower for intervention subjects after the program. *Conclusions:* A 6-month cluster visit group model of care for adults with diabetes improved glycemic control, self-efficacy, and patient satisfaction and resulted in a reduction on healthcare utilization after the program.

Types: Clinical trial. Randomized controlled trial.
PMID: 10587835

Yoga

Damodaran, A., Malathi, A., Patil, N., Shah, N., Suryavansihi, and Marathe, S. (2002). Therapeutic potential of yoga practices in modifying cardiovascular risk profile in middle aged men and women. *Journal of the Association of Physicians of India, 50*(5), 633–640.

Aims of Study: To study effect of yoga on the physiological, psychological well-being, psychomotor parameter and modifying cardiovascular risk factors in mild to moderate hypertensive patients. *Methods:* Twenty patients (16 males, 4 females) in the age group of 35 to 55 years with mild to moderate essential hypertension underwent yogic practices daily for one hour for three months. Biochemical, physiological and psychological parameters were studied prior and following period of three months of yoga practices, biochemical parameters included, blood glucose, lipid profile, catecholamines, MDA, Vit. C cholinesterase and urinary VMA. Psychological evaluation was done by using personal orientation inventory and subjective well-being. *Results:* Results showed decrease in blood pressure and drug score modifying risk factors, i.e., blood glucose, cholesterol and triglycerides decreased overall improvement in subjective well-being and quality of life. There was decrease in VMA catecholamine, and decrease MDA level suggestive [of] decrease sympathetic activity and oxidant stress. *Conclusion:* Yoga can play an important role in risk modification for cardiovascular diseases in mild to moderate hypertension.

Type: Clinical trial.
PMID: 12186115

Malhotra, V. Singh, S., Singh, K.P., Gupta, P., Sharma, S.B., Madhu, S.V., and Tandon, O.P. (2002). Study of yoga asanas in assessment of pulmonary function in NIDDM patients. *Indian Journal of Physiology and Pharmacology, 46*(3), 313–320.

Certain yoga asanas if practiced regularly are known to have beneficial effects on the human body. These yoga practices might be interacting with various, somato-neuro-endocrine mechanisms to have therapeutic effects. The present study done [with] twenty-four NIDDM patients of 30–60 years old provides metabolic and clinical evidence of improvement in glycaemic control and pulmonary functions. These middle-aged subjects were Type II diabetics on antihyperglycaemic and dietary regimen. Their baseline fasting and postprandial blood glucose and glycosylated Hb were monitored along with pulmonary function studies. The expert gave these patients training in yoga asanas and were pursued 30–40 minutes per day for 40 days under guidance. These asanas consisted of thirteen well-known postures done in a sequence. After 40 days of yoga asanas regimen, the parameters were repeated. The results indicate that there was significant decrease in fasting blood glucose levels (basal 190.08 ± 90.8 in mg/dl to 141.5 ± 79.8 in mg/dl). The post prandial blood glucose levels also decreased (276.54 ± 101.0 in mg/dl to 201.75 ± 104.1 in mg/dl), glycosylated hemoglobin showed a decrease ($9.03 \pm 1.4\%$ to $7.83 \pm 2.6\%$). The FEV1, FVC, PEFR, MVV increased significantly (1.81 ± 0.4 lt to 2.08 ± 0.4 lt, 2.20 ± 0.6 lt to 2.37 ± 0.5 lt, 3.30 ± 1.0 lt/s to 4.43 ± 1.4 lt/s and 64.59 ± 25.7 lt/min to 76.28 ± 28.1

lt/min respectively). FEV1/FVC% improved ($85 \pm 0.2\%$ to $89 \pm 0.1\%$). These findings suggest that better glycaemic control and pulmonary functions can be obtained in NIDDM cases with yoga asanas and pranayama. The exact mechanism as to how these postures and controlled breathing interact with somato-neuro-endocrine mechanism affecting metabolic and pulmonary functions remains to be worked out.

Type: Clinical trial.
PMID: 12613394

Malhotra, V., Singh, S., Tandon, O.P., Madhu, S.V., Prasad, A., and Sharma, S.B. (2002). Effect of yoga asanas on nerve conduction in Type 2 diabetes. *Indian Journal of Physiology and Pharmacology, 46*(3), 298–306.

Twenty Type 2 diabetic subjects between the ages of 30–60 years were studied to see the effect of 40 days of yoga asanas on the nerve conduction velocity. The duration of diabetes ranged from 0–10 years. Subject suffering from cardiac, renal and proliferative retinal complications were excluded from the study. Yoga asanas included Suryanamskar, Tadasan, Konasan, Padmasan, Pranayam, Paschimottansan Ardhmatsyendrasan, Shavasan, Pavanmukthasan, Sarpasan and Shavasan. Subjects were called to the cardiorespiratory laboratory in the morning time and were given training by the yoga expert. The yoga exercises were performed for 30–40 minutes every day for 40 days in the above sequence. The subjects were prescribed certain medicines and diet. The basal blood glucose, nerve conduction velocity of the median nerve was measured and repeated after 40 days of yogic regime. Another group of 20 Type 2 diabetes subjects of comparable age and severity, called the control group, were kept on prescribed medication and light physical exercises like walking. Their basal and post 40 days parameters were recorded for comparison. Right hand and left hand median nerve conduction velocity increased from 52.81 ± 1.1 m/sec to 53.87 ± 1.1 m/sec and 52.46 ± 1.0 to 54.75 ± 1.1 m/sec respectively. Control group nerve function parameters deteriorated over the period of study, indicating that diabetes is a slowly progressive disease involving the nerves. Yoga asanas have a beneficial effect on glycaemic control and improve nerve function in mild to moderate Type 2 diabetes with subclinical neuropathy.

Type: Clinical trial.
PMID: 12613392

About the Author

Cynthia Mascott, MS, CTRS, RTC, has been a Certified Therapeutic Recreation Specialist since 1986, after graduating with a Master's Degree in Therapeutic Recreation from the University of Oregon. She currently is the Acting Clinical Supervisor in the Psychiatric Recreation Therapy Department at Los Angeles County & University of Southern California Healthcare Network.

She previously worked as the Senior Recreation Therapist at the Center for Chemical Dependency at Cedars Sinai Medical Center and as the Department Head of the Therapeutic Recreation Department at Windemere Nursing and Rehabilitation on Martha's Vineyard Island in Massachusetts.

Cynthia has written several travel guides about the New England region and wrote a weekly health column for the *Martha's Vineyard Times*. She also produced an Oral History Project for the paper using the life stories of the residents of the nursing home.

Other Books by Venture Publishing, Inc.

A Social Psychology of Leisure
by Roger C. Mannell and Douglas A. Kleiber

Special Events and Festivals: How to Organize, Plan, and Implement
by Angie Prosser and Ashli Rutledge

Steps to Successful Programming: A Student Handbook to Accompany Programming for Parks, Recreation, and Leisure Services
by Donald G. DeGraaf, Debra J. Jordan, and Kathy H. DeGraaf

Stretch Your Mind and Body: Tai Chi as an Adaptive Activity
by Duane A. Crider and William R. Klinger

Therapeutic Activity Intervention with the Elderly: Foundations and Practices
by Barbara A. Hawkins, Marti E. May, and Nancy Brattain Rogers

Therapeutic Recreation and the Nature of Disabilities
by Kenneth E. Mobily and Richard D. MacNeil

Therapeutic Recreation: Cases and Exercises, Second Edition
by Barbara C. Wilhite and M. Jean Keller

Therapeutic Recreation in Health Promotion and Rehabilitation
by John Shank and Catherine Coyle

Therapeutic Recreation in the Nursing Home
by Linda Buettner and Shelley L. Martin

Therapeutic Recreation Programming: Theory and Practice
by Charles Sylvester, Judith E. Voelkl, and Gary D. Ellis

Therapeutic Recreation Protocol for Treatment of Substance Addictions
by Rozanne W. Faulkner

Tourism and Society: A Guide to Problems and Issues
by Robert W. Wyllie

A Training Manual for Americans with Disabilities Act Compliance in Parks and Recreation Settings
by Carol Stensrud

Venture Publishing, Inc.
1999 Cato Avenue
State College, PA 16801
Phone: (814) 234-4561
Fax: (814) 234-1651